JOURNAL FOR THE STUDY OF THE NEW TESTAMENT
SUPPLEMENT SERIES
116

Executive Editor
Stanley E. Porter

Editorial Board
Richard Bauckham, David Catchpole, R. Alan Culpepper,
Margaret Davies, James D.G. Dunn, Craig A. Evans, Stephen Fowl,
Robert Fowler, Robert Jewett, Elizabeth Struthers Malbon

Sheffield Academic Press
Sheffield

Luke's Literary Achievement

Collected Essays

C.M. Tuckett

Journal for the Study of the New Testament
Supplement Series 116

BS
2589
.L84
1995

Copyright © 1995 Sheffield Academic Press

Published by
Sheffield Academic Press Ltd
Mansion House
19 Kingfield Road
Sheffield, S11 9AS
England

Typeset by Sheffield Academic Press
and
Printed on acid-free paper in Great Britain
by Bookcraft
Midsomer Norton, Somerset

British Library Cataloguing in Publication Data

A catalogue record for this book is available
from the British Library

ISBN 1-85075-556-6

CONTENTS

Preface	7
List of Abbreviations	12
List of Contributors	15

LOVEDAY ALEXANDER
   'In Journeyings Often': Voyaging in the Acts of the Apostles
   and in Greek Romance   17

MARTINUS C. DE BOER
   God-Fearers in Luke–Acts   50

GEORGE BROOKE
   Luke–Acts and the Qumran Scrolls: The Case of MMT   72

GERALD DOWNING
   Theophilus's First Reading of Luke–Acts   91

JEAN-DANIEL KAESTLI
   Luke–Acts and the Pastoral Epistles: The Thesis of a Common
   Authorship   110

DANIEL MARGUERAT
   Saul's Conversion (Acts 9, 22, 26) and the Multiplication
   of Narrative in Acts   127

DAVID PARRY
   Release of the Captives: Reflections on Acts 12   156

ANDRIANJATOVO RAKOTOHARINTSIFA
   Luke and the Internal Divisions in the Early Church   165

THOMAS RÖMER AND JEAN-DANIEL MACCHI
   Luke, Disciple of the Deuteronomistic School 178

ROGER TOMES
   Why did Paul Get his Hair Cut? (Acts 18.18; 21.23-24) 188

CHRISTOPHER TUCKETT
   The Lukan Son of Man 198

Index of References 218
Index of Authors 229

PREFACE

The essays in this volume represent papers which were given at a colloquium held in the University of Manchester in May 1994 as part of the link established between the Department of Religions and Theology in the University of Manchester and the Faculté de Théologie in the Université de Lausanne, Switzerland. The meetings were also opened to any interested members of the Department of Biblical Studies in the University of Sheffield, and a group from Sheffield attended a large number of the sessions held, one of their number, Dr Loveday Alexander, contributing a main paper. The rest of the papers were given by staff, students and other members of the graduate seminars of the respective biblical sections of the institutions of Manchester and Lausanne. As many as 40 people attended one or more of the sessions, and the discussion after the papers was invariably stimulating and added to the value of the meeting.

The meeting had originally been planned as a symposium on the Lukan writings in general, with a number of scholars invited to prepare and submit papers. It was perhaps striking that the great majority of the papers focused almost exclusively on Acts, rather than on Luke's Gospel. It was also striking that many of the contributions focused on a more 'literary' approach to Luke's text. New Testament studies in the last 20 to 30 years have been dominated by two major trends: one is the application of techniques and insights from the fields of sociology and anthropology to understanding more about the New Testament texts and the communities and individuals who lie behind them; the other is the growing awareness of the insights which can be gained by applying the methods and results from other 'literary' studies to the New Testament texts. The latter area can of course cover a vast field, and an enormous variety of different, though related, approaches. Some of these can contribute to a more traditional 'historical-critical' approach to the study of the text (in that some attempt is made to throw light on some aspect of the 'original' situation of the text, be it the author or the audience); other approaches can be quite ahistorical, bracketing off any questions about the 'original' situation (of authors or readers) as irrelevant, or unattainable, or some combination of the two. The general approach in all the essays in this volume was to preserve a 'historical' dimension to the study of the text, but sometimes to use all the riches of a more 'literary-critical' approach in seeking to illuminate aspects of the history to which the text gives us access. Yet for the most part, the aim was not to recover the historical events which Luke himself narrates so much as to ascertain what Luke himself was concerned with in telling the story in the way he has done, or alternatively, to ascertain how the first readers/hearers of Luke might have read/heard the text.

The one essay to focus primarily on the Gospel, rather than on Acts, was the essay of Tuckett, devoted to Luke's references to Jesus as Son of Man. The essay addressed the specific question of the meaning of the phrase 'Son of Man' for Luke, as well as the more general question of what this evidence might indicate about Luke's use of his source materials. The essay is thus primarily a 'redaction-critical' study, though also arguing that Luke's 'redaction' is perhaps at times not as extensive as has sometimes been suggested. The model of Luke as a 'conservative redactor' by no means commanded universal assent, though it would clearly have implications for other study of the Gospel and Acts.

A more overtly literary approach is adopted by Marguerat in his study of the three accounts of Saul's conversion in Acts 9, 22 and 26, where he seeks to analyse why there is more than one account, and also what the peculiar features of each account are. The essay shows very well the contribution which insights from literary critical studies can make to a more traditional 'historical-critical' approach. The two approaches are clearly not mutually antagonistic, but can be used fruitfully together. Methodologically similar is the essay of Parry on the story of Peter's release from prison in Acts 12, where Parry shows how the story forms an important part of the wider Lukan narrative, with many parallels elsewhere to individual elements in the story.

Approaches which are in one way more overtly 'historical' (though equally 'literary' in another) are adopted by Downing and Alexander, both of whom seek to locate Luke's writing, especially Acts, within the context of a wide body of literature from the Greco-Roman world. So often in the past, attention had been focused on Jewish writings of the period as providing 'the' background for the New Testament. But Luke's audience/readers were not necessarily Jewish and hence one should perhaps be looking at other, non-Jewish texts as the 'literary' context in which Luke's work would have been first heard and read. Thus Downing draws in a wide range of other literature to make suggestions about the way in which Luke's work might have been first received and also about the kind of expectations which his audience might have had in terms of other similar literature of the period.

Alexander's approach is in one way more limited in that she focuses on a narrower body of possible comparable material, namely the Greek Romances. These stories share with Acts the motif of voyaging over the sea as an integral part of the story. Alexander does not suggest (as others have done) that Acts is itself a 'novel', or a 'romance'. Nevertheless, the use of this body of material does throw important light on Luke's narrative in Acts, sometimes as much by contrast as by similarity, but also by illustrating well some of the presuppositions (the 'mental map') which the first readers of Acts may well have brought to the story and which would then significantly affect the reading of it.

Two of the essays do address more 'historical' issues. De Boer's essay surveys the vexed question of the existence of a group of people known as 'godfearers' in first century Judaism. There is the problem of whether Luke himself thought that such a group with a 'title' of this nature existed (i.e. the problem of existence within Luke's story world), and *if* so, whether there is evidence for such a group of people in other writings of this period. The problem, or rather problems (i.e. both within and outside Luke's story world) are immensely complicated, and, as de Boer shows at the end of his essay, can have far-reaching effects for assessing Luke's overall purposes and aims in many respects. A smaller historical problem is the subject of the essay of Tomes, although the ramifications can reach far and wide. Tomes discusses the question of whether, and why, Paul cut his hair in Acts 18. Within Lukan studies, the incident is by no means a trivial one since it is one of the stock examples used by modern critics to argue that Luke's portrait of Paul, showing Paul to be a law-abiding Jew par excellence, cannot be historically accurate since it clashes so strongly with the picture which emerges from Paul's own letters. Tomes gives a detailed analysis of the story and argues that the vow in question is unlikely to be a Nazirite vow; more importantly, he argues that Paul's behaviour here can be squared with the principles he himself enunciates elsewhere in his letters. The relevance of the argument to much modern Lukan study needs no highlighting here.

A similar background of scholarly discussion underlies the study of

Rakotoharintsifa, examining the stories of conflicts in Acts. Taking his point of departure from a 'standard' view of Luke as one who regularly covers over disputes and arguments in the church to present a gloriously united and happy community, Rakotoharintsifa shows that conflicts are present in the church in Acts. And whereas there is more than an element of truth in the standard critical view that Luke plays down any disputes within the church, the fact remains that in many instances Luke's account is the only evidence we possess for the existence of such conflicts. Thus the Acts account is far more complex that the Tübingen school would have us believe.

If the importance of the Greco-Roman background is stressed by Downing and Alexander, the Jewish background of Luke is the focus of attention in the essay of Römer and Macchi. The authors discuss the wide influence of so-called deuteronomistic thought and ideas in Judaism across a long period of time; and they show that Stephen's speech in Acts 7 (taken by them to be a Lukan product) shows a significant level of deuteronomistic influence. Given the peculiarity of Stephen's speech within Luke–Acts as a whole, it would obviously repay further study to see if such deuteronomistic influence can be demonstrated so strongly elsewhere in the Lukan writings.

In this respect the essay of Brooke has particular significance. Like Römer and Macchi, Brooke looks at Jewish literature, focusing in particular on the Qumran literature to see how this might throw light on Luke–Acts. Brooke's particular interest in this study is the newly published 4QMMT text. He argues that there is no question of direct literary dependence between 4QMMT and Luke–Acts, but nevertheless the two do display some striking similarities in common interests and concerns (including some associated with deuteronomistic writers). There has been a great flood of newly available texts from Qumran in recent years, and they will clearly take a long time to digest and assimilate for their full and proper significance to be determined. Brooke's essay is an important step in what will no doubt be a very full discussion in years to come.

A rather different approach is offered in the essay of Kaestli. Luke is famous, or infamous, for having almost every (possibly) pseudonymous text of the New Testament ascribed to him by one scholar or another. The possibility that the Pastoral Epistles might have been written by Luke has been suggested by a number of critics in the past. Kaestli gives a searching critical analysis of such theories and finds them wanting. But he does show how the author of the Pastorals could have constructed many of the personal details in these letters by a reading of the text of Acts. In one sense then Kaestli's essay is an example of an application of reader-response theory, arguing for a plausible *reading* of Acts by a first-century reader. He thus presents a powerful case which does justice both to Acts and the Pastorals respectively, explaining both their similarities to each other and also their significant differences.

A colloquium of New Testament scholars rarely produces unanimity. Nevertheless, the papers presented here did make all those present at the discussion acutely aware of many of the problems of contemporary Lukan studies and of the uncertain nature of many of the 'standard' solutions currently on offer. Certainly all were very conscious of the need to take a full range of 'background' material into account in seeking to read and understand Luke's work, and of the gains which are to be had if one uses the insights of other literary critics and those involved in reading other stories and narratives as one attempts to read and understand Luke's narrative.

All those whose papers are printed here are grateful to Professor Stanley Porter for agreeing to publish them in the JSNT Supplement Series, and to Webb Mealy and the staff at Sheffield Academic Press for their help in the production process. The colloquium was also assisted by a generous grant from the Research Support Fund of the University of Manchester, and this generosity is very gratefully acknowledged.

Christopher Tuckett

ABBREVIATIONS

AB	Anchor Bible
ABD	Anchor Bible Dictionary
AnBib	Analecta Biblica
ANRW	*Aufstieg und Niedergang der römischen Welt*
ATANT	Abhandlungen zur Theologie des Alten und Neuen Testaments
BARev	*Biblical Archaeology Review*
BET	Beiträge zur biblischen Exegese und Theologie
BETL	Bibliotheca ephemeridum theologicarum lovaniensium
Bib	*Biblica*
BJRL	*Bulletin of the John Rylands University Library of Manchester*
BK	Biblischer Kommentar
BTS	*Bible et vie chrétienne*
BWANT	Beiträge zur Wissenschaft vom Alten und Neuen Testament
BZ	*Biblische Zeitschrift*
BZAW	Beihefte zur ZAW
CBQ	*Catholic Biblical Quarterly*
CRINT	Compendia rerum iudaicarum ad novum testamentum
DJD	Discoveries in the Judaean Desert
EB	Etudes bibliques
EH	Europäische Hochschulschriften
EHPhR	Etudes d'histoire et de philosophie religieuse
EKK	Evangelisch-katholischer Kommentar zum Neuen Testament
EncJud	*Encyclopaedia Judaica* (1971)
FRLANT	Forschungen zur Religion und Literatur des Alten und Neuen Testaments
HNT	Handbuch zum Neuen Testament
HSM	Harvard Semitic Monographs
HTKNT	Herders theologischer Kommentar zum Neuen Testament
HTR	*Harvard Theological Review*
HUT	Hermeneutische Untersuchungen zur Theologie
JAC	*Jahrbuch für Antike und Christentum*
JBL	*Journal of Biblical Literature*
JJS	*Journal of Jewish Studies*
JRelS	*Journal of Religious Studies*
JRS	*Journal of Roman Studies*
JSNTSup	*Journal for the Study of the New Testament* Supplement Series

JSJ	*Journal for the Study of Judaism*
JSNT	*Journal for the Study of the New Testament*
JSOTSup	*Journal for the Study of the Old Testament* Supplement Series
JSP	*Journal for the Study of the Pseudepigrapha*
JSS	*Journal of Semitic Studies*
JTS	*Journal of Theological Studies*
KEK	Kritisch-exegetischer Kommentar über das Neue Testament
LCL	Loeb Classical Library
LD	Lectio divina
NedTT	*Nederlands theologisch tijdschrift*
NICNT	New International Commentary on the New Testament
NovT	*Novum Testamentum*
NRT	*Nouvelle revue théologique*
NTA	Neutestamentliche Abhandlungen
NTD	Das Neue Testament Deutsch
NTS	*New Testament Studies*
OBO	Orbis biblicus et orientalis
OTL	Old Testament Library
ÖTKNT	Ökumenischer Taschenbuchkommentar zum Neuen Testament
PW	Pauly–Wissowa, *Real-Encyclopädie der classischen Alterthumswissenschaft*
RB	*Revue biblique*
REJ	*Revue des études juives*
RevQ	*Revue de Qumran*
RevThom	*Revue thomiste*
RivB	*Rivista biblica*
RTP	*Revue de théologie et de philosophie*
SBAB	Stuttgarter biblische Aufsatzbände
SBL	Society of Biblical Literature
SBLSPS	Society of Biblical Literature. Sources for Biblical Study
SBLSP	Society of Biblical Literature Seminar Papers
SemBi	Sémiotique et bible
SNTSMS	Society of New Testament Studies Monograph Series
SBS	Stuttgarter Bibelstudien
ST	*Studia theologica*
STDJ	Studies on the Texts of the Desert of Judah
TAPA	Transactions of the American Philological Association
TDNT	Theological Dictionary of the New Testament
ThW	Theologische Wissenschaft
ThWNT	*Theologisches Wörterbuch zum Neuen Testament*
TNTC	Tyndale New Testament Commentaries
TOTC	Tyndale Old Testament Commentaries
TRE	*Theologische Realenzyklopädie*
TZ	*Theologische Zeitschrift*
UTB	Uni-Taschenbücher

VT	*Vetus Testamentum*
WBC	Word Biblical Commentary
WMANT	Wissenschaftliche Monographien zum Alten und Neuen Testament
WUNT	Wissenschaftliche Untersuchungen zum Neuen Testament
ZAW	*Zeitschrift für die alttestamentliche Wissenschaft*
ZNW	*Zeitschrift für die neutestamentliche Wissenschaft*

LIST OF CONTRIBUTORS

Loveday Alexander is Lecturer in New Testament in the Department of Biblical Studies, University of Sheffield.

George J. Brooke is Senior Lecturer in Intertestamental Literature in the University of Manchester and Co-Director of the Manchester–Sheffield Centre for Dead Sea Scroll Research.

Martinus C. de Boer is Lecturer in New Testament Studies in the University of Manchester.

Gerald Downing is Vicar of the Anglican Parish of St Simon and St Jude, Bolton.

Jean-Daniel Kaestli is Professor and Director of the *Institut des Sciences bibliques* at the University of Lausanne. He is also General Secretary of the Association pour l'étude de la littérature apocryphe chrétienne (ALEAC).

Jean-Daniel Macchi is Assistant in Old Testament in the Faculté de Théologie, University of Lausanne.

Daniel Marguerat is Professor of New Testament in the Faculté de Théologie, University of Lausanne.

Andrianjatovo Rakotoharintsifa is Assistant in the *Institut des Sciences bibliques* at the University of Lausanne.

Thomas Römer is Professor of Old Testament in the Faculté de Théologie, University of Lausanne.

David T.N. Parry is Team Rector of the Parish of East Farnworth and Kearsley.

Roger Tomes is Honorary Lecturer in Biblical Studies in the University of Manchester.

Christopher M. Tuckett is Rylands Professor of Biblical Criticism and Exegesis, and Director of the Centre for Biblical Studies, in the University of Manchester.

'IN JOURNEYINGS OFTEN': VOYAGING IN THE ACTS
OF THE APOSTLES AND IN GREEK ROMANCE*

Loveday Alexander

Voyaging is integral to the plot of both Acts and Greek romance. In Acts, right through from the opening mission statement at 1.8, geographical movement is a central component in the narrative: travel is not an optional extra for Jesus' followers, and especially not for Paul. For the Greek novels,[1] too, it may justly be claimed that the voyage is not simply one adventurous element among others that may befall the hero and heroine: it is *the* adventure which undergirds the plot of ancient romance. In Reardon's words, 'In the novel, the obstacles that circumstance puts in the way of a happy union are those consequent upon extensive travel in the Eastern Mediterranean and its hinterland—from Sicily to Babylon, from the Bosporus to Ethiopia'.[2] The travel motif

* Versions of this paper have been read at the Centre for East Roman Studies, University of Warwick, at the Manchester–Lausanne Colloquium, and at the International Meeting of the SBL, Leuven 1994. I am grateful to friends and colleagues in all these places for their many helpful comments.

1. There is a growing and vigorous scholarly literature on the Greek novel. For translations and fundamental bibliography, see B.P. Reardon (ed.), *Collected Ancient Greek Novels* (Berkeley: University of California Press, 1989 [hereinafter: Reardon, *Novels*]). T. Hägg, *The Novel in Antiquity* (English edn [revised]; Oxford: Blackwell, 1983), provides a readable and insightful introduction to the genre; J.R. Morgan and R. Stoneman (eds.), *Greek Fiction: The Greek Novel in Context* (London: Routledge, 1994), is a wide-ranging and stimulating collection of essays. The most concerted and convincing comparison with Acts to date may be found in R.I. Pervo, *Profit with Delight: The Literary Genre of the Acts of the Apostles* (Philadelphia: Fortress Press, 1987).

2. B.P. Reardon, 'The Greek Novel', *Phoenix* 23 (1966), pp. 291-309 [hereinafter: Reardon, 'Greek Novel']) (292-93); cf. also *idem*, *The Form of Greek Romance* (Princeton: University Press, 1991 [hereinafter: Reardon, *Form*]), pp. 15-16, 25. The obvious exception is Longus's *Daphnis and Chloe,* but even this is described by Reardon as 'a journey in time' (*Form*, p. 33).

thus provides a good starting point for a comparative analysis of Acts and the Greek novels: good, because it is a motif essential to the plot of both; but also manageable in that it makes it possible to select salient narrative features for analysis. We are beginning to make great strides in the understanding of the literary environment of the New Testament texts;[3] but if this form of literary analysis is to make any progress, I believe, it is time to move beyond the often vague and general observations of the pioneers and undertake serious and concerted comparative studies with an eye to the differences as much to the similarities between texts.

In a single paper only a limited amount of such study can be attempted, and the texts chosen will perforce be selective. Greek romance is a large and complex phenomenon; here I have chosen to focus on the earliest of the full novel texts we possess, Chariton's story of *Chaereas and Callirhoe*[4] and the *Ephesiaca* of Xenophon of Ephesus.[5] These are not only the closest in date to Acts but also (by common consent) the least 'sophistic': which is not to say that they lack literary art, but that they are the closest of the novels to the popular roots of Greek romance. And even within the theme of 'voyaging' I cannot hope to do justice to all its possible ramifications. For this reason I have largely (though not entirely) avoided the 'shipwreck' theme, which has received its fair share of attention. Instead I have tried to isolate three areas for concerted comparison within the broader theme: the structure of the voyage in terms of plot; the mental maps which the narrative presupposes; and the significance of the sea as a mode of travel.

---

3. Notably (for example) D.E. Aune, *The New Testament in its Literary Environment* (Cambridge: James Clarke, 1988); K. Berger, 'Hellenistische Gattungen im neuen Testament', *ANRW*, II. 25. 2 (1984), pp. 1034-1380.

4. Chariton: see Reardon, *Novels*, pp. 17-124. Greek text with French translation in the Budé series: *Chariton: Le Roman de Chairéas et Callirhoé* (ed. G. Molinié; Paris: 'Les Belles Lettres', 1979). Reardon (*Novels*, p. 17) dates the text 'around the middle of the first century A.D.', Molinié (p. 2) between the third quarter of the first century and the first quarter of the second.

5. Xenophon: see Reardon, *Novels*, pp. 125-69. Greek text with French translation in the Budé series: *Xénophon d'Ephèse: Les Ephésiaques* (ed. G. Dalmeyda; Paris: 'Les Belles Lettres', 1962). Xenophon is generally dated around the beginning of the second century CE.

The Voyage as Plot

'This book will make a traveller of thee.'[6]

The use of a voyage, real or imaginary, to provide the essential structure for a narrative must be one of the oldest plot devices in literature, and is certainly not unique to Greek romance. The journey is a simple means of providing momentum and maintaining interest. Movement in space carries the story line forward in 'alternating marches and halts', and provides a thread on which a whole series of adventures can be hung: as Philip Stadter has observed in a different context, 'It is one of the features of a journey narrative, whether *periplus* or land journey (such as those of Xenophon and Alexander), that it may be expanded at will at any point'.[7] The travelling itself may simply serve as a linking device which transports the characters from one scene to another, so that the exotic location (and the adventures which take place there) are more important in narrative terms than the route by which it is reached; or the travel may itself become the focus of attention.

The travel plot in Chariton is relatively simple. In the opening scene the lovers meet, marry and are divided: Chaereas' baseless jealousy of his pregnant wife causes him to give her a kick, which leads to her apparent death and (real) burial. Pirates break in to rob the tomb, find Callirhoe recovering consciousness, and abduct her as part of their booty. The rest of the narrative recounts the separate adventures of the parted lovers: when they meet again, we know we have reached the climax of the story and the expected 'happy ending'. But before this can happen, the pair have to travel from Sicily in the far west of the Greek world to Babylon beyond its eastern frontiers: Chaereas follows the trail of Callirhoe to Miletus, where he is himself captured and enslaved in nearby Caria; both are then taken by circumstances beyond their control to Babylon, where a sensational trial scene reveals them to each other but fails to resolve the complex situation that prevents their reunion; war with Egypt takes both to Syria and Phoenicia, where Chaereas's military prowess finally rewards him with the recapture of his wife on the island of Aradus. The final scene recounts their return to Syracuse to live 'happily ever after' (Figure 1).

---

6. John Bunyan, *The Pilgrim's Progress* (from 'The Author's Apology for his Work').

7. P. Statder, *Arrian of Nicomedia* (Chapel Hill: University of North Carolina Press, 1980), pp. 76, 126

Xenophon follows essentially the same plot structure, but with more complicated travels. His hapless pair, Anthia and Habrocomes, are likewise married in the opening scene (in Ephesus), set out on a honeymoon voyage (by which means their parents unaccountably hope to escape the perils prophesied by an oracle), are captured by pirates, sold as slaves, and separated. The rest of the narrative recounts Habrocomes' search for Anthia in Syria and Cilicia, then in Egypt and Ethiopia, finally in Sicily and Italy, before the two are reunited in Rhodes and sail back to Ephesus to begin their married life (Figure 2).

In a sense, then, both plots follow the familiar *nostos* structure of the Odyssey, in which the voyage achieves its closure with a return to the point of departure. By comparison with the Odyssey, however, Chariton devotes far more attention to the voyage out than to the homeward journey, which takes up only a few lines of narrative. Xenophon's structure is a little more symmetrical, though his chaotic management of narrative time makes it hard to be dogmatic.[8] In both the primary motivation for the voyage is the separation of the hero and heroine, which means that both are also committed to following the simultaneous adventures of two protagonists, not one—a problem which Chariton solves with characteristic grace and economy, Xenophon rather more creakily: 'Xenophon can think of no very effective means of conducting the parallel actions, and ends up moving his characters more and more wildly around the Mediterranean, like demented chessmen'.[9] In Chariton's narrative, Chaereas and Callirhoe actually are never very far from one another: geographically, Chaereas succeeds in dogging his wife's footsteps fairly closely throughout, and the barriers to their reunion are as much social as geographical (a possibility exploited much more fully later in *Daphnis and Chloe*[10]). Xenophon's more complex plot is still worked out in terms of paired voyages (tripled at times where the robber chief Hippothous becomes a third major character), but the underlying shape of a single journey, with the movement following a

---

8. Part or all of the text may be an epitome: see T. Hägg, 'Die *Ephesiaka* des Xenophon Ephesius: Original oder Epitome?', *Classica et Mediaevalia* 27 (1966), pp. 118-61.

9. Reardon, *Form*, p. 36. Cf. T. Hägg, *Narrative Technique in Ancient Greek Romances: Studies of Chariton, Xenophon Ephesius, and Achilles Tatius* (Skrifter Utgivna av Svenska Institutet i Athen, ser. 8, VIII; Uppsala: Almqvist & Wiksell, 1971), ch. 4.

10. Reardon, *Form*, pp. 30-34.

fundamental loss + search + finding structure, is clearly visible in both.

The overall motivation of the voyaging is thus tied to the essential plot motif of separation, and in the hands of a competent narrator like Chariton this aspect of the plot is generally managed in a plausible fashion. In Xenophon, the travels of the protagonists are noticeably less well motivated: in other words it becomes more obvious with Xenophon that the voyage is a plot necessity which overrides the novelist's 'literary conscience'.[11] Some journeys are completely unmotivated (like Habrocomes' trip to Italy), others simply puzzling (like the original honeymoon trip, which seems precisely the wrong response to an oracle predicting disaster at sea).[12] Sometimes it is simply not clear whether travel is undertaken for the sake of adventure, or whether adventures occur in order to provide an excuse for travel: Habrocomes' trial 'before the prefect of Egypt' seems to be little more than a device for getting the hero to Alexandria after he has inconveniently got himself shipwrecked at the wrong end of the Delta (3.12.6). Even in Chariton, where motivation is generally speaking more plausible, the referral of the trial to the Persian King (4.6-7) can be seen as a device for creating geographical movement to an exotic location; and travel is clearly seen as an adventure in its own right, as part of the *pathos* which the characters have to endure before they can be reunited. Thus Chariton's last book begins,[13]

> Now that Chaereas had made honourable amends to Love, in that he had wandered the world from west to east and gone through untold suffering, Aphrodite took pity on him; having harassed by land and sea the handsome couple she had originally brought together, she decided now to reunite them. (8.1)

What happens if we try to read Acts against this background? The use of the voyage motif shows both similarities with and differences from its use in the novels. The surface motivation for the journeyings of Acts is of course different: the underlying plot, with a series of voyages motivated by a divinely inspired mission to preach the word, suggests a

---

11. The phrase is Reardon's: 'Greek Novel', p. 297.
12. Honeymoon: 1.6-7; Italy: 4.4 (cf. note *ad loc.*, Reardon, *Novels*, p. 157 and n. 2).
13. In the New Testament, the idea of travel as *pathos* is perhaps best exemplified not in Acts but in Paul's own account of his travels in 2 Cor. 11.23-27. It is a salutary reminder that Acts is not the only, and not even the most romantic, New Testament narration of the travels of the apostle.

parallel rather with philosophical biography[14] than with the romance plot of the separation of lovers. But the journey narrative, as we have observed, has its own structural logic irrespective of motivation, and the novels provide an unparalleled resource for understanding the management of this structure in popular narrative (roughly) contemporary with Acts—something which cannot be matched in philosophical biography.[15] It is worthwhile, therefore, to proceed with the comparison on a 'compare and contrast' basis without at this stage raising questions of sources or influence.

It is not difficult, as we have observed, to view the whole narrative of Acts as a voyage, that is, as a description of the geographical expansion of the Gospel message outwards from Jerusalem 'to the end of the earth' (1.8). These words already imply a divine bird's-eye view of the world, and Luke's continued use of the Greek term *oikoumenē* reinforces the sense of a mission with a strong territorial imperative.[16] In Robert Maddox's words, 'the story of Jesus and of the church is a story full of purposeful movement'.[17] But structurally this voyage plot differs in two important ways from the plot of romance. First, if the whole narrative is viewed as a voyage, there is no single traveller to act as focus. If we ask who (or what) travels in this narrative, we are left with many named and nameless individuals (8.4), working under the guidance of a divine spirit (chs. 13, 16): stirring stuff, but not easily paralleled with the plot of romance.[18] The hero of this relentless expansion is not any single individual, but 'the church' (8.1) or perhaps 'the

---

14. Cf. L.C.A. Alexander, 'Acts and Ancient Intellectual Biography', in B.W. Winter and A.C. Clarke (eds.), *The Book of Acts in its First Century Setting*. I. *Ancient Literary Setting* (Grand Rapids: Eerdmans, 1993), pp. 31-63.

15. Alexander, 'Biography', pp. 43-48, on the lack of 'real' narration in Diogenes Laertius. The travel element is best paralleled in the life of Pythagoras, and reappears later in Philostratus's *Life of Apollonius of Tyana*, but it is not typical of the philosophical *bios*.

16. The word occurs more often in Luke–Acts than in the rest of the New Testament put together. Paul uses it only once (Rom. 10.18), in an Old Testament quotation.

17. R. Maddox, *The Purpose of Luke–Acts* (Göttingen: Vandenhoeck & Ruprecht, 1982), p. 11.

18. The parallelism between Peter and Paul does not extend to parallel travel narratives: Peter has only two trips to Joppa, and disappears from the main narrative line after ch. 12, reappearing only briefly in ch. 15 as a secondary character in a scene in which Paul is still the protagonist.

Word'.[19] And secondly, the thrust of this expansive movement is centrifugal: Acts, seen as a whole, does not share the outward-and-return structure of the novels.

Luke's predilection for structuring his narrative in terms of journeying has already been demonstrated in the 'travel-narrative' of the Gospel. In Acts it is of course seen most clearly in the Paul narrative, and it is this which has most obviously attracted comparison with Greek romance. Here too we are struck at first sight by the centrifugal thrust of the plot: in geographical terms (as in much else) Acts is much more open-ended than the classic *nostos*. Paul's final destination is not Jerusalem but Rome. But the narrative significance of this final move may be thrown into relief by the predominantly outward-and-return structure of the Pauline journeys up to the climactic arrest in Jerusalem. What we seem to have is a series of shorter trips out and back from the Antioch base enfolded (in a kind of multiple *inclusio*) in a broader journey which begins and ends in Jerusalem (7.58; 21.17) (Figure 3).

The narrative pull exerted by Jerusalem in Luke's story has often been observed,[20] and it is particularly strong in the closing stages of the travel narrative, where from 19.21 onwards Paul, like his master before him, has firmly 'set his face to go to Jerusalem'.[21] The importance of this structure for Luke is highlighted by a comparison with Paul's own account of his mission in Rom. 15.17-29, which has a much simpler outward momentum 'from Jerusalem as far round as Illyricum', capped by prospective visits to Rome and Spain. For Paul, the impending visit to Jerusalem (15.25) is a temporary detour which he had hoped to be able to avoid (1 Cor. 16.3-4). Luke's different emphasis may be no more than the inevitable result of hindsight.[22] But what is important for our purposes is that this return to Jerusalem gives the journey narrative in Acts a distinctive shape which is much closer to the shape of voyaging

---

19. Cf. Lk. 3.2—the first actor in Luke's account of Jesus' ministry is 'the word of the Lord'.

20. Cf. commentaries and standard works on Pauline chronology: R. Jewett, *A Chronology of Paul's Life* (Philadelphia: Fortress Press, 1979); G. Lüdemann, *Paul, Apostle to the Gentiles: Studies in Chronology* (London: SCM Press, 1984).

21. Lk. 9.51. Cf. Maddox, *Purpose*, pp. 66-67, 76-80, for a cautious overview of the parallelism between Paul and Jesus in Luke–Acts.

22. I would agree with Ed Sanders that it is unlikely Luke could have written a totally fictitious account of events which must have been public knowledge: E.P. Sanders, *Paul* (Past Masters series; Oxford: Oxford University Press, 1991), p. 15.

in the novels than in the Epistles. Moreover Luke notoriously (and puzzlingly) fails to pick up on the practical motivation for the last Jerusalem visit which is explicit in the Epistles: the 'collection' is never mentioned in Acts, and as a result Paul's conviction that he must return (and that he must 'see Rome') is left without motivation. As so often in the novels, it seems that the voyage is predetermined by the author (in this case, Luke implies, by the divine author) before the plot has had chance to provide sufficient motivation. Paul has already indicated that this journey is a 'necessity', and has received divine confirmation in a dream (23.11), long before he calls into play the legal mechanism which actually motivates the journey.[23]

It may be objected that Luke's Pauline narrative is much less neat than those of Chariton and Xenophon, each of which, for all their convolutions, may be viewed as a single voyage. On the traditional reckoning Acts narrates four Pauline journeys (3 'missionary journeys' plus the final trip to Rome), which contrasts not only with the novels but with the single geographical sweep of Rom. 15.19. The contrast may be more apparent than real, however. Clearly Acts gives detail where Paul summarizes, and it is the reconstruction of the geographical data which has led to the accepted schema of 'missionary journeys'. But in narrative terms (i.e. in terms of what the narrator signals in the text) the three-journey structure is much less obvious. There is only one formal commissioning by the church and only one 'sending out' by the Spirit (13.1-4), followed by a second divine intervention in the call to Macedonia (16.6-10), which is not a new voyage but a decision made *en route*. The first voyage is brought to a clear closure with the return to the place 'from which they had been committed to the grace of God for the work which they fulfilled' (14.26), but there is no corresponding closure between the 'second' and the 'third' jouneys: within the space of a few verses, Paul is refusing speaking engagements in Ephesus, promising to return, sailing to Caesarea, going up and greeting 'the church',[24] visiting Antioch, and off again strengthening disciples in Phrygia and Galatia (18.20-23). A much more obvious narrative closure marks the end of Paul's whole missionary activity with the (multiply-signalled) return to Jerusalem, which dovetails with the equally clear

---

23. I am grateful to Cheol-Won Yoon for the observation that the appeal to Caesar functions (in plot terms) as the motive force to get Paul to Rome.

24. Perhaps in Jerusalem, but the text does not say so. Cf. Lüdemann, *Chronology*, pp. 141-57.

signals of the impending journey to Rome. Note also that both the opening stages of the missionary journey (13.4) and its decisive change of direction (16.11) are marked by the fact that the party immediately puts to sea—for the Greek reader, a sure sign that real voyaging is under way. We shall return to this point below.

Mental Maps

'... from the map to learn up painted worlds'[25]

It is an index of the centrality of the voyage motif that the reading of both Acts and the novels seems to demand a map: as Tomas Hägg puts it,[26] 'A map of the Mediterranean region showing the routes of the hero and heroine of a novel inevitably brings to mind the school-bible's map of the travels of St Paul'. But the juxtaposition immediately raises another question: what kind of geographical conceptions would have been shared by the authors and readers of these texts?[27] What kind of mental maps do the narratives presuppose? A 'mental map' in this sense is not simply a chart of the areas of a reader's knowledge or ignorance (a concept which itself assumes that the familiar modern map of the Mediterranean is 'the real map': it is of course itself a construct).

> Human beings appear to have a fundamental need to project order onto the space in which they live and move: they process spatial data received through the senses, relating one element to another and abstracting a mental map or model which functions as a constant frame of reference for all their activities.[28]

In the words of cognitive geographers Gould and White,

> Man exists in what the psychologist David Stea has called 'invisible landscapes', which shape quite strongly his mental images and his behaviour... We are slowly realizing that people's perception of places is

---

25. *e tabula pictos ediscere mundos* (Propertius 4.3.33-40).
26. See the endpapers to Tomas Hägg, *The Ancient Novel*.
27. I have not attempted to provide a full bibliography of the geographical perspectives of biblical and Graeco-Roman literature. For a fuller discussion of the former, see P.S. Alexander, 'Geography and the Bible, Early Jewish', *ABD*, II, pp. 977-88 and now J.M. Scott, 'Luke's Geographical Horizon', in D.W.J. Gill and C. Gempf (eds.), *The Book of Acts in its First Century Setting*. II. *Graeco-Roman Setting* (Grand Rapids: Eerdmans, 1994), pp. 483-544. Scott's paper (which I did not see until after the completion of my own) confirms a number of the points made here.
28. P.S. Alexander, 'Geography and the Bible, Early Jewish', p. 978.

one of the things we must consider as we try to understand the pattern of man's work on the face of the earth.[29]

A cognitive map in this sense does not have to be drawn out on paper, but it can be projected from the patterns of behaviour and language of an individual or group; conversely, pictured maps can be used to illuminate a group's worldview and frame of reference.

The mental map underlying Chariton's voyage narrative is highly schematic and mirrors rather precisely the old Ionian map which dominated the Greek world (and this is very definitely a Greek world, not a Greco-Roman one).[30] Like the Ionian map, Chariton's mental map is an oblong shape much longer than it is wide—or it has breadth but no depth, if you prefer.[31] The action swings from one end of this oblong to the other and finally back again, and its dramatic centre is also the geographical centre, at Miletus, plumb on the Ionian meridian which ran down the western coast of Asia Minor from Lysimachia on the Propontis to Alexandria.[32] The sea is at the centre of this view of the world, and its major routes are sea-routes. Most of the action happens along a longitudinal axis drawn along the Mediterranean from Sicily in the West to the crossing of the Euphrates at Zeugma or Thapsacus—though, as we shall see, Chariton's knowledge of the East beyond the Euphrates is distinctly woolly. This axis corresponds closely to Dicaearchus' *diaphragma*, which was, according to Agathemerus,

> a straight line drawn from the Pillars through Sardinia, Sicily, Peloponnessus, Ionia, Caria, Lycia, Pamphylia, Cilicia, and the Taurus, one after another, up to the Imaus mountains.[33]

---

29. P. Gould and R. White, *Mental Maps* (Harmondsworth: Penguin, 1974), pp. 141, 45.

30. On ancient maps in general see O.A.W. Dilke, *Greek and Roman Maps* (London: Thames & Hudson, 1985). On the Ionian map, see W.A. Heidel, *The Frame of the Ancient Greek Maps* (New York: Arno Press, 1976, repr. of original edn, New York: American Geographical Society, Research Series no. 20, 1937).

31. Heidel, *Frame*, p. 17.

32. Heidel, *Frame*, pp. 124-5

33. Heidel, *Frame*, pp. 111-12, citing Agathemerus 1.5 (GGM 472). Heidel continues, 'This line, we know, was adopted by Eratosthenes as the main longitudinal axis of his chart (Strabo II,i,1)... [I]t practically coincided with the equator of the Ionian map between the Pillars and Asia Minor. From thence the text of Herodotus based on the 'Persian map' indicates a line, marking the boundary between the tract (*akte*) of Asia Minor and that of Syria, in the same direction as far as the Eastern limits of Persia.'

Although this line is roughly parallel with the Equator, it produces an elongation of the Mediterranean (and especially of the 'Ionian Sea' which figures so large in Chariton's narrative) which can clearly be seen in reconstructions of the world map of Eratosthenes. According to Strabo, Eratosthenes placed even Athens on the same parallel (*Geog.* 67-68 [II.i.1]):

> In the third book of his Geography Eratosthenes, in establishing the map of the inhabited world, divides it into two parts by a line drawn from west to east, parallel to the equatorial line... He draws the line from the Pillars through the Strait of Sicily and also through the southern capes both of the Peloponnesus and of Attica, and as far as Rhodes and the Gulf of Issus... and indeed our whole Mediterranean Sea itself extends, lengthwise, along this line as far as Cilicia... then the line is produced in an approximately straight course along the whole Taurus range as far as India... so that in like manner both the Taurus and the Sea from the Pillars up to the Taurus lie on the parallel of Athens (Figures 4, 5).

If we trace Callirhoe's journey on one of these maps rather than on a modern projection, it becomes clear that the whole of her journey (including the stop 'opposite Athens') is along this same west–east axis, and she scarcely deviates from it on her return when she is incarcerated on Aradus. Chaereas is allowed a little more north–south movement, but not much: the initial search party taking him toward North Africa is narrated in the briefest of summaries and does not really form part of the narrative at all; and the Egyptian king is well into Phoenicia before Chaereas catches up with him.

But what of the great set-piece journey to Babylon, which (as we all know) is well to the south of this line? We may know it, and Chariton's contemporary Arrian knows it, as his acount of Alexander's expedition makes clear, but I am not sure that Chariton does. There is nothing in the text to indicate that Dionysius's party turn south (or 'down-river') after the crossing of the Euphrates, and I suspect that for Chariton, Babylon (which represents the Oriental world) is simply 'East of the River'.[34] This is why Mithridates and his party, travelling from Caria via Armenia, actually arrive in Babylon faster than Dionysius travelling through Cilicia—which is a little surprising on any cartographic projection. Chariton's knowledge of the route to Babylon is a classic example

---

34. Contrast Arrian's detailed knowledge of the topography of the river crossings and the approach to Babylon: cf. *Anab.* 3.7-8, 15-16.

of what Gould and White call travelling 'through a tube of ignorance', illustrated by overheard conversations of the form:

> 'We went to Majorca for our holidays'
> 'Where is Majorca?'
> 'I don't know exactly, we flew'.[35]

Habitual motorway drivers experience a similar phenomenon, in which geographical space is understood not as territory on a two-dimensional map projection but as a series of points on a one-dimensional itinerary: as in the *Peutinger Tafel*, the spatial relations of points on different itineraries are distorted because they are not important (Figure 6). The Euphrates crossings at Zeugma and Thapsacus are, as it happens, more or less due East of Syracuse and Miletus—therefore to all intents and purposes Babylon is 'in the East' (since you get to it by travelling East), and Callirhoe's trial takes place on the eastern limits of Chariton's Greek world (Figure 7).

Xenophon's narrative world is equally centred on the Mediterranean, though its proportions are slightly different from Chariton's: this mental map has depth as well as breadth. Again, the Ionian meridian forms its primary axis, with the action starting and finishing in Ephesus. The couple's disastrous honeymoon trip is heading due south down this meridian to Alexandria when it is rudely interrupted by pirates: the maritime location of the disaster is undefined (1.13.3), but its source is identified as Rhodes, where the pirates first catch sight of their prospective booty (1.13.1). Fittingly, the final resolution also takes place in Rhodes (5.10-15), which as the point of intersection between the prime meridian and Dicaearchus's longitudinal axis qualifies as the geographical centre of this particular mental map (cf. Figure 4). Before that point, however, the lovers have travelled East, South and then West in a hectic tangle of separate journeys. The Orient for Xenophon is represented by Syria, with Cilicia and Cappadocia as extensions of the eastern voyage, I think, rather than a separate northern expedition.[36] After failing to meet in the East, the lovers follow separate sea-ways south to Egypt and Ethiopia, followed doggedly on land by the bandit chief Hippothous who has fallen for Habrocomes. Both thus eventually reach Alexandria, the destination of their original voyage, but separately and in various harrowing circumstances. Habrocomes gives up at this point and heads off

35. Gould and White, *Mental Maps*, pp. 119-20.
36. North is represented by Hippothous's story of his own origins at Perinthus (3.2), but this is not part of the primary narrative.

to the West: it is left to Anthia and Hippothous to explore Ethiopia, the traditional southern extremity of the Ionian maps[37] (and an area fruitfully exploited by the later novelist Heliodorus). Anthia is threatened with an even longer voyage, as she leaves Egypt en route for India (4.3.1). On Xenophon's mental map, India is 'south' in the same sense as Chariton's Babylon is 'east': the important fact is that the route to India (at least one of the major trading routes) runs south through Egypt and Ethiopia before heading for the Indian Ocean at Coptos.[38] The final phase of this exercise in 'boxing the compass' is westward, when the three all find themselves (for different reasons) in Greater Greece (Sicily and southern Italy) before heading back to the centre for their reunion in Rhodes (Figure 8).

Xenophon's map, then, seems best explained in terms of travel routes rather than territorial overview. As with Chariton the patterns of movement are highly schematic, but Xenophon's pattern is triangular rather than linear. Some of these routes are better known than others. Xenophon knows of three routes from Cilicia to Egpyt (though details along the way are decidedly sketchy[39]); and it is interesting that he knows the trade-route to India via Coptos, which, as he tells us himself, attracts 'a great crowd of merchants passing through for Ethiopia and India'.[40] But the sea-route from Alexandria to Italy is described in the minimum of words (4.4.2; 5.1.1), and Habrocomes's final route home (Sicily–Crete–Cyprus–Rhodes) looks like a nonsense, except perhaps on the assumption that the list represents a well-known list of destinations for ships heading into the eastern Mediterranean from Sicily (cf. the return voyage of Cheareas and Callirhoe) in which the order of the ports of call has been muddled.

The predominance of the Ionian mental map and the centrality of the sea for the voyages of Greek romance throw into relief the rather

37. Strabo, *Geog.* 3 (1.1.6); Heidel, *Frame*, pp. 26-28.
38. 4.1.5. For the importance of this route, cf. L. Casson, *The Periplus Maris Erythraei* (Princeton: University Press, 1989), pp. 13-14.
39. Cf. Dalmeyda on 4.1.1-5, 'Cet itinéraire d'Hippothous est d'une aimable fantaisie. Rohde dit avec raison que ce sont là proprement dit des μυρμήκων ἀτραποί. Xénophon se pique de géographie, mais sa science ne va pas très loin et il semble ici jouer avec des noms de localités égyptiennes' (Dalmeyda, *Xénophon*, p. 49 n. 2)
40. 4.1.5; Schedia (4.1.3, 5.2.7) must have been also well known to traders: Strabo, *Geog.* 800 (17.1.16) describes it as 'the station for paying duty on the goods brought down [sc. down-river] from above it and brought up from below it'.

different geographical perspectives of Acts. Luke's story really has two mental maps, one centred on Jerusalem and one on the Mediterranean, and the movement from the one to the other enables us to chart a profound cultural shift within early Christianity. The geographical importance of the list of nations in Acts 2.9-11 has long been recognized. Whether or not the table has affinities with 'astrological geography',[41] it is clear that it presupposes a vision of the world centred on Jerusalem, like the later mediaeval Christian maps and like the contemporary map presupposed by the book of *Jubilees*.[42] Richard Bauckham in a recent lecture argues rightly, I think, that the names in the table are best understood as representative of different directions viewed from Jerusalem: the East (Parthians, Medes, Elamites and residents of Mesopotamia), the centre (Judaea), the North (Cappadocia, Pontus, Asia, Phrygia and Pamphylia), the South-West (Egypt and Libya), the West (Rome and Crete) and the South (Arabia).[43] Rome stands for the West because that is the direction from which its representatives appear—and Crete is on their direct route. Luke resists the temptation to take his primary narrative into these unexplored regions, though the episode of the Ethiopian eunuch allows the reader to feel that the narrative has touched the exotic at one remove (much as Chariton is able to bring a southern dimension into his tale through the secondary narrative of the Egyptian king). But the implied narratives of the other, unnamed travellers of Acts 2 serve to back up the claim that the preaching of the gospel is a world-wide event: the charge of 'turning the world upside down' (17.6, 24.5) is welcomed rather than refuted (26.6).

Viewing the world from this Jerusalem-centred perspective has some interesting side-effects. It means that the Aegean is masked from sight, an unexplored backwater into which the westward-bound traveller has no need to penetrate (an effect which is exaggerated in later Christian

41. S. Weinstock, 'The Geographical Catalogue in Acts II,9-11', *JRS* 38 (1948), pp. 43-46; J.A. Brinkman, 'The Literary Background of the "Catalogue of the Nations"', *CBQ* 25 (1963), pp. 418-27; B.M. Metzger, 'Ancient Astrological Geography and Acts 2.9-11', in W.W. Gasque and R.P. Martin (eds.), *Apostolic History and the Gospel: Biblical and Historical Essays presented to F.F. Bruce on his 60th Birthday* (Exeter: Paternoster Press, 1970), pp. 123-33; Scott, 'Luke's Geographical Horizon', pp. 527-30.

42. P.S. Alexander, ' Geography and the Bible, Early Jewish', pp. 980-82; Scott, 'Luke's Geographical Horizon', pp. 524-44.

43. R. Bauckham, 'James at the Centre: A Jerusalem Perspective on New Testament History and Canon' (Inaugural Lecure, University of St Andrews, 1994).

maps, where it has shrunk to the size of a creek) (Figures 10, 11). This may be one reason for the puzzling omission from Luke's list of Macedonia and Achaia, the areas where Paul is to spend so much of his time. But the omission may also be precisely *because* Paul is to spend his time there: it allows Luke to present these areas as virgin territory unreached by the gospel (unlike Rome, which already has a church when Paul arrives), and to assign to Paul an exploratory role which reverses the presuppositions of the Greek geographers. To explore is to travel beyond the boundaries of the known world. For Greek romance with its Ionian worldview, this means pressing beyond the known world of the Aegean to the unknown East (Syria, Phoenicia, Babylon) or South (Egypt, Ethiopia) or West (Sicily, Italy). But to a worldview centred on Jerusalem, the Aegean may be equally unknown territory, and its penetration by the emissaries of the gospel is a geographical achievement worthy of celebration. Paul's ministry in Macedonia and Greece simply does not fit into the world-map of Acts 2: his crossing of the Bosporus marks a breaking out of the known world, a new step carefully signalled in the narrative by a series of false moves successively blocked by the Spirit (16.6-8). It is hardly surprising that the decisive move requires the explicit guidance of a dream (16.9-10).

The voyages of Acts 16 and onwards, then, have already extended the boundaries of the mental map of Acts 2. By the final phases of the narrative the perspective has shifted decisively to a Mediterranean-centred map whose co-ordinates reflect those of Chariton and Xenophon. Jerusalem is the place where Paul's story begins (for narrator and readers—it is only later that we learn of his birth in Tarsus) and the goal to which it has been reverting from 19.21 onwards. But Paul's final voyage takes him by carefully charted stages in a new direction (also announced in 19.21) from which the narrative offers no return: Jerusalem is no longer the centre of a circle but the eastern edge of a westerly voyage which follows the sea-routes more familiar to the Greek reader than to the Bible.

The Significance of Sea-Travel

—As some grave Tyrian trader, from the sea,
Descried at sunrise an emerging prow...
And knew the intruders on his ancient home [44]

---

44. Matthew Arnold, *The Scholar-Gipsy*.

This shift in geographical perspective is reflected in an equally significant shift in the mode of travel. We noted above that decisive stages in Paul's missionary journey are marked not only by divine guidance but also by the fact that the journey becomes (however briefly) a sea-voyage. The commissioning of the Spirit in Acts 13.4 leads the party directly to the port of Seleucia, from where they sail (ἀπέπλευσαν) to Cyprus; the same verb marks their return to Antioch with the commission fulfilled (14.26). Similarly the crossing from Asia Minor to Macedonia in Acts 16.11 is described in terms which emphasize the nautical nature of the voyage (ἀναχθέντες, εὐθυδρομήσαμεν). Indications of sea-travel recur at intervals throughout the Aegean ministry, clustering particularly around the return to Jerusalem, and reaching a climax in the final voyage to Rome.[45] The narrative of ch. 27 is (as commentators have long observed[46]) richly embellished with nautical terms, and full of realistic detail which ensures that the reader cannot forget that Paul's last journey is a *plous*, a sea-voyage.

To appreciate the full force of the lexical choices made here by Luke, we have only to look at Paul's own vocabulary of travel. Paul never uses the verb πλέω or any of its cognates, but speaks of his extensive journeys in non-specific terms (ἔρχομαι, πορεύομαι): it would be hard to tell from Romans 15, for example, that any sea-travel at all was involved in the projected trip to the West. This may be because from Corinth, where Paul is writing, it is more natural to contemplate the short crossing to Italy via Brundisium,[47] or it may be that Paul simply did not like the sea (his attitude to it in 2 Cor. 11 certainly suggests that[48]). But it is not the possible authorial motives that interest us here so

---

45. 20.6, 13-16, 38; 21.1-3, 6-7; 27 *passim*.

46. See on this passage E. Norden, *Agnostos Theos: Untersuchungen zur Formengeschichte religiöser Rede* (Stuttgart: Teubner 1956 [1913]), pp. 313-27; M. Dibelius, *Studies in the Acts of the Apostles* (ed. H. Greeven; London: SCM Press, 1956), pp. 7-9, 204-206; V.K. Robbins, 'By Land and by Sea: The We-passages and Ancient Sea-Voyages', in C.H. Talbert (ed.), *Perspectives on Luke–Acts* (Edinburgh: T. & T. Clark, 1978), pp. 215-42. Cf. further note 50.

47. The mention of Illyricum in the same passage suggests that the land routes were in his mind.

48. Paul uses θάλασσα only in Old Testament allusions apart from 2 Cor. 11.26, which speaks in lurid terms of 'danger by sea'. This passage also includes (v. 25) the dramatic ἐναυάγησα and ἐν τῷ βυθῷ, which echoes LXX Ps. 106. (I am indebted to Brian Dodd for this observation.) Does Acts 20.3, 13 reflect a known apostolic distaste for sea travel?

much as the effects on the reader. Acts foregrounds an aspect of Paul's travels which Paul himself prefers to ignore, or at least (except in the notoriously rhetorical passage 2 Cor. 11) to downplay. Moreover Luke has carefully prepared the ground in such a way that Paul (and his party) are the only characters who travel by sea in the whole two-volume narrative: Galilee for Luke is a 'lake' (λίμνη), not the sea (θάλασσα or πέλαγος), so that, in Vernon Robbins's words, 'Only Paul and his associates face the challenge, adventure, and destiny of voyaging across the sea'.[49] It is well known that this proliferation of nautical terms is almost (but not quite) coextensive with the 'we-passages'. But again, it is no part of my purpose here to explore the many theories about the possible reasons for this odd phenomenon.[50] Rather than speculating about the author and/or his sources, I am interested to explore its effects on the readers, and especially on readers acquainted with Greek romance.

The theme of journeying by sea is not of course unique to the novel in Greek literature. Its obvious and ever-present archetype is the *Odyssey*, which has its Roman counterpart in the *Aeneid*. For both these foundational narratives, the hero reaches his goal via a sea-voyage, in which islands are more familiar than the continental interior, and whole regions are known solely by their coastlands and ports. The popularity of this kind of voyage narrative among the Greeks (as among the Irish and the Scandinavians) must reflect the importance of the sea, and especially of the coastal voyage, in the Greek perception of the world. For much of Greek history, sea travel was quicker and more convenient than land travel. Thus, for Xenophon's mercenaries, in a famous scene, a distant glimpse of the sea means release from a nightmare and the prospect of homecoming (*Anabasis* 4.7.20-27). Travellers' tales appeared in prose as well as in verse: the *periplous* and the *periegesis* provided a convenient and durable format for scientific exploration, for merchant handbooks, as a basis for mapping, and (increasingly under the Empire) for a growing public of armchair travellers which enjoyed reading lengthy

49. Robbins, 'By Land and by Sea', p. 216. The nearest any other character gets to the sea is Acts 10.6, where we are told that Peter is staying 'by the sea' at the point when he receives his horizon-extending dream.

50. See, in addition to the literature cited in n. 46, S.M. Praeder, 'The Problem of First Person Narration in Acts', *NovT* 29 (1987), pp. 193-218; J. Wehnert, *Die Wir-Passagen der Apostelgeschichte: Ein lukanisches Stilmittel aus jüdischer Tradition* (Göttingen: Vandenhoeck & Ruprecht, 1989); S.E. Porter, 'Excursus: The "We" Passages', in D.W.J. Gill and C. Gempf (eds.), *The Book of Acts in its First Century Setting*. II. *Graeco-Roman Setting* (Grand Rapids: Eerdmans, 1993), pp. 545-74.

geographical descriptions in the form of a voyage around the coasts of the Mediterranean.[51]

This literary context is important to bear in mind when we consider the role of the sea in the novels of Chariton and Xenophon. For both, voyaging begins with embarkation, and ends with a triumphant landfall.[52] Nautical terminology defines the means of travel: these adventurers 'sail' from one theatre of action to another; 'finding a ship' is an important event.[53] The sea is a potential source of danger and disaster: crossing it is an adventure in itself, yet it unites the lovers as well as separating them.[54] And, as Chariton especially makes clear in a number of set-piece speeches, the Mediterranean is seen as 'the Greek sea', the area where his Greek characters feel at home and where they can effortlessly triumph over the massed forces of oriental despotism.[55] This feeling is made explicit on Callirhoe's inland journey to Babylon, when the narrator tells us that

> Callirhoe was distressed to be taken far from the Greek sea; as long as she could see the harbors of Miletus, she had the impression that Syracuse was not far away; and Chaereas' tomb in Miletus was great comfort to her (4.7.8).

As 'an island woman' (νησιῶτις) she expresses poignantly her feelings on crossing the Euphrates, 'beyond which there is a vast stretch of unending land':

---

51. Dilke, *Greek and Roman Maps*, ch. 6, gives a useful survey of the genre. For the *periplous* format in exploration, cf. Hanno, Scylax, Arrian, Nearchus; for merchant handbooks, cf. the *Periplus Maris Erythraei* (above n. 38). For the (sometimes uneasy) relationship between these accounts and the mapmakers, cf. F.W. Walbank, 'The Geography of Polybius', *Classica et Mediaevalia* 9 (1948), pp. 155-82; C. van Paassen, *The Classical Tradition of Geography* (Groningen, 1957); P. Pédech, *La méthode historique de Polybe* (Paris, 1964), ch. 12; and compare the extensive discussion in book two of Strabo's *Geography* (e.g. 71 [2.1.11]: even the astronomer Hipparchus 'trusted the sailors'). For armchair travellers, cf. Aelius Aristides, *Or.* 14 = 1.226.7 (395), Dindorf edn. For *Periegeseis* of the Mediterranean, cf. Pseudo-Scymnus, Dionysius Calliphontis (C. Müller, *Geographi Graeci Minores* [Paris: Didot, 1855], I, pp. 196-237, 238-39).

52. Chariton: 1.10.8–11.1; 3.3.8, 4.17, 5.1-9; 8.6.1-12. Xenophon: 1.10.3–11.6; 5.15.1.

53. E.g. Xenophon 3.10.4; 5.10.2.

54. E.g. Chariton 3.5.9, 6.6, 10.8; 4.1.5-6, 7.8; and cf. 1.14.9, where Reardon accepts Hercher's conjecture πελάγει.

55. Cf. e.g. 7.5.8, 6.1-2; 8.2.12.

Now it is not Ionia where you [Fortune] keep me exiled; the land you allotted to me up to now was admittedly a foreign country, but it was Greek, and there I could take comfort in the thought that I was living by the sea. Now you are hurling me from my familiar world—I am at the other end of the earth from my own country. This time it is Miletus you have taken from me; before, it was Syracuse. I am being taken beyond the Euphrates, shut up in the depths of barbarian land where the sea is far away—I, an island woman! What ship can I hope will come sailing after me from Sicily now? (5.1.5-6)

The sea, then, is an important mode of travel in the novels and provides the opportunity for many of their adventures. Despite its dangers it is seen as a natural route of communication, linking the Greek cities and islands across the Mediterranean seaboard. Inland are no cities (no Greek cities, that is) but the lands of the barbarians, peopled with bandits—and foreigners. Beyond the Euphrates, as we have seen, lie the 'unending lands' of 'the king's great empire' (5.1.3); but even Caria, in Chariton's historical imagination, is a citiless desert, the territory of a Persian satrap worked by chain-gangs (3.7.3; 4.2.1ff.). Chariton's Babylon is rather like Mozart's *Seraglio*, a stereotype of the oriental court, characterized by the scheming of eunuchs and the 'kow-towing' of courtiers;[56] this is a thoroughgoing case of 'Orientalism',[57] redeemed only by the humanity and irony of this author's characterization.[58] Xenophon is less concerned than Chariton with creating a 'historical' setting for his tale, but his view of the lands travelled by his characters is equally depressing. Phoenicia is 'a barbarian land' peopled by 'lustful pirates' (2.1.2), and Syria is little better: Anthia spends her time there with a country goatherd. Egypt, despite the endeavours of the 'prefect', is overrun with bandits; and Psammis, the Indian merchant-prince, is not only naturally lustful (the collocation with ἄνθρωπος βάρβαρος suggests that the two facts are connected) but also 'superstitious like all barbarians' (δεισιδαίμονες δὲ φύσει βάρβαροι, 3.11.4).[59]

---

56. Reardon's apt equivalent for *proskunēsis* (p. 79 n. 79). The 'orientalism' of the Babylonian court is carefully conveyed through the use of stock characters (the satraps, the eunuch, the queen and her ladies) and behaviour (e.g. 5.9.1; 6.3.1–7.10) as well as by set-piece descriptions (5.4.5-6; 6.4).

57. I owe the term to E. Said, *Orientalism* (London: Routledge & Kegan Paul, 1978).

58. E.g. 5.3.1-10; 8.3.1-11.

59. The identical reaction of Polyidus to Anthia at 5.4.5-7 is not described as

Against this background we may begin to appreciate the full effects of Luke's presentation of Paul as a sea-voyager. We have already noted that the Jerusalem-centred perspective of the first half of Acts entails a reversal of the usual Greek perspective on the world: for Luke's hero, Syria and Phoenicia are home ground, while the Aegean is unexplored territory. The reversal is highlighted by occasional touches of regional characterization. The only 'barbarians' in Acts are in the West, not in the East (28.2); and it is the Athenians, in the heartland of Greek culture, who are described as 'superstitious' (δεισιδαιμονεστέρους, 17.22).[60] For the Greek reader, this is 'turning the world upside down' (17.6) with a vengeance.

The cultural significance of the Athens episode has been well analysed by a number of commentators: here Paul is presented as a new Socrates, beating the philosophers at their own game.[61] Paul's sea-voyages, I would suggest, represent a parallel act of narrative aggression. Chariton claims the sea as Greek cultural territory (much as the British used to do), and it is a claim with which readers of the Greek classics could easily identify.[62] Moreover it is not a claim which many readers of the Bible would care to dispute: in the book of Jonah, which offers the only parallel narrative in the Hebrew Bible, the hero's sea-trip is a disastrous mistake; and in the New Testament the book of Revelation notoriously (and to the lasting regret of that very British poet Rudyard Kipling) looks forward to an eschatological future in which 'the sea was no more' (Rev. 21.1). Paul himself, as we have seen, describes his experiences of sea-travel in lurid terms scarcely bettered by the novelists (2 Cor. 11), and carefully avoids drawing attention to the practicalities of his journeys. Like a presidential candidate on the campaign trail, the apostle travels from venue to venue without having to think about the means of travel at all, relying on his team to study the timetables and make the reservations. For the narrator of Acts, by contrast, sea travel is a matter of consuming interest. This narrator

---

'barbarian'. For a similar combination (φύσει...τὸ βάρβαρον γυναιμανές), cf. Chariton 5.2.6.

60. Chariton's picture of Athens is also slightly ironic: compare 1.11.6-7 with Acts 17.21.

61. For full discussion and bibliography, cf. Alexander, 'Ancient Intellectual Biography', pp. 31-63.

62. For a full collection of texts, cf. A. Lesky, *Thalatta: Der Weg der Griechen zum Meer* (New York: Arno Press, 1973 [1896]).

(note the association of 'we-narration' with the sea) is perfectly at home on the sea, able to find seagoing connections with ease, familiar with the names of winds and harbours, alert to the complexities of shipping traffic in the Aegean and the Mediterranean.[63] The sea is presented as a proper sphere of activity for the emissaries of the gospel.[64] The hero on his last voyage is calm in the face of the storm, better at forecasting wind and weather than helmsman and captain, able to dominate the panic-stricken crew in the shipwreck.[65] Jonah's situation is reversed: far from being the cause of the ship's peril, Paul is the reason for its salvation. It is because of his mission, and his destined arrival in Rome, that its 276 souls will be delivered 'all safe to land'.[66] Clearly, as many commentators have seen, there is a theological claim implicit in the shipwreck narrative of Acts 27. Paul's God dominates and controls the sea crossing for him just as Aphrodite and Isis do for the heroines of the novels:[67]

> Just before she went on board, Callirhoe made an obeisance to Aphrodite. 'I thank you, lady', she said, 'for what is happening now. You are reconciled to me now; grant that I see Syracuse too! A great stretch of sea separates me from there; an ocean is waiting for me that is frightening to cross; but I am not frightened if you are sailing with me' (8.4.10).

But a comparison with the geographical perspectives of the novels also makes it clear, I would suggest, that the narrator is implicitly laying claim to a cultural territory which many readers, both Greek and Judaeo-Christian, would perceive as inherently 'Greek'.[68]

---

63. Acts 20.13-16; 21.1-3; 27.1-2, 4-8, 12-16; 28.11-13.
64. For this concept, cf. V.K. Robbins, 'Luke–Acts: A Mixed Population Seeks a Home in the Roman Empire', in L.C.A. Alexander (ed.), *Images of Empire* (Sheffield: JSOT Press, 1991), pp. 202-21; but I would be inclined to see the relationship with Greek aspirations here as more aggressive, less 'symbiotic' than Robbins does.
65. 27.9-10, 21-26, 30-36.
66. Cf. nn. 46, 50 above for bibliography on Paul's shipwreck.
67. On the identification of Aphrodite with the sea, cf. Lesky, *Thalatta*, pp. 279-82. For the parallel role of Isis in the *Ephesiaca*, cf. Dalmeyda, *Xénophon*, pp. xvi-xvii, and esp. 5.13.2-4.
68. The Romans also had an interest in claiming dominance of the sea (and the claim was asserted in imperial monuments found in Chariton's home town of Aphrodisias: C. Nicolet, *Space, Geography, and Politics in the Early Roman Empire* [Jerome Lectures, 19; Ann Arbor: University of Michigan Press, 1991 (ET of

Conclusions

It is time to try to draw some tentative conclusions. It seems clear from this preliminary exploration at least that the comparison between Acts and the novels is well worth pursuing: even the limited topic of voyaging has thrown up a variety of leads which could be pursued at greater depth than has been possible here. But the exercise must also take note of differences as well as similarities, and should ideally be pursued in full awareness of the broader cultural context: romance does not have a monopoly on voyage narratives. I would like to finish by making some observations on this broader context.

Frederick Brenk has demonstrated in a recent article[69] how the wall paintings of the temple of Isis at Pompeii suggest ways in which the Roman worshipper could be

> successively drawn deeper and deeper into the profundities of Egyptian religion and thus transformed... The painting, like the architecture, innocently Greco-Roman in appearance, becomes more dangerously religious as one 'zooms in' on a world continually more mysterious and Egyptian in imagery and theme.

The comfortable and familiar landscapes of 'romantic Hellenism' are seen on closer inspection to be dotted with Egyptian buildings and symbols, so that 'seemingly innocent and innocuous iconography, veiled in familiar garb, only gradually begins to reveal its deeper meaning'. At one level we may legitimately, I think, compare Luke's use of the narrative techniques of romance with the 'innocuous iconography' of these wall paintings, a device to introduce the Greek or Roman reader to a new and 'exotic' religion by easy stages. But at the level of the narrative itself the position is reversed. Luke cannot dot the romantic landscape with 'Christian' buildings and symbols because such things do not exist. Even the 'synagogues' which form the most prominent feature of his cities are community groups rather than architectural features rivalling the temples of the Greek gods. Instead, we have suggested, Luke structures his narrative in such a way that his hero is

---

L'inventaire du monde: Geographie et politique aux origines de l'Empire Romain [Libraire Arthème Foyard, 1988])], pp. 45-47): but we cannot pursue this important topic here.

69. F.E. Brenk, 'A Gleaming Ray: Blessed Afterlife in the Mysteries', *Illinois Classical Studies* 18 (1993), pp. 147-64 (157-64).

presented as 'invading' Greek cultural territory: first the 'hidden' ports of the Aegean, then the 'Greek sea' itself. It is as daring in its way as the paintings of the Iseum, and potentially—at least for the Greek reader—much more disturbing.

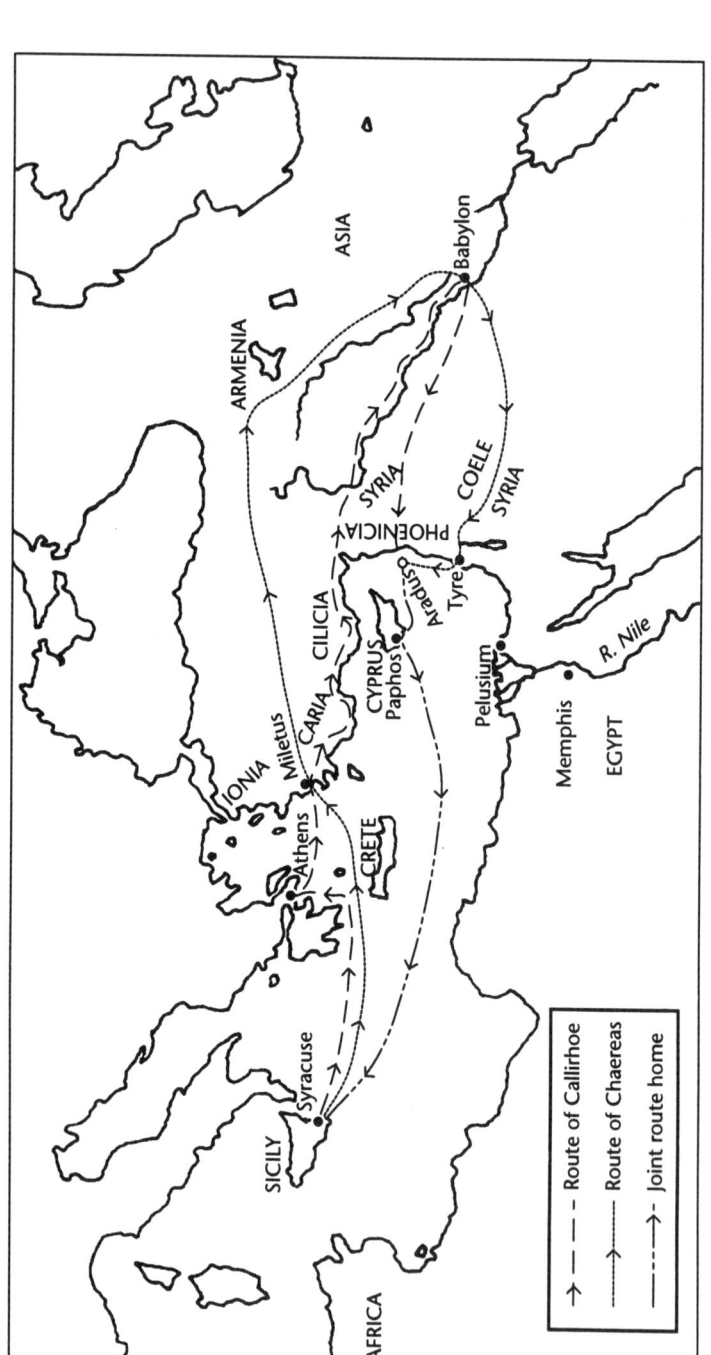

Figure 1. *Chariton: The Travels of Chaereas and Callirhoe.*

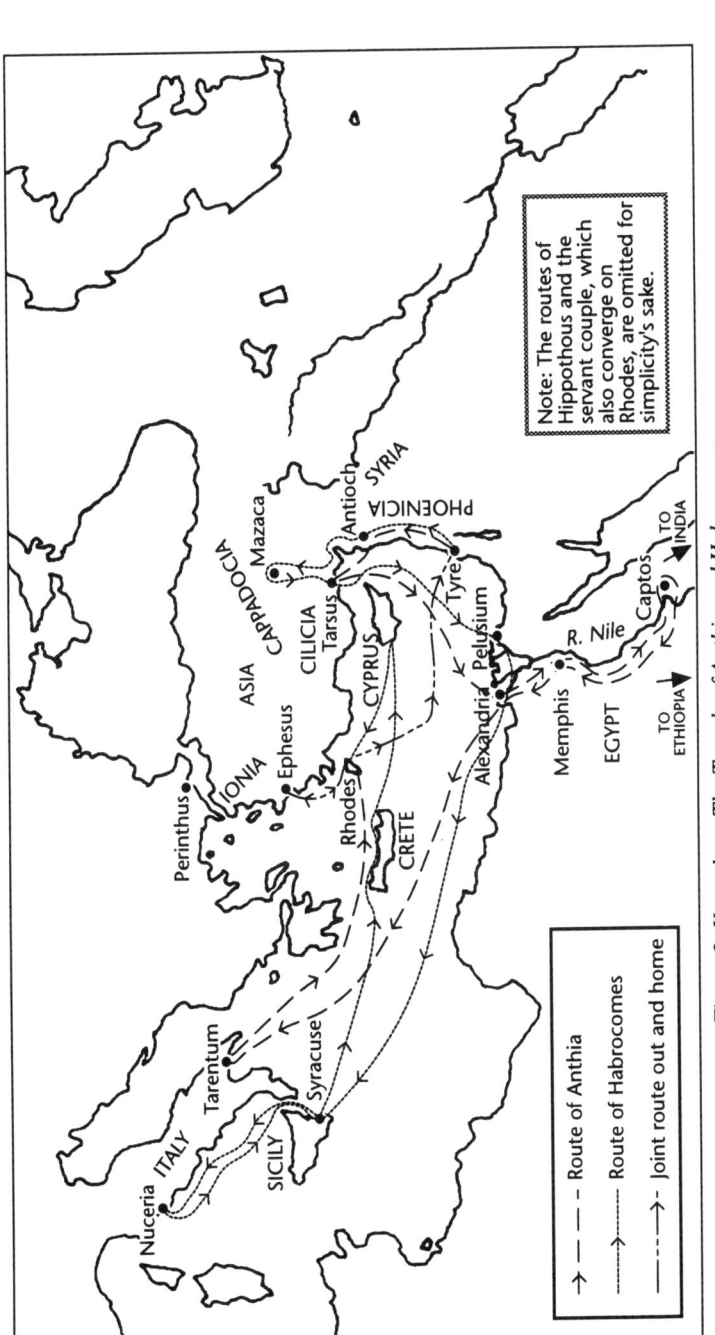

Figure 2. Xenophon: The Travels of Anthia and Habrocomes.

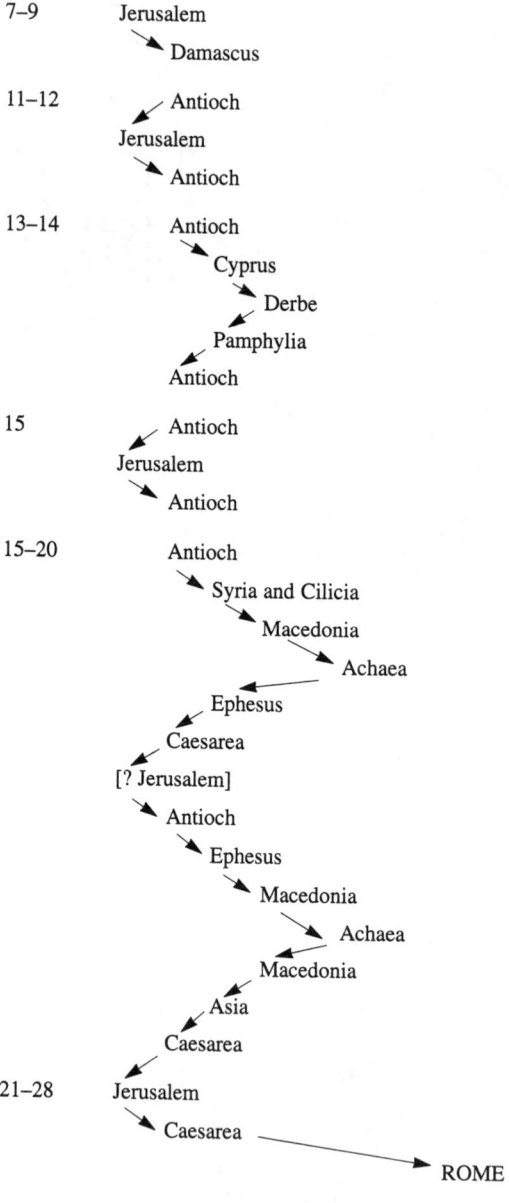

Figure 3. *Inclusio Diagram*

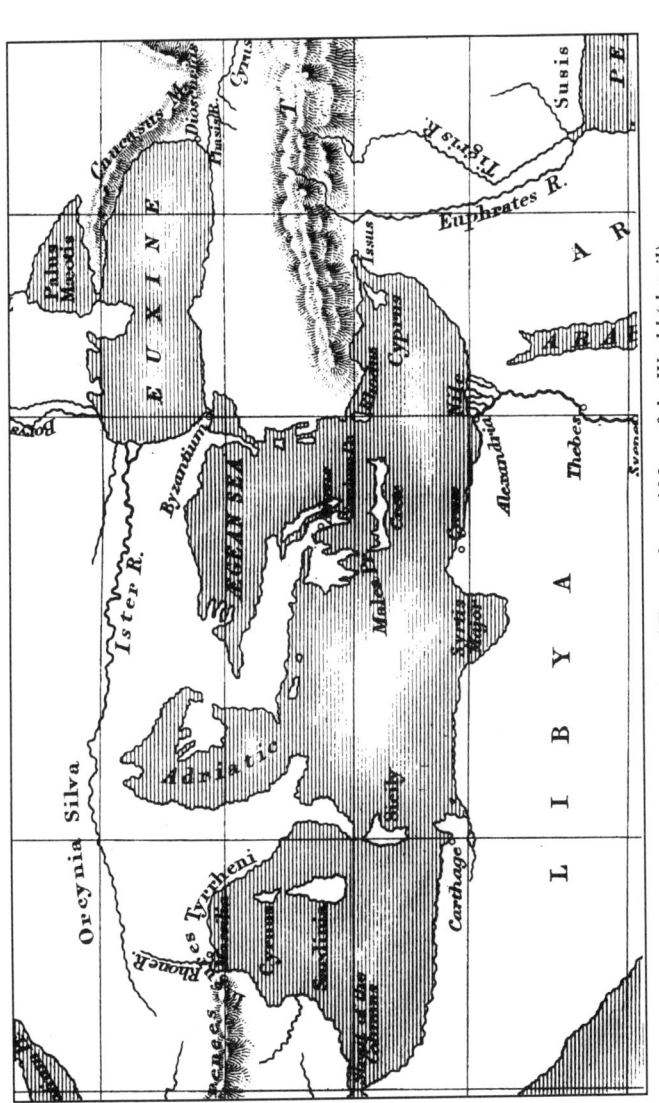

Figure 4. *Reconstruction of Eratosthenes' Map of the World (detail).*
From E.H. Bunbury, *A History of Ancient Geography*, I (London: John Murray, 2nd edn, 1883), after p. 660.

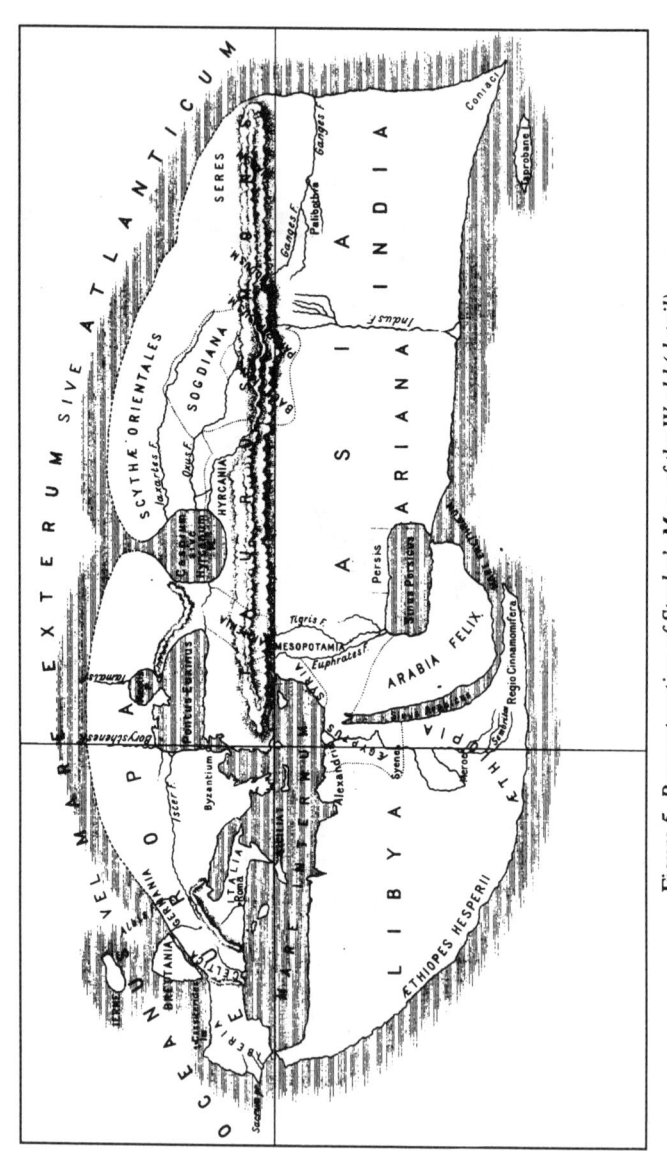

Figure 5. *Reconstruction of Strabo's Map of the World (detail)*.
From H.F. Tozer, *A History of Ancient Geography*, (Cambridge: Cambridge University Press, 1897), facing p. 239.

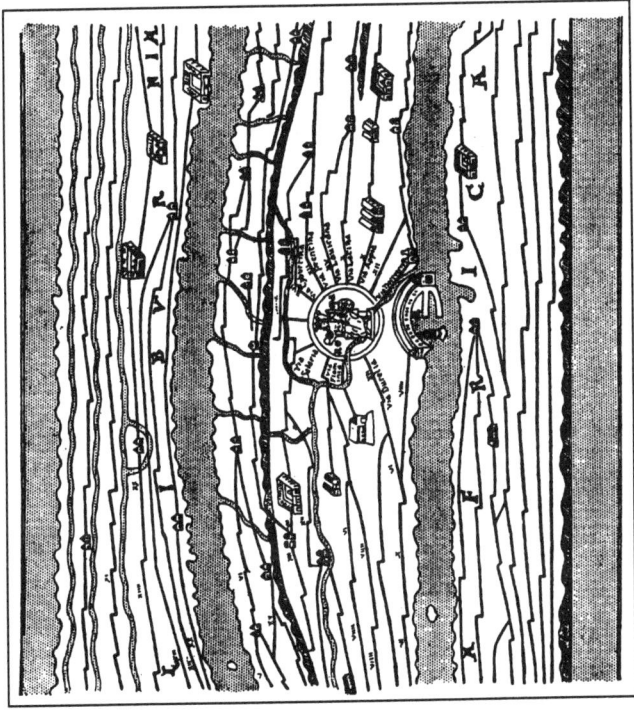

Figure 6. *Detail from the Peutinger Tafel (fourth cent. CE), Showing Roads Leading to Rome.* From M.B. Synge, *A Book of Discovery* (London: T.C. & E.C. Jack, n.d.), p. 62.

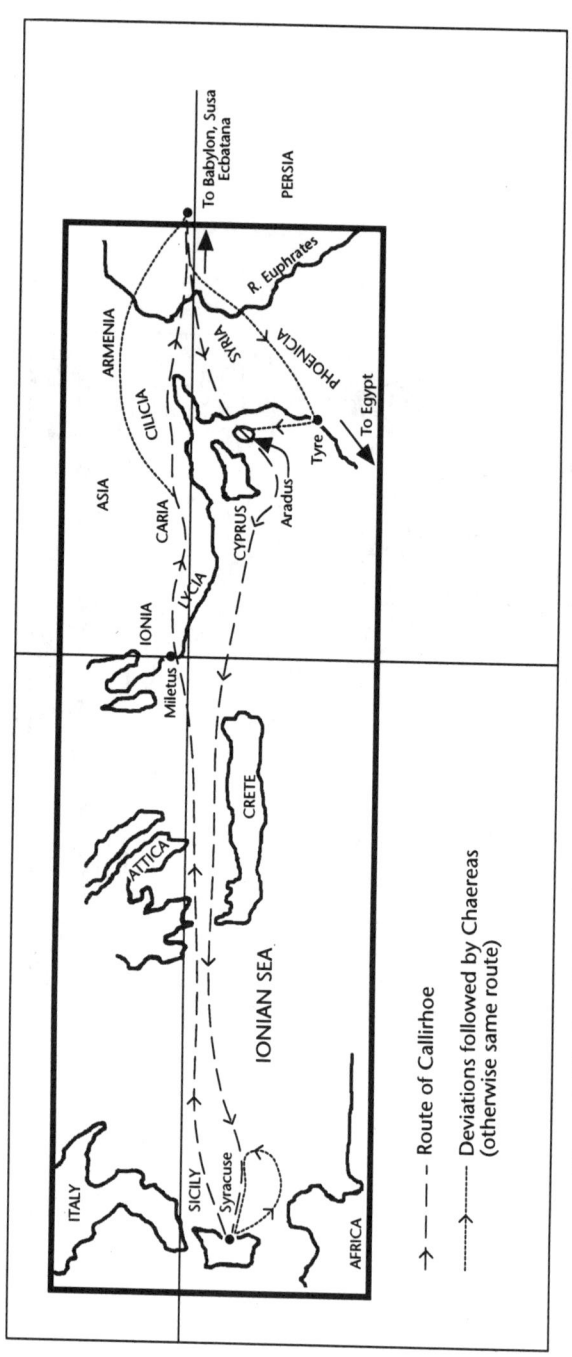

Figure 7. *Chariton: Schematic Route Maps for Main Characters Based on Eratosthenes' Projection.*

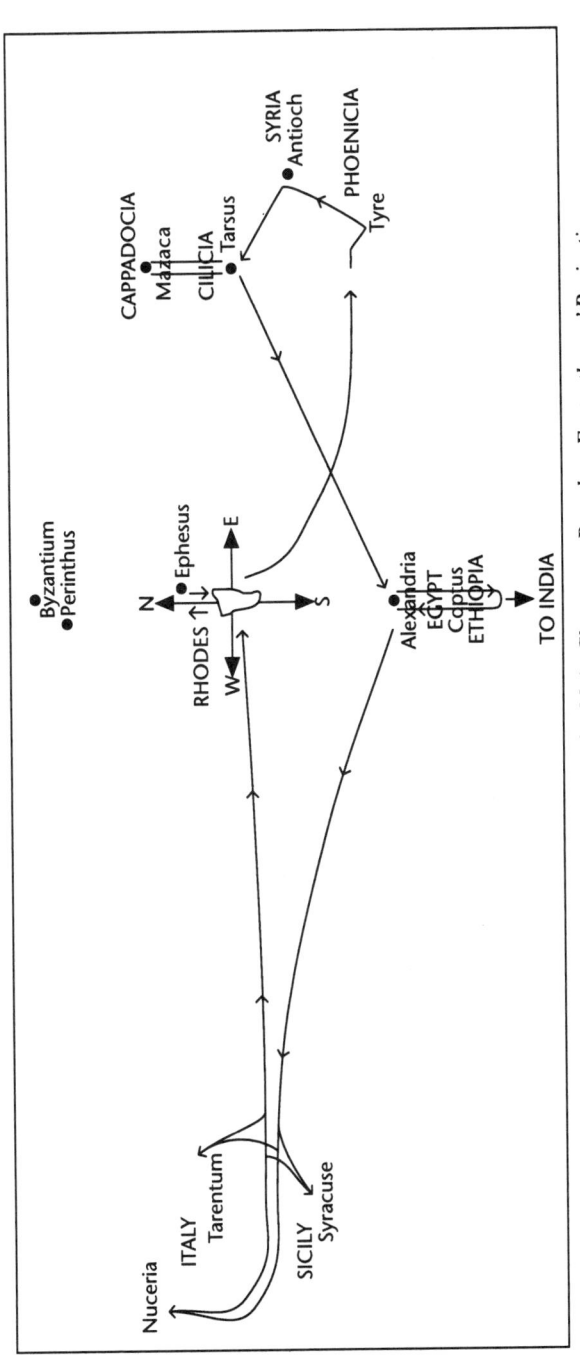

Figure 8. *Xenophon: Schematic Route Maps for Main Characters Based on Eratosthenes' Projection.*

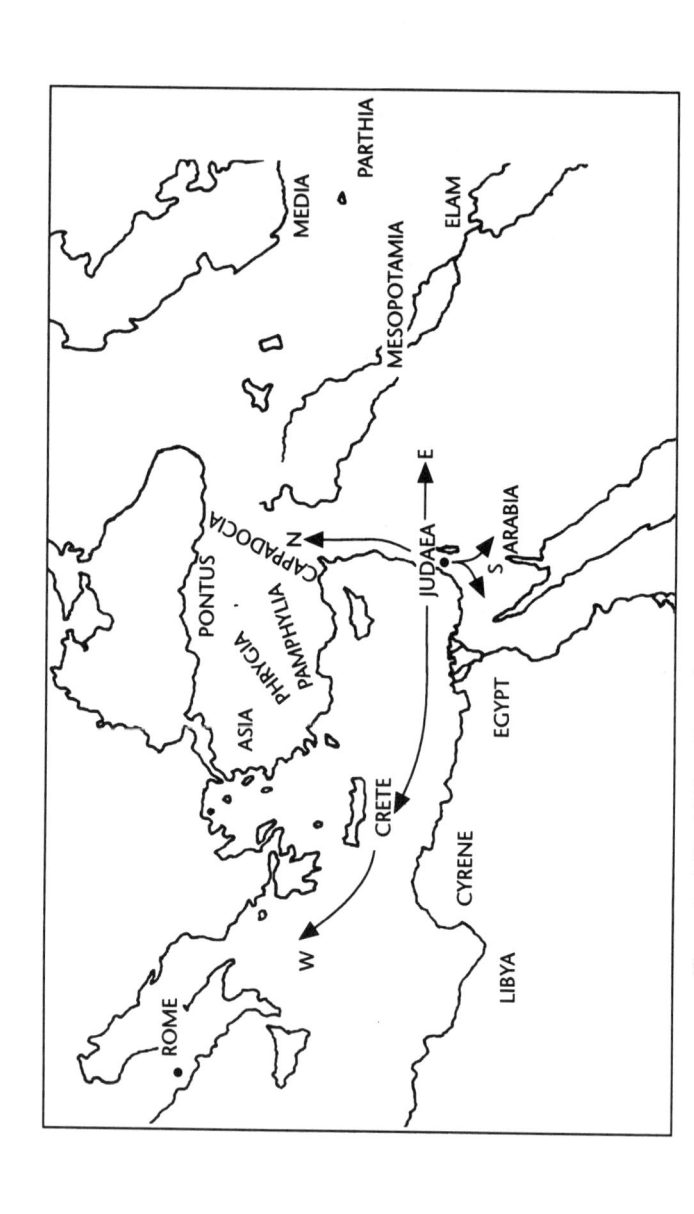

Figure 9. *A World View Centred on Jerusalem: The Regions of Acts 2.9-11.*

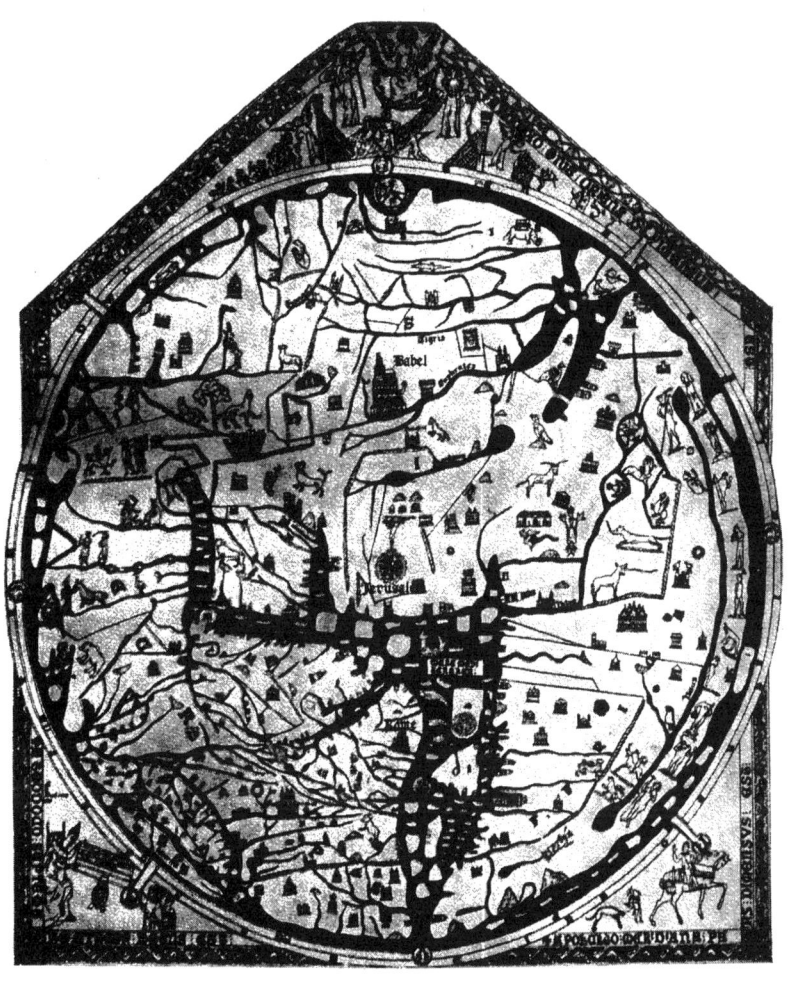

Figure 10. *The Hereford World Map,* drawn by Richard de Haldingham and Lafford in 1280 CE.
Jerusalem lies at the centre of this Christian map, which is orientated with East at the top. Note how Babylon, Jerusalem and Rome all appear on the same (vertical) E-W parallel, and how the Aegean and Adriatic have shrunk in size. From M.B. Synge, *A Book of Discovery* (London: T.C. & E.C. Jack, n.d.), after p. 134.

GOD-FEARERS IN LUKE–ACTS

Martinus C. de Boer

Are there God-fearers in Luke–Acts? And if so, are they an invention of the author? What do they disclose about the community, audience and purpose of Luke–Acts? Such questions have been much debated,[1] in part because such questions do not even emerge in connection with the remainder of the New Testament—there are no God-fearers (at least not explicitly) in the other books of the New Testament. What then are we to make of Luke–Acts?

I

Two issues need to be distinguished in this debate about God-fearers in Luke–Acts:

1. Does Luke–Acts depict Gentiles who were in some way or another 'sympathetic' to Jews and to Judaism, who may thus have adopted certain Jewish customs or practices (prayer directed to the God of Israel, synagogue attendance, Sabbath observance, alms-giving, food laws, etc.), but who stopped short of becoming proselytes to Judaism (a step that would involve, for male converts, circumcision)?[2] We may consider the following bits of evidence.

1. The modern debate began with an article by J. Bernays (1877). In 1933, K. Lake could write about God-fearers in Acts, 'This has been the centre of a long and complicated discussion of which the outcome is not clear as yet and perhaps never will be' (1933: 84). More recent discussion began with the essays by Kraabel (1981) and Wilcox (1981), both of whom cast doubt on the value of Luke's evidence about God-fearers; see n. 18 below. Cf. Finn 1985; Collins 1985: 179-85; Gager 1986; Kraabel 1986, 1991; Esler 1987: 36-45, 162-63; Overman 1988; Jervell 1988; Trebilco 1991: 145-66, 246-55; McKnight 1991: 110-14; Sanders 1991; Tyson 1992: 35-39, 181-83; Lieu 1994b.

2. For proselytes in Acts, see 2.10; 6.5; 13.43; for circumcision and its function as a boundary marker dividing Jew from Gentile (both religiously and socially), see

a. Cornelius, a Roman centurion (10.1), and uncircumcised (cf. 11.3), is described in Acts 10 as 'a devout man (εὐσεβής) and one fearing God with all his household, giving many alms to the people [i.e. the Jews] and praying to God constantly' (10.2; cf. 10.33). He receives a vision of an angel of God at 'the ninth hour' (10.3; cf. 10.30), that is, 'the ninth hour of prayer' (3.1) for Jews (or Christian Jews like Peter and John) present at the Temple for the afternoon *tāmîd* sacrifice. He is told that his prayers and alms have, like the fragrance of the sacrifice in the Temple, 'ascended as a memorial before God' (10.4; cf. 10.31, 35).[3] Cornelius is described as 'a righteous man and one fearing God, well-spoken of by the whole nation of the Jews' (10.22). One of his soldiers is also described as 'devout' (εὐσεβής) (10.7).

b. Another centurion, in Luke 7, who wants Jesus to heal his slave, sends 'Jewish elders' to Jesus to plead on his behalf, and they tell Jesus that the centurion 'is worthy of having you do this for him, for he loves our nation and he built the synagogue for us' (Lk. 7.4-5). The parallel account in Mt. 8.5-6 does not have these details.[4]

c. Three passages in Acts depict Paul in diaspora synagogues (Iconium, Thessalonica, Corinth), seeking to persuade not only Jews but also 'Greeks' ("Ελληνες) attending Sabbath services (14.1; 17.4; 18.4).[5]

d. The answer to the first question, then, would seem to be affirmative: Luke does portray Gentiles sympathetic to Jews and to Judaism, but who are not proselytes (2.10; 6.5; 13.43).

7.8; 10.45; 11.2; 15.1, 5; 16.3; 21.21 (cf. Collins 1985). See Trebilco (1991: 150, 248 n. 24) for Acts' seemingly technical use of the term προσήλυτος to mean full convert to Judaism (cf. Kuhn 1968), involving circumcision for men and the concomitant obligation to observe the Law to the same extent as those who were born Jews (cf. Philo, *Spec. Leg.* 1.9 §51; Mt. 23.15). For women converts, see Cohen 1987: 430; 1990; Lieu 1994a: 364-67. By the second century, immersion may have sufficed for woman proselytes (*b. Yeb.* 47a), but the situation is unclear for the first century.

3. Esler (1987: 162) points to Lev. 2.2, 9; 6.15; Sir. 45.15 to explain the sacrificial imagery of this verse: Luke wants to show that 'the prayers and the alms of this Gentile were accepted by God in lieu of the sacrifices which he was not allowed to enter the Temple to offer himself'.

4. See Gagnon 1994, arguing that Luke's differences from Matthew are Lukan additions to Q, not Q material which Matthew deleted.

5. 'Jews and Greeks' (14.1; 18.4) is a stereotyped phrase in Acts (19.10, 17; 20.21). There are further references to 'Greeks' in 11.20 (*v.l.*); 16.1, 3; 17.4, 12; 21.28. These passage indicate clearly that 'Greeks' are not proselytes (i.e. 'Jews') for the author of Acts (see n. 2 above and n. 51 below).

2. But does Luke–Acts itself use *technical* terms to describe such Gentiles? Two terms are at issue.

a. οἱ φοβούμενοι τὸν θεόν, those fearing God, the fearers of God, the God-fearers.

As just noted, Cornelius is described as 'one fearing God' or 'a God-fearer' (φοβούμενος τὸν θεόν) in 10.2 and 10.22. The term appears once again later in ch. 10 on the lips of Peter. After encountering Cornelius, he speaks of 'the one fearing him (God) (ὁ φοβούμενος αὐτόν) and doing righteousness *in every nation*' (10.35). Cornelius is thus a representative instance of 'a person who fears God'.

The two remaining instances of the term, both in ch. 13, confirm this claim. Paul is at a synagogue on a Sabbath in Pisidian Antioch (13.14). After the reading of the Law and the prophets, he is invited to say a word of exhortation to 'the people' (13.15). He begins his address with the words, 'Men Israelites and the fearers of God (οἱ φοβούμενοι τὸν θεόν), listen' (13.16). Later in the same address, Paul says, 'Men, brothers (cf. 13.15), sons of the race of Abraham and[6] the fearers of God among you (οἱ ἐν ὑμῖν φοβούμενοι τὸν θεόν)...' (13.26).[7] The 'men Israelites/sons of the race of Abraham' are clearly Jews; the fearers of God are a different group ('among you').

b. οἱ σεβόμενοι (τὸν θεόν), those worshipping (God), the worshippers (of God), the devout ones.

According to ch. 17, Paul 'argued in the synagogue (in Athens) with the Jews and the worshipping ones (οἱ σεβόμενοι)' (17.17; NRSV: 'the devout persons'). Earlier in ch. 17, Paul goes to 'a synagogue of the Jews' in Thessalonica where 'on three Sabbaths' he engages Jews in midrashic debate about Jesus as the Messiah (17.1-3). According to 17.4, 'Some of them (the Jews) were persuaded and joined Paul and Silas, [as were] both (τε) a large crowd of the worshipping Greeks (σεβομένων Ἑλλήνων)[8] and (τε) not a few of the leading women' (17.4).

---

6. This word (καί) is omitted by 𝔓[45] and B, but with no impact on the meaning (note ἐν ὑμῖν in what follows).

7. These texts are presumably behind the use of the term 'God-fearer' in biblical scholarship as a convenient label for Gentiles who are sympathetic (to one degree or another) to Jews and to Judaism, even when this precise term is absent.

8. Following ℵ B E Ψ 0120 *et al.* (NRSV: '...of the devout Greeks'). Other witnesses insert καί (𝔓[74] A D 33 *et al.*), thus reading, '...of the worshipping ones *and* of Greeks' (see n. 10 below). The full reading of D for 17.4b must be translated as follows: '...many (πολλοί) of the worshipping ones, both (καί) a large crowd of Greeks and (καί) not a few of the women (wives) of the leading men'. (D omits

According to 13.50, 'the Jews' of Pisidian Antioch 'incited the worshipping women (αἱ σεβόμεναι γυναῖκες) of high standing and the leading men of the city, and stirred up persecution against Paul and Barnabas'. In the same chapter, at the conclusion of Paul's long sermon in the synagogue at Pisidian Antioch (13.16-41), the reader is told that 'many of the Jews and of the worshipping proselytes (οἱ σεβόμενοι προσήλυτοι) followed Paul and Barnabas' (13.43).

In 16.14, Lydia, a woman from Thyatira and a dealer in purple cloth, is described as 'a worshipper of God' (σεβομένη τὸν θεόν). Paul encounters her 'on a Sabbath day', with other women, 'outside the gate by the river, where we supposed there to be a place of prayer (προσευχή)' (16.13). In Corinth, Paul testifies in a synagogue 'to the Jews that the Messiah is Jesus' (18.5) and declares that because of their rejection of his testimony he would 'from now on go to the Gentiles' (18.6). He then leaves the synagogue and goes next door to 'the house of someone by the name of Titius (or Titus) Justus', who is described as 'a worshipper of God' (σεβόμενος τὸν θεόν) (18.7).

c. From this brief survey of the pertinent material, the answer to the second question (whether Luke uses technical terms to describe Gentiles sympathetic to Jews and Judaism) is less clear than the answer to the first question.

When looked at together, the first group of passages discussed above (Acts 10.2, 22, 35; 13.16, 26) encourages us to surmise that at least for *Luke* (= the author of Luke–Acts) the expression οἱ φοβούμενοι τὸν θεόν is a technical or formal designation for a special group of persons, Gentiles who 'feared' the God of Israel and did so in concrete, visible ways (i.e. attend synagogue on the Sabbath, or, like Cornelius, give alms and pray to the God of Israel when Jews do).[9]

both instances of τε, found in the other witnesses, substituting καί in each case). The reading of D seems to be an attempt to clarify the meaning: 'the worshipping ones' are now clearly identified as comprising both Greeks and prominent women. Cf. 13.50.

9. Wilcox (1981) is right to point out that 10.2, 22, 35 are insufficient to establish that 'fearer of God' was 'a technical term or even an embryonic technical term for non-Jewish synagogue adherents' (p. 107). In his view (pp. 104-105), Luke only wants to stress Cornelius's piety, 'his personal quality of devotion and not his being a synagogue-adherent (if in fact he was)'. Luke is certainly stressing Cornelius's piety, but this does not mean he was not an adherent of the synagogue, nor that Luke himself is not using the term in a technical way. Wilcox attempts, without much success, to get around the implications of Acts 13.16, 26, grudgingly

But would the intended reader (or readers) of Luke–Acts have so understood the term? One could certainly argue that such a reader, after having read the account of Cornelius in ch. 10, would have understood 'the God-fearers' addressed by Paul in his synagogue sermon (13.16, 26) as Luke's formal designation for Gentiles who had adopted certain Jewish customs, including going to synagogue on the Sabbath to venerate the God of Israel. Yet we probably have to cast our nets wider than Luke–Acts to increase the probability of that conclusion, especially in light of Lk. 1.50. Luke has Mary, the mother of Jesus, speak in her song of praise (Lk. 1.46-55) of God's mercy to 'those who fear him' (οἱ φοβούμενοι αὐτόν) (1.50). It is not obvious that the φοβούμενοι αὐτόν are pious Gentiles; they may in fact be pious Israelites.

What then about οἱ σεβόμενοι (τὸν θεόν)? Acts 17.17 and 17.4 together encourage the conclusion that this expression is interchangeable with οἱ φοβούμενοι τὸν θεόν: people described as οἱ σεβόμενοι are seemingly distinguished from 'the Jews' in 17.17, while 17.4 refers to 'the worshipping Greeks'[10] alongside 'not a few of the leading women'. An intervening verse, Acts 17.12 (where Paul is in a synagogue in Beroea), reports that 'Many of them (the Jews) believed, and (καί) not a few Greek women of high standing and men'. Similarly, in 13.50, 'the worshipping women of high standing' are distinguished, along with 'the leading men of the city', from 'the Jews', while 13.43 refers to 'worshipping proselytes', presumably Gentile (or Greek) σεβόμενοι who have gone a step further and converted to Judaism (cf. 2.11; 6.5),[11] but

---

acknowledging that the God-fearers referred to may be 'Gentile adherents to the synagogue' while immediately adding, 'but the text does not require it' (pp. 107-108). Yet Paul is depicted as addressing a gathering of God-fearers in a synagogue on the Sabbath after the reading from the Law and the prophets (13.14-15). What, then, does the text require?

10. But see n. 8. If the alternate reading is adopted, presumably the 'worshipping ones' could be referring to devout Jews. But 17.17 (with 17.12) suggests that with N–A[26,27] we are to read 'worshipping Greeks'.

11. See n. 2 above for Luke's technical use of the term 'proselyte' to mean full convert to Judaism. McKnight (1991: 112) understands Acts 13.43 to mean that for Luke a God-fearer is 'a kind of proselyte', but the reverse appears to be the case, a proselyte is a kind of God-fearer, i.e., a proselyte is a God-fearing Gentile who has gone on to become a Jew. The proselytes in 2.11 and 6.5 are best understood as full converts and thus as Jews (contrast Overman 1988: 18-20). Haenchen (1971: 413 n. 50) wonders whether 'proselytes' may be 'an ancient gloss' to distinguish the God-worshippers from the Gentiles who are not mentioned until v. 47. One could

whose prior condition as Gentile (or Greek) σεβόμενοι has not yet been forgotten or entirely effaced (from a Jewish point of view) at the level of social intercourse and religious status.[12] This evidence would indicate that Lydia, a woman of considerable social standing (cf. 13.50; 17.4, 12), in 16.14 is also a Gentile (not a Jewish[13]) 'worshipper of God', as is Titius Justus in 18.7.

Lake (1933: 88) correctly suggests that σεβόμενος, which is a participial form of the verb, can in some instances in Acts be understood to describe an activity that is going on and not an abiding characteristic of the persons engaged in that activity. For example, he claims that 'the worshipping proselytes' (οἱ σεβόμενοι προσήλυτοι) in 13.43 really means 'the proselytes who were (at that moment) worshipping'. This argument could also (perhaps more convincingly) apply to the instance in 17.4 ('the worshipping Greeks'). But it is difficult to maintain elsewhere. In 13.50, the reference to 'the worshipping women' (αἱ σεβόμεναι γυναῖκες) occurs *after* Luke has reported that some of 'the Gentiles' who had heard Paul's words (spoken on a Sabbath) came to believe (13.48) and *after* he has observed that 'the word of the Lord [subsequently] spread through the whole region' (13.49). It is just possible that the phrase σεβομένη τὸν θεόν in 16.14 is to be taken adverbially ('Lydia, while worshipping God, was listening'), though it seems more natural to take it as a noun in apposition to those that precede ('a certain woman, Lydia by name, a dealer in purple cloth of the city of Thyatira, a worshipper of God, was listening'). The clearest evidence that *Luke* himself may regard the expression 'worshipper of God' as a

---

just as well attribute such a motive to Luke. See next note.

12. Cohen (1989: 29) observes that it is doubtful whether 'the proselyte received real equality with the native born. The proselyte probably had an ambiguous status in the Jewish community. Many epitaphs and synagogue inscriptions attach the label 'proselyte' after the name of the person being commemorated', including the famous inscription from Aphrodisias. Pertinent are the remarks of Philo, *Virt.* 21 §108: 'And if any of them should wish to pass over into the Jewish community, they must not be spurned with an unconditional refusal as children of enemies, but be so far favoured that the *third generation* is invited to the congregation and made partakers in the divine revelations, to which the native born, whose lineage is beyond reproach, are rightfully admitted' (cf. *m. Bikk.* 1.4). To *outsiders*, a proselyte would of course have been considered a Jew, as he or she in fact was according to rabbinic law (*b. Yeb.* 47b): 'In the eyes of outsiders a proselyte "became" and could be called a Jew' (Cohen 1989: 28, citing *Acts of Pilate* 2.1-4).

13. So, without argument, Witherington 1992: 422-23.

formal or technical designation for a special class of persons (Gentile devotees of the God of Israel, like οἱ φοβούμενοι τὸν θεόν), is provided by 18.7. The phrase σεβόμενος τὸν θεόν in 18.7 is difficult to construe as an activity in which Titius Justus is at that moment engaged (he is manifestly not in the synagogue, worshipping, but next door, welcoming Paul into his house).[14] The phrase defines what sort of a person he is: He is a God-worshipper. Acts 17.17 lends further, if less certain, support to this conclusion.[15]

It may also be pertinent to observe here that Luke never uses this verb to describe the worshipping attitudes and activities of Jews or Christians. With them, he favours the verb λατρεύω (Lk. 1.74; 2.37; 4.8; Acts 7.7, 42; 24.14; 26.7; 27.23).[16] Luke uses σεβόμενοι to describe the attitudes and actions of Gentiles who venerate the God of Israel but who remain *outside* the Jewish and Christian communities.[17]

But would the original, intended readers have so understood the term? The first occurrence of the verb in Acts (there are none in Luke)

---

14. One could, I suppose, translate as follows: 'He (Paul) moved on from there (the synagogue) and went into the house of someone by the name of Titius Justus *while he (Titius Justus) was (still) worshipping God*, whose house was next-door to the synagogue'. This would mean that Paul went next door while Titius Justus stayed behind in the synagogue worshipping! This is not the most natural way to understand the situation (cf. 18.6) or the grammar.

15. Lake (1933: 87) rather grudgingly concedes the point in connection with 17.17 and 18.7.

16. The verb προσκυνέω also occurs (Lk. 4.7-8; 24.52; Acts 7.42, 43; 8.27; 10.25; 24.11) and is used to describe acts of worship (prostration) directed to the God of Israel on the part of Jews (Lk. 4.8), Christians (Acts 24.11 [Paul]) and God-fearers (8.27 [Ethiopian eunuch]; cf. Jn 12.20 [Greeks]; Josephus, *Ant.* 20.2.5 §49 [Queen Helena of Adiabene]). In the last four texts listed, worship involves going up to Jerusalem and the Temple; like devout Jews or Christians, σεβόμενοι may or may not go up to Jerusalem to worship in the sense of προσκυνέω. Luke can also use this verb for worship that is not directed to God, as in Lk. 4.7 (the devil); Acts 7.42, 43 (false gods); 10.25 (Peter, by Cornelius!). In these cases, the worship that is properly to be given to God alone, or perhaps also to Jesus (Lk. 24.52), is wrongly directed elsewhere (cf. Acts 3.12 and 14.11-15 for parallels to the situation depicted in 10.25-26).

17. In one instance, Luke uses the verb σέβομαι to refer to Gentile worship of the goddess Artemis (Acts 19.27). A cognate noun is also used in connection with 'pagan objects of worship' (σεβάσματα) in Acts 17.23. The immediate literary context is obviously important for determining what the object of worship is in each case; see previous note.

is to be found in 13.43, where it describes proselytes (Gentile God-fearers who had 'become' Jews, but whose Gentile origins were not forgotten). The second instance, in 13.50, describes women who clearly are Gentiles. These initial references to Gentile 'worshippers of God' come shortly after references to Gentile 'fearers of God' in the same chapter (vv. 16, 26). Indeed, at this juncture of the narrative, Luke has seemingly intentionally (or because of his sources?) changed his terms; he drops 'God-fearers' (last used in 13.26, in the midst of Paul's sermon) in favour of 'God-worshippers' (first used in 13.43, at the conclusion of the same sermon). One could once again argue that an attentive reader would have understood the subsequent references to σεβόμενοι (τὸν θεόν) to mean Gentile worshippers of God (16.14; 17.4, 17; 18.7), whether or not they had known of it previously as a supposedly technical or formal label for such Gentiles. This conclusion is further encouraged by 18.13, where the Jews of Corinth tell Gallio that Paul is 'persuading ἄνθρωποι (not the Jewish λαός of 10.2 and *passim*) to worship God (σέβεσθαι τὸν θεόν) contrary to the Law'. Luke's own usage, therefore, indicates that the σεβόμενοι are, like the φοβούμενοι, Gentiles who venerate the God of Israel.

We may still wonder, however, whether there is evidence outside of Luke–Acts that would explain these peculiar Lukan uses of the term. In short, did Luke himself *coin*, or invent, one or perhaps two technical, or semi-technical, expressions for Gentiles who venerate the one God of Israel, or did he in fact *adopt* existing terms?[18]

---

18. Kraabel's 1981 article began a furious debate in some quarters about the existence of God-fearers in the ancient world. He argued that the God-fearers to be found in Acts are the author's invention, a device that serves his theological programme of showing 'how Christianity had become a Gentile religion legitimately and without losing its Old Testament roots' (1981: 120). In the same year, there appeared the article by Wilcox, arguing that the two expressions are basically Lukanisms, i.e., features of Lukan style (the first one under the influence of LXX). More recently, Kraabel has sought to question the value of Luke's evidence, even as he concedes that there is 'some historical basis for these characters in Luke's story'. He concludes, 'If their numbers were low and their occurrence scattered, as I suspect, then as evidence they are not sufficient to bear the weight of Luke's argument, and the few details that Luke provides about them should not be accepted uncritically as historical data. Their importance has been greatly inflated by Luke to serve the purposes of his narrative' (1991: 280). A good critique of Kraabel is that of Overman (1988).

II

Is there evidence outside of Luke–Acts for the existence of God-fearers? As in the case of Luke–Acts, there are two ways to answer this question.

1. Do other ancient writers give accounts of Gentiles who are sympathetic to Jews and Judaism, but who are not proselytes? We may take some soundings from Philo and Josephus.

a. According to Philo, 'not only Jews but almost every other people, particularly those which take more account of virtue, have so far grown in holiness as to value and honour our laws. In this they have received a special distinction which belongs to no other code' (*Vit. Mos.* 2.17). He goes on to claim that Jewish customs and institutions 'attract and win the attention of all, of barbarians, of Greeks, of dwellers on the mainland and islands, of nations of the east and the west, of Europe and of Asia, of the whole inhabited world from end to end' (2.20). Philo singles out the observance of the Sabbath (2.21-22) and of the annual Day of Atonement (2.23-24).[19]

b. Josephus makes similar sweeping claims in Book 2 of *Contra Apionem*: 'our laws...have to an ever increasing extent excited the emulation of the world at large' (279). 'The masses have long since shown a keen desire to adopt our religious observances' (282). Josephus here mentions the Sabbath, 'the fasts and the lighting of lamps',[20] and food laws. He claims that 'as God permeates the universe, so the Law has found its way among all humankind' (284). Josephus also claims that Moses welcomes 'all who desire to come and live under the same laws with us' (210).

c. In some passages, Josephus refers specifically to 'Greeks' in connection with the adoption of Jewish customs, as does the author of Acts (14.1; 17.4; 18.4). In *Apion* 2.123, for example, he writes that 'many of them (the Greeks) have agreed to adopt our laws'. In *Ant.* 3.217, he writes of 'Greeks who revere our practices (ἔθη)'. According to *War* 7.45, the Jews of Antioch 'were constantly attracting to their

---

19. Translations of Philo and Josephus follow (with occasional modification) those found in the Loeb Classical Library.

20. Cohen, commenting on this passage, writes, 'In the city of Rome, at least, in the latter part of the first century BCE and throughout the first century CE, pagans of both the upper and lower classes observed the Sabbath by lighting lamps and fasting. In the following centuries Sabbath observance extended to gentiles in Egypt and Asia Minor as well' (1989: 20).

religious ceremonies a large crowd of Greeks (πολὺ πλῆθος Ἑλλήνων; Acts 17.4 has similar wording), and these they in some measure incorporated with themselves'. This latter clause (literally, 'these they made in some measure a part [μοῖραν] of themselves') may imply conversion,[21] though not necessarily. In 2.463, Josephus refers to Gentile 'Judaizers' in Syria.

d. As in the case of Luke–Acts, the answer to our first question must be affirmative. Gentiles sympathetic to Jews and Judaism and adopting at least some of its customs and laws are not unique to Luke–Acts. Even allowing for some obvious exaggeration by Philo and Josephus, it would seem that such Gentiles were not all that exceptional. Pagan authors also testify to the existence of such Gentiles.[22]

Cohen (1989: 14-15) has usefully classified and described seven forms of behaviour discernible in the ancient sources whereby a Gentile could 'show respect or affection for Judaism' in the ancient world:

1. admiring some aspect of Judaism;
2. acknowledging the power of the god of the Jews or incorporating him into the pagan pantheon;
3. benefitting the Jews or being conspicuously friendly to Jews [cf. Lk. 7.4-5 above];
4. practicing some or many of the rituals of the Jews;
5. venerating the god of the Jews and denying or ignoring the pagan gods;
6. joining the Jewish community [through, e.g., marriage to a Jew];
7. converting to Judaism and 'becoming a Jew' [a proselyte].

Cohen suggests that the term 'sympathizers' ought to be used to cover all these different categories, 'precisely because it is so vague and does not imply the existence of a homogeneous category', while the term 'adherents' (used by A.D. Nock) could apply to those in categories 4 and 5 (1989: 31). These two categories apply to the God-fearing/God-worshipping Gentiles in Acts. 'Proselytes' or 'converts' would describe those in category 7, although in this case Cohen's term 'sympathizer' seems not to go far enough. A proselyte is a sympathizer or an 'adherent' who has become a Jew (cf. Acts 13.43) and is thus more than a sympathizer.

21. Cohen 1989: 27.
22. See e.g., Tacitus, *Hist.* 5.5 (Stern 1980, §281); Juvenal, *Sat.* 14.96-107 (Stern 1980, §301). These and numerous other pagan authors are analyzed by Cohen (1989).

2. But do ancient writers use supposedly 'technical' terms to describe such 'sympathetic' Gentiles? Are there parallels to Luke's usage? Lake (1923: 87-88) formulated the issue as follows:

> The question is merely whether φοβούμενος τὸν θεόν and σεβόμενος τὸν θεόν were technical terms to describe this class and whether it had a recognized status. In favour of such a theory is the fact that the words are applied at least most often to this class in Acts. Against it is the fact that they are perfectly well known Old Testament phrases which do not bear any technical meaning.

But the Old Testament evidence may not be the most relevant.

a. οἱ φοβούμενοι τὸν θεόν? Lk. 1.50 refers in a general way to those who fear God and this verse echoes OT usage (cf. esp. LXX Ps. 102.11, 13, 17),[23] where it describes pious Israelites. The Hebrew counterpart (יראי אל) is found in the Dead Sea Scrolls, referring not to Gentile sympathizers but to devout Jews.[24]

But there is other evidence supporting Luke's usage, though it is not strong. LXX 2 Chron. 5.6 (ca. 200 BCE) lists οἱ φοβούμενοι (which has no counterpart in MT) as a group distinct from 'the whole congregation of Israel'.[25] Stanton (1994) has recently argued that two passages in Justin are relevant. The expression οἱ φοβούμενοι τὸν θεόν occurs in Justin's *Dial. Tryph.* 10.4 and 24.3 and, according to Stanton, refers to Gentiles sympathetic to Judaism. In the first passage, Trypho complains that while Christians claim to know God they do not keep the commandments, something which οἱ φοβούμενοι τὸν θεόν do. In the second, Justin appeals to such people to 'come with me'. Stern (1980: 105), however, points out that Justin may be dependent upon Acts for this term.

Many scholars have pointed to Juvenal (*Sat.* 14.96-107), who writes (in Latin) of a father sympathetic to Judaism as one who 'fears (*metuentem*) the Sabbath' (and abstains from eating pork), in contrast to his son who becomes a proselyte to Judaism by undergoing circumcision. Then there is *Mekhilta de Rabbi Ishmael* which refers (as do many later rabbinic texts) to יראי שמים, fearers of Heaven.[26] All of this evidence, to be sure, is second-century or later.

b. οἱ σεβόμενοι (τὸν θεόν)? The Hebrew expressions just surveyed could also be cited here, since the LXX employs both Greek expressions

---

23. Wilcox 1981: 104.
24. So Wilcox 1981: 115-16.
25. See Reynolds 1987: 65; Callan 1993: 293.
26. Cf. Wilcox 1981: 116; Lake 1923: 82; Stern 1980: 104; Reynolds 1987: 48.

to translate the same Hebrew terms (יראי אל or יראי יהוה).²⁷

More important, however, is Josephus. In *Ant.* 14.110, he writes that 'all the Jews throughout the habitable world (τῶν κατὰ τὴν οἰκουμένην Ἰουδαίων) *and those who worshipped God* (καὶ σεβομένων τὸν θεόν), even those from Asia and Europe, had been contributing to it (the Temple) for a very long time'. This is very similar to Acts 17.17, where we are told that Paul 'argued in the synagogue with the Jews and the worshipping ones (οἱ σεβόμενοι)' (the direct object, τὸν θεόν, occuring in Acts 16.14; 18.7). Both passages seem to distinguish between 'the Jews' on the one side and σεβόμενοι on the other. It is possible, however, to understand σεβόμενοι in the Josephus passage to refer to the behaviour of Jews, perhaps of the Jews mentioned in the text,²⁸ but this has seemed unlikely to many interpreters.²⁹ It seems superfluous to specify the Jews to whom Josephus here refers as 'worshipping God' (the same applies to Lk. 17.17). The geographical notations further encourage the view that Josephus is writing of two distinct groups: (1) all the Jews throughout the habitable world, and (2) those worshipping God, even those from Asia and Europe. The parallel with the material in Acts also seems to speak against taking σεβομένων τὸν θεόν as referring to Jews.³⁰

According to *Ant.* 20.34-35, part of Josephus's account of Izates and his mother Helena, the queen of Adiabene (20.17), 'a certain Jewish merchant named Ananias visited the king's wives and taught them to worship God (τὸν θεὸν σέβειν). It was through their agency that he was brought to the notice of Izates, whom he similarly won over with the co-operation of the women.' Helena herself 'had likewise been instructed by another Jew and had been brought over to their laws'. Interestingly, Izates himself 'considered that he would not be genuinely a Jew unless he was circumcised' (20.38). Ananias attempts to convince him otherwise: 'The king could, he said, worship God (τὸν θεῖον [sic]

---

27. See Reynolds 1987: 49. Cf. LXX Dan. 3.90.

28. Lake (1923: 85) thinks that 'the Greek surely makes it plain that σεβομένων is a further description of those who are called Ἰουδαίων, and καί connects it with κατὰ τὴν οἰκουμένην, so that the meaning of the whole phrase is "all the Jews worshipping throughout the world"'. The other reading, he thinks, would 'require τῶν before σεβομένων'. This grammatical argument is not impossible, though it seems forced. The absence of the article is also not decisive; see Trebilco 1991: 148.

29. For the discussion, see Trebilco 1991: 148, 247 nn. 14, 15.

30. Cf. Collins 1985: 181.

σέβειν) even without circumcision' (20.41).³¹

c. θεοσεβής? This term, meaning 'God-worshipping, devout' (as an adjective) or 'God-worshipper' (as a noun), does not occur in Luke–Acts,³² but as Gager (1986: 92) observes, 'θεοσεβής is in effect little more than an adjectival contraction of the Lukan phrase, σεβόμενος τὸν θεόν (16.14; 18.7)'.³³ We may also note that εὐσεβής is used to describe Cornelius and his soldier in Acts 10.2, 7 (no further instances in Luke–Acts).³⁴

θεοσεβής has become prominent in the discussion because of the inscription from Aphrodisias in Asia Minor (c. 210 CE). This two-sided stele lists the names of contributors to a memorial building, sponsored by a group within the synagogue (*dekanias*, a burial society? a society to help the poor?). The stele distinguishes between Jews, proselytes and God-worshippers (θεοσεβίς [sic]). More than fifty such God-worshippers are listed,³⁵ and their names are nearly all clearly Greek or Graeco-Roman (nine of them city councillors, listed at the beginning!), in contrast to the names of those labeled Jews (at least 69)³⁶ or proselytes (3).³⁷ Trebilco (1991: 153) sums up the implications, widely shared, as follows:

---

31. This does not mean, as some intimate (cf. recently Callan 1993: 291), that Izates was a proselyte without circumcision (see Collins 1985: 178-79). As the context shows, the attitude of Ananias, who is motivated by political caution and personal safety, is that it is acceptable for Gentiles to 'worship God' precisely as Gentiles. In the sequel, another Jew, a Galilean by the name of Eleazer, perhaps a Pharisee, tells Izates that he must be circumcised if he wants to be a Jew (*Ant.* 20.43-48), which is exactly what Izates himself believes (20.38), as well as his mother, who seeks to dissuade Izates from circumcision on the grounds that his subjects would not want 'a Jew' to rule over them (20.39). Apart from circumcision, in short, Izates is not a Jew, no matter how 'zealous' he may be 'for the ancestral traditions of the Jews' (20.41). The same is true of the argument around circumcision in Acts.

32. There is only one instance of the term in the New Testament, Jn 9.31 (cf. 1 Tim. 2.10 for a cognate).

33. In the LXX (Exod. 18.21; Job 1.1), it translates יראי אלהים, one who fears God (see Siegert 1973: 109-12; Reynolds 1987: 49).

34. Luke seems to prefer εὐλαβής for Jews and Christians (Lk. 2.25; Acts 2.5; 8.2; 22.12). But cf. Acts 3.12.

35. Reynolds (1987: 54) counts 54.

36. Reynolds 1987: 54. See further van der Horst 1989.

37. Cf. Sanders 1991: 440-41; McKnight 1991: 112-13; Trebilco 1991: 152-55. Other pertinent inscriptions are analysed by Trebilco (1991: 152-64).

The conclusion that they are all Gentile 'God worshippers' seems unavoidable. They are attached in some definite way to the Jewish community as a distinct, separate and formal category of people who are neither Jews nor proselytes. They have all been allowed to belong, seemingly as enrolled members of a subsection of the whole community. We now know that at least at Aphrodisias there was a group of Gentile God-worshippers involved with the Jewish community who are given the title θεοσεβεῖς.

Josephus already seems to use the term in a similar way in *Ant.* 20.195, in connection with Poppaea Sabina, consort of Nero. She 'pleaded (with Nero) on behalf of the Jews, for (so Josephus explains) she was a God-worshipper (θεοσεβής)'.[38]

d. This survey of some of the pertinent evidence is enough to indicate that Luke was not creating terms *de novo* to characterize, or to label, Gentiles who were sympathetic to Jews and to Judaism. The Josephus evidence is particularly important, since Josephus and Luke were contemporaries and were probably not familiar with each other's writings,[39] though it must be noted that, in contrast to Acts (or Justin), Josephus does not seem to use φοβούμενος for Gentile sympathizers, only σεβόμενος (and θεοσεβής).

But can we speak of 'technical' terms for such Gentiles outside of Acts itself? The Aphrodisias inscription suggests that at least by the third century in one city of Asia Minor θεοσεβής was probably a technical term for such Gentiles among Jews. According to Gager (1986: 98), this word 'designates a separate category of persons associated with the synagogue; it is used in a technical fashion as a title; the category itself is distinct from both proselytes and other Jews; it appears to cover Gentiles, whether exclusively or not'. With respect to earlier material, scholars are less certain and, in fact, most of them explicitly deny that the terms found in earlier material are properly 'technical' ones.[40] But the matter is perhaps not so clear.

Cohen's discussion of the pertinent Josephus material is instructive. He writes (1987: 419):

---

38. Whether and to what extent she actually was such a God-worshipper is of course an open question. See Reynolds 1987: 50.

39. On this question, see now Mason 1992: 185-229.

40. Callan (1993: 294), for example, has recently written that 'there was no technical term for Gentiles attracted to Judaism'.

Neither *theosebēs* nor *sebomenos*, of course, is a technical term for a Gentile who 'adheres' to Judaism. In Josephan Greek the adjective *theosebēs* can describe pious Israelites and Jews who venerate the true God of Israel as well as pious Gentiles who venerate the false gods of the nations. Similarly, the verb *sebein*, in both the active and middle voices, has for its subjects both Gentiles and Jews, and for its objects both the true God of Israel and the false gods of the nations. In sum: neither *sebomenos* nor *theosebēs* is a technical term for 'adherent' (even after his 'conversion' Izates can be said to 'venerate God', *Ant.* 20.4.2 §88)...[41]

However, Cohen also observes that 'when a *Jew* describes a *Gentile* as "pious" or "reverent" without further qualification, the reference is probably *not* to the Gentile's selfless dedication to Isis or Heracles. The Jew is probably calling the Gentile an "adherent"' (emphasis added). For this reason, he concludes, 'one of the possible applications of the terms [θεοσεβής, σεβόμενος] is to a Gentile with an unusual attachment to the God of the Jews, an 'adherent' [i.e. someone belonging to Cohen's categories 4 and 5 of sympathizers above] and it is this meaning which best fits the language of both *Ant.* 14.7.2 §110 and 20.8.11 §195'. Similarly, Gager (1986: 93) writes that sympathetic Gentiles 'appear to have been designated by a recurrent, if unofficial set of terms'. Such statements come very close to regarding these terms as technical ones, at least when used by Jews, for a certain class of people, Gentiles who by their behaviour (esp. going to synagogue on the Sabbath) were known to be sympathetic to Jews and to Judaism to a greater or a lesser extent.[42]

Lake may perhaps point to a proper, or at least useful, assessment of the matter. He writes (1923: 88), 'The epithets themselves could have been given to a pious Jew, and it is only when they are applied to a non-Jew that *the context* gives them a peculiar meaning' (emphasis added). In short, the terms, when applied to sympathetic Gentiles, are

---

41. Just like the proselytes in Acts 13.43 (see n. 12 above). Elsewhere (1989: 31), Cohen claims that 'In the eyes of the Jewish community any gentile benefactor, any gentile well disposed towards Jews or Judaism, might be called a "venerator of God"'.

42. In a similar way the terms 'God-fearers' and 'sympathizers' have become technical (or semi-technical) terms among biblical scholars and historians of Judaism. These words can mean other things, but in context (e.g. the article titles of Feldman, Lifshitz and Siegert) they refers to Gentiles in the ancient world who had a friendly attitude toward Jews and Judaism, often to the point of adopting Jewish customs and beliefs.

'contextually technical', that is, while the terms can be used in a variety of contexts to mean a variety of things in those contexts (a statement which is true of all words or phrases), there are contexts in which the terms are used to describe, or to label, what McKnight (1991: 113) calls 'a socially distinct group in their relationship to Judaism'.

III

It is evident that Luke was not inventing new terminology to describe, or to label, this socially distinct group, and also then that his first-century readers would probably have understood the 'technical' (or, at least, 'semi-technical') import of the terms in the contexts in which Luke uses them. This conclusion is perhaps more certain in the case of σεβόμενος than in the case of φοβούμενος. The latter is always followed by τὸν θεόν (or αὐτόν), and accompanied by further explanatory phrases (e.g. giving alms, doing righteousness), whereas the former is not. It requires more knowledge on the part of the reader. This fact is consistent with the evidence from Josephus since, as we noted above, Josephus uses σεβόμενος (and θεοσεβής) but *not* φοβούμενος for Gentile sympathizers.

What sort of readers would be likely to have such knowledge about the meaning of σεβόμενος? Clearly, Jews (especially of the Greek-speaking diaspora) and/or σεβόμενοι themselves would have such knowledge. Such readers would learn from Luke's shift in terminology in the middle of ch. 13 that the φοβούμενοι of 10.2, 22, 35 and 13.16, 26 were in fact the same as the Gentile σεβόμενοι with which they were already familiar. In view of Paul's final declamation against Jewish unbelief in Acts 28.25-28, however, it would seem very unlikely that (non-Christian) Jews were part of Luke's intended (or implied) audience. What then of σεβόμενοι?

This question touches upon the crucial issue of the community, audience, and purpose of Luke–Acts. Obviously we cannot do justice to this vexed matter in the space available. We can only pay brief attention to aspects of the debate among some scholars of Luke–Acts in recent years.

Jervell (1988) has argued that Luke did not seek to welcome or to convert Gentiles as such ('the idolators and people without knowledge of the Torah', p. 11) to Christianity, but only *God-fearing* Gentiles. Paul's mission to 'the Gentiles' (τὰ ἔθνη) is in reality a mission to God-fearers, as shown by the Cornelius episode with its conclusion in 11.18

('then also to τὰ ἔθνη has God granted repentance unto life').[43] Luke's church consists of Jews and God-fearers who have come to faith in Jesus, not of pagan Gentiles. Esler (1987: 36-45) has mounted a similar argument: the concern of Luke–Acts is to legitimize harmonious relations between Jewish Christians and Gentile Christians in Luke's community; those Gentile Christians were primarily God-fearers.[44] The Cornelius episode is also crucial for Esler (pp. 37-38): the 'qualities' Cornelius manifests as a God-fearing Gentile are 'presented as essential prerequisites for the conversion of Gentiles to Christianity'. This 'little-noticed but highly important fact', Esler claims, becomes evident in Peter's statement in 10.34-35 that 'in every nation (ἔθνει) the person who fears God and does righteousness is acceptable to him'.[45]

In response to Jervell and Esler, Sanders (1991) has surveyed the letters of Paul, LXX, Josephus, Mark and Q and concludes that there is no evidence to indicate that the readers of Luke–Acts would have understood the many references to τὰ ἔθνη to be references to God-fearers. More importantly, argues Sanders, Lk. 21.24-25 ('Jerusalem will be trodden underfoot by τὰ ἔθνη') and 24.47 (the preaching of 'repentance of sins for the forgiveness of sins to all τὰ ἔθνη') do not favour understanding τὰ ἔθνη to mean God-fearers in Acts. Indeed, Gentiles as such, not God-fearing Gentiles, must be meant in Acts 9.15 (where Paul is to go to 'τὰ ἔθνη and kings and the sons of Israel'), 21.21 (where Paul is charged with teaching apostasy from Moses to 'all the Jews among τὰ ἔθνη'), and 22.21 (where Paul is sent by Jesus 'to ἔθνη far away'). Sanders finds no evidence that Jews of Luke's time distinguished between Gentiles and God-fearers when discussing salvation or the life of the world to come. It thus seems implausible to

---

43. On Acts 10.1–11.18, see Bovon 1970.
44. In the Gospel, the key passage for Esler is Jesus' synagogue sermon in Luke 4.16ff. Acts 10.38, part of the Cornelius episode, seems to allude to Lk. 4.18. Esler (1987: 34-35) sees God-fearers in the figures of the widow of Zarephath in Sidon and Naaman the Syrian (Lk. 4.26-27).
45. Callan (1993) moves along similar lines, arguing that the Apostolic Decree (15.20, 29; 21.25) actually derives from and specifies 'the minimal requirements [derived from Lev. 17–18] for the Gentiles who wish to associate themselves with Judaism without fully converting' (p. 296). This in turn implies that 'the core of the church' consists of Jews who believe Jesus to be the Messiah; such believing Jews are the 'restored Israel'. Gentile Christians 'are incorporated into [this restored] Israel in some way' (Callan is not sure they should be considered converts or adherents) by means of the stipulations of the Apostolic Decree (p. 297). See Reynolds 1987: 61.

him that Luke would be positing such a distinction in 11.18, as Jervell's interpretation would require. Against Esler he asserts that 'τὰ ἔθνη in Luke–Acts does not mean God-fearers, unless they are so designated' (1991: 450). Sanders does not, however, address Esler's claim that 10.34-35 posits the 'conditions' (1987: 38) under which Gentiles may be included within Luke's Christian community.

This debate assumes that Luke's primary audience is a Christian community, seeking to defend or to establish its identity over against criticisms and suspicions coming from Jews, Jewish Christians, and/or Roman officials.[46] Tyson's recent study (1992) has called this assumption into question. Using a literary and rigorously non-historical approach, Tyson attempts to give a portrait of the implied reader of Luke–Acts, surveying what the implied reader is supposed to know about geographical locations, persons, languages, events, measurements and money, religious practices, and literature. He concludes that the implied reader fits the profile of a literate Gentile God-fearer, familiar with Jewish literature and practices. The two centurions in Luke 7 and Acts 10, he surmises, are 'intratextual representations of the implied reader' of Luke–Acts, 'righteous Gentiles who are acquainted with and attracted to Judaism' (p. 37). The Ethiopian eunuch (Acts 8.27-39) who visits Jerusalem to worship there and is familiar with at least one passage of Scripture also 'fits the profile of the implied reader' (p. 38).

Tyson then goes on to argue that 'Theophilus' (Lk. 1.3; Acts 1.1) may also be placed among the intratextual representations of the implied reader, though he is technically the narratee. As a 'lover of God' (θεόφιλος), he should be understood as a Gentile favourably disposed toward Jewish religious life. This Theophilus also knows something about Christianity, as Lk. 1.4 shows, but it is limited and in need of 'amplification and correction' (1992: 38).[47] According to Tyson, the implied reader (apart from Theophilus) can also be shown to have some limited acquaintance with Christianity. The implied author's aim is to show the implied reader that 'what is good about Judaism may be found in Christianity without the burden of circumcision and full Torah obedience' (p. 182). In short, the purpose of Luke–Acts is to persuade God-fearers to accept Christianity instead of Judaism:[48] 'Christianity is

---

46. See the recent survey of opinions in Gagnon 1994: 129-31.
47. Tyson declines, however, to 'say anything specific about his social or political position or his existence outside the text' (p. 38).
48. See also for Luke, Nolland 1989. Gagnon (1994: 131) does not agree,

shown to be the fulfilment of the Hebrew Scriptures and long-held Jewish hopes and expectations' (p. 182).[49]

It lies beyond the scope of this essay to enter into a detailed critical evaluation of these various proposals, but they show the importance of coming to an adequate understanding of the God-fearers within both the narrative and the social worlds of Luke–Acts.[50] In my view, three aspects of the God-fearers in Luke–Acts need further investigation and clarification:

(1) The God-fearers in Luke 7 and Acts 10 are both centurions. What is the significance of this?[51]

(2) The God-fearers of Luke–Acts are often people (esp. women) of considerable social standing (Lk. 7.1-10; Acts 8.27-28; 10.1-2, 7; 13.50; 16.14; 17.4, 12; 18.7). This is also true of other evidence (Aphrodisias, Josephus on the royal family of Adiabene). What is the significance of this for understanding the God-fearers of Luke–Acts and the setting of the book?

(3) Those identified as 'Greeks' ("Ελληνες) in Acts often seem to be God-fearers (cf. esp. 14.1; 16.1, 3; 17.4, 12; 18.4; less clearly in 11.20?;

---

arguing that it cannot hold for Lk. 7.3-6a (though it might for 7.9-10): 'why would a non-Christian God-fearer need confirmation from the Jews that it was okay for Christians to minister to God-fearers?' He adds that 'the motif of Jewish intercessors in 7.3-5 would undercut any attempt on Luke's part to present Christianity as an alternative to Judaism'. But one can read this scene differently. The scene could be informing God-fearers that (some) Jews in *Jesus*' day (as in that of the early church) did acknowledge his special authority and status, that such Jews had no qualms about seeking Jesus' attention for a God-fearer, and that a God-fearer was indeed 'worthy' of Jesus' attention.

49. Tyson's study is mainly concerned with seeking to understand the ambivalent images of Judaism in Luke–Acts. He concludes, 'If one intent of the implied author is to wean the implied reader away from Judaism and convince him to accept the Christian message, the ambivalence in Luke–Acts in regard to the images of Judaism can be understood. The positive images are consistent with the assumed attitudes of a Godfearer. Negative images both show the inferiority of Judaism to Christianity and help to explain Jewish rejection of the Chritian message' (p. 183). See also Tyson 1995.

50. See Lieu 1994b.

51. See Tyson (1992: 37), who points out that centurions as a group are presented favourably in Luke–Acts (cf. Acts 21.32; 22.25-29; 23.17, 23; 24.23; 27.1, 6, 31, 43). Acts 27.11 presents the only exception. According to Tyson, the implied author attempts to lead 'the implied reader to a positive commitment about Jesus, a commitment similar to the centurion in Luke 23.47' (p. 38). See also Esler 1987.

19.10, 17; 20.21; 21.28).⁵² The same seems to be true of several passages in Josephus (see above, *Apion* 2.123, *Ant.* 3.217, *War* 7.45). If Luke uses the term ἔθνη to designate pagan Gentiles, as Sanders argues, is it possible that "Ελληνες is another technical (or quasi-technical) term for God-fearing/God-worshipping Gentiles in Acts?⁵³ And what would that tell us about them and about Luke–Acts?

BIBLIOGRAPHY

Bernays, J.
1877 'Die Gottesfürchtigen bei Juvenal' (originally 1877), in H. Usener (ed.), *Gesammelte Abhandlungen von Jacob Bernays* (Berlin: Hertz, 1885. Reprint: Hildesheim: Georg Olms, 1971), pp. 71-80.

Bovon, F.
1970 'Tradition et rédaction en Actes 10,1–11,18', *TZ* 26: 22-45.

Callan, T.
1993 'The Background of the Apostolic Decree (Acts 15.20, 29; 21.25)', *CBQ* 55: 284-97.

Cohen, S.J.D.
1987 'Respect for Gentiles in the Writings of Josephus', *HTR* 80: 409-30.
1989 'Crossing the Boundary and Becoming a Jew', *HTR* 82: 13-33.
1990 'The Rabbinic Conversion Ceremony', *JJS* 41: 177-203.

Collins, J.J.
1985 'A Symbol of Otherness: Circumcision and Salvation in the First Century', in J. Neusner and E. Frerichs (eds.), *'To See Ourselves as Others See Us': Christians, Jews, 'Others' in Late Antiquity* (Chico, CA: Scholars Press), pp. 163-86.

---

52. In 16.1, 3, Timothy's problem is that his father was 'a Greek' (unlike his mother who was a 'Jewish woman'), which means that his father was not circumcized nor then a Jew. He may, then, have been a God-fearer, as were the 'Greeks' to be found in the synagogue on the Sabbath in 14.1; 18.4. In 21.28, Jews from Asia object that Paul has brought 'Greeks' (God-fearers?) into the temple. The charge would make little sense if proselytes were meant, since proselytes were, for religious purposes and privilege, Jews (cf. 2.11; 6.5; 13.43). See further Trebilco 1991: 150.

53. See McRay (1992: 1093), who writes that in NT times 'the term Greek became somewhat of a cultural designation, referring to anyone who also accepted Greek culture and spoke the language', and that 'Luke probably reserves the term "Greeks" for non-Jews who worship the one true God (Acts 14.1; 16.1, 3; 17.4, 12; 19.17), also calling them Godfearers..., and designates as 'Gentiles' those who were polytheistic pagans...' See Reynolds 1987: 51 for a similar view. Note that in John 12.20 "Ελληνες come to Jerusalem 'to worship at the feast'.

Esler, P.F.
1987 *Community and Gospel in Luke–Acts: The Social and Political Motivations of Lucan Theology* (SNTMS, 57; Cambridge: Cambridge University Press).

Feldman, L.H.
1950 'Jewish "Sympathizers" in Classical Literature and Inscriptions', *TAPA* 81: 200-208.
1989 '"Proselytes" and "Sympathizers" in the Light of the New Inscriptions from Aphrodisias', *REJ* 148: 265-305.
1993 'Proselytism by Jews in the Third, Fourth and Fifth Centuries', *JSJ* 24: 1-58.

Finn, T.M.
1985 'The God-Fearers Reconsidered', *CBQ* 47: 75-84.

Gager, J.J.
1986 'Jews, Gentiles, and Synagogues in the Book of Acts', *HTR* 79: 91-99.

Gagnon, R.
1994 'Luke's Motives for Redaction in the Account of the Double Delegation in Luke 7.1-10', *NovT* 36: 122-45.

Horst, P.W. van der
1989 'Jews and Christians in Aphrodisias in the Light of Their Relations to other Cities in Asia Minor', *NedTT's* 43: 106-21.

Jervell, J.
1988 'The Church of Jews and Godfearers', in J.B. Tyson (ed.), *Luke–Acts and the Jewish People: Eight Critical Perspectives* (Minneapolis: Fortress Press), pp. 11-20.

Kraabel, A.T.
1981 'The Disappearance of the "God-Fearers"', *Numen* 28: 113-26.
1986 'Greek, Jews, and Lutherans in the Middle Half of Acts', *HTR* 79: 147-57.
1991 'The God-Fearers Meet the Beloved Disciple', in B.A. Pearson (ed.), *The Future of Early Christianity: Essays in Honor of Helmut Koester* (Minneapolis: Fortress Press), pp. 276-284.

Kuhn, H.G.
1968 'προσήλυτος', *TDNT*, VI, pp. 727-44.

Lake, K.
1933 'Proselytes and God-Fearers', in F.J. Foakes Jackson and K. Lake (eds.), *The Beginnings of Christianity*. V. *The Acts of the Apostles* (5 vols.; London: Macmillan), pp. 74-96.

Lieu, J.
1994a 'Circumcision, Women and Salvation', *NTS* 40: 358-70.
1994b 'Do God-Fearers Make Good Christians?', in S.E. Porter, P. Joyce and D.E. Orton (eds.), *Crossing the Boundaries: Essays in Biblical Interpretation in Honour of Michael D. Goulder* (Leiden: Brill), pp. 329-34.

Lifshitz, B.
1970 'Du nouveau sur les "Sympathisants"', *JSJ* 1: 77-84.

Mason, S.
1992 *Josephus and the New Testament* (Peabody, MA: Hendrickson).

McKnight, S.
1991 *A Light among the Gentiles. Jewish Missionary Activity in the Second Temple Period* (Minneapolis: Fortress Press).

McRay, J.
1992 'Greece', *ABD*, II, 1092-98.

Millar, F.
1986 'Gentiles and Judaism: God-Fearers and Proselytes', in E. Schürer, rev. G. Vermes, F. Millar, and M. Goodman, *The History of the Jewish People in the Age of Jesus Christ*, III.1 (Edinburgh: T. & T. Clark), pp. 150-76.

Nolland, J.
1989 *Luke 1–9:20* (WBC 35A; Dallas: Word Books).

Overman, J.A.
1988 'The God-Fearers: Some Neglected Features', *JSNT* 32: 17-26.

Reynolds, J., and R. Tannenbaum
1987 *Jews and God-Fearers at Aphrodisias: Greek Inscriptions with Commentary* (Cambridge Philological Society, Supplementary Volume 12. Cambridge: Cambridge Philological Society).

Sanders, J.T.
1991 'Who is a Jew and who is a Gentile in the Book of Acts?', *NTS* 37: 434-55.

Siegert, F.
1973 'Gottesfürchtigen und Sympathisanten', *JSJ* 4: 109-64.

Stanton, G.N.
1994 'Justin Martyr's *Dialogue with Trypho*: Group Boundaries, "Proselytes", and "God-Fearers"', paper presented at the British–Israeli Colloquium, 'Tolerance and Intolerance in Early Judaism and Christianity', Hebrew University, Jerusalem, April 1994 (forthcoming).

Stern., M. (ed.)
1980 *Greek and Latin Authors on Jews and Judaism* (2 vols.; Jerusalem: Israel Academy of Sciences and Humanities).

Trebilco, P.R.
1991 *Jewish Communities in Asia Minor* (SNTSMS, 69; Cambridge: Cambridge University Press).

Tyson, J.B.
1992 *Images of Judaism in Luke–Acts* (Columbia, SC: University of South Carolina Press).
1995 'Jews and Judaism in Luke–Acts: Reading as a Godfearer', *NTS* 41: 19-38.

Wilcox, M.
1981 'The God-Fearers in Acts: A Reconsideration', *JSNT* 13: 102-22.

Witherington, B.
1992 'Lydia', *ABD*, IV, 422-23.

LUKE–ACTS AND THE QUMRAN SCROLLS: THE CASE OF MMT

George J. Brooke

1. *Luke–Acts and the Scrolls*

Since the early days of research into the meaning and significance of the scrolls found at Qumran, parallels with the Gospel of Luke and the Acts of the Apostles have been pointed out frequently and in detail. It is intriguing to note that apart from the Sermon on the Mount, neither Matthew's supposed Jewishness nor Mark's early date have resulted in those Gospels having more than their fair share of parallels with the forms of Palestinian Judaism represented in the Qumran scrolls. In fact, of the Synoptics, it is the third Gospel that has featured most in discussions of literary parallels. The *locus classicus* of this distinctiveness has been the parable of the unjust steward, unique to Luke (Lk. 16.1-9), in which the term 'sons of light' (Lk. 16.8) occurs. It has been noted that this term does not occur in either the Hebrew Bible or rabbinic literature, and so may be considered in some way particular to those who preserved and composed the scrolls found at Qumran.[1]

For the Acts of the Apostles the story has been the same. Numerous parallels have been noted.[2] Among the most important has been the

---

1. See J.A. Fitzmyer, 'The Story of the Dishonest Manager', *Essays on the Semitic Background of the New Testament* (London: Chapman, 1971), pp. 161-84, esp. pp. 167-68 n. 10. Together with others Fitzmyer observes that Luke 16.8b is part of the Lukan conclusion to the story in which comment is made about Christian disciples as the children of light. The phrase also appears in Jn 12.36; Eph. 5.8; 1 Thess. 5.5. In those instances it clearly refers to Christian believers. On the phrase generally, see J.A. Fitzmyer, 'Qumran and the Interpolated Paragraph in 2 Cor. 6.14-7', *Essays on the Semitic Background of the New Testament*, pp. 208-10; on the use of the phrase in 1 Thessalonians see most recently H.-W. Kuhn, 'The Impact of the Qumran Scrolls on the Understanding of Paul', in D. Dimant and U. Rappaport (eds.), *The Dead Sea Scrolls: Forty Years of Research* (STDJ, 10; Leiden: Brill, 1992), pp. 328-29.

2. Most neatly summed up by J.A. Fitzmyer in 'Jewish Christianity in Acts in

common ownership of property by the respective communities. In the Community Rule membership of the community is by voluntary association but the surrender of property is obligatory (1QS 6.13-23). According to Acts 4.36–5.11 it is not clear that the surrender of property was obligatory, though clearly it characterized the ideal community and was expected, as the story of Ananias and Sapphira exemplifies. Just as important as the general parallel are the technical details in common. Most significantly Acts 4.32 is the first place in Acts in which πλῆθος is used in the specific sense of the Christian congregation.[3] This terminology is remarkably close to the use of רב and רבים of the community in 1QS.[4] Indeed there is also some overlap in the terms יחד as used in many of the texts reflecting the life and practices of the community and κοινωνία (Acts 2.42).[5] In light of the important role played by Levites in some of the scrolls,[6] worth noting also is that the positive example provided in the matter of community of goods in Acts is the Levite Barnabas.[7]

Since the unpublished scrolls became generally available in 1991, there has been renewed interest in parallels between the scrolls and the New Testament. In several instances the study of certain fragmentary texts is in its infancy; here it is common for the New Testament evidence to be used for the better understanding of the Qumran material in itself, rather than there being any interest in drawing out the literary parallels for a better understanding of the New Testament. In almost every case it has been the Gospel of Luke which has been the subject of the comparison. For example, though known before 1991, the so-called 'Son of

Light of the Qumran Scrolls', in L.E. Keck and J.L. Martyn (eds.), *Studies in Luke–Acts* (London: SPCK, 1968), pp. 233-57.

3. See E. Haenchen, *The Acts of the Apostles: A Commentary* (Oxford: Blackwell, 1971), p. 230 n. 1. It is also used in this way in Acts 6.2, 5; 15.12, 30; 19.9; 21.22.

4. See especially H.W. Huppenbauer, 'רב, רוב, רבים in der Sektenregel (1QS)', *TZ* 13 (1957), pp. 136-37.

5. Cf. εἶχον ἅπαντα κοινά (Acts 2.44) and ἦν αὐτοῖς πάντα κοινά (Acts 4.32).

6. See most recently R.C. Stalman, 'Levi and the Levites in the Dead Sea Scrolls', *JSP* 10 (1992), pp. 163-89.

7. For more detail see G.J. Brooke, 'Levi and the Levites in the Dead Sea Scrolls and the New Testament', in Z.J. Kapera (ed.), *Mogilany 1989: Papers on the Dead Sea Scrolls Volume I* (Qumranica Mogilanensia, 2; Kraków: Enigma Press, 1993), pp. 105-29, esp. pp. 122-23.

God' text (4Q246) has been the cause of much recent debate.[8] The text is fragmentary and it is not easy to understand. The principal argument lies between those who see the Son of God and Son of the Most High as epithets used of a wicked figure and those who see the title referring to some messianic or angelic figure.[9] It is not difficult to see why those in the latter camp refer to the positive use of the title in Lk. 1.32-35 to assist in their interpretation of 4Q246.[10]

Another instance of Luke playing a role in the better understanding of scrolls material concerns the so-called 'Pierced Messiah' text. In this case R.H. Eisenman made the unlikely suggestion that והמיתו נשיא העדה should be translated as 'and they will put the Prince of the Congregation to death'.[11] Because of the place of Isa. 11.1 at the start of the disputed fragment, support for insisting that the most likely and therefore preferred rendering should be 'and the Prince of the Congregation will kill him', included reference to the use of Isa. 11.1-5 elsewhere. Since it was claimed that 11QMelchizedek supported the interpretation of 4Q285 as

8. E. Puech has published the text in full: 'Fragment d'une apocalypse en araméen (4Q246 = pseudo-Dan[d]) et le "royaume de Dieu"', *RB* 99 (1992), pp. 98-131; he relates it to other texts in *La croyance des Esséniens et la vie future: Immortalité, résurrection, vie éternelle. II. Les données qumraniennes et classiques* (EB, 22; Paris: Gabalda, 1993), pp. 570-72.

9. See the convenient summary of positions on this text in F. García Martínez, 'The Eschatological Figure of 4Q246', *Qumran and Apocalyptic: Studies on the Aramaic Texts from Qumran* (STDJ, 9; Leiden: Brill, 1992), pp. 162-79.

10. See, e.g., J.J. Collins, 'The "Son of God" Text from Qumran', in M.C. de Boer (ed.), *From Jesus to John: Essays on Jesus and New Testament Christology in Honour of Marinus de Jonge* (JSNTSup, 84; Sheffield: JSOT Press, 1993), pp. 65-82: 'Luke is dependent in some way, whether directly or indirectly, on this long lost text from Qumran' (p. 66). See also J.A. Fitzmyer, 'The Aramaic "Son of God" Text from Qumran Cave 4', in M.O. Wise, N. Golb, J.J. Collins and D.G. Pardee (eds.), *Methods of Investigation of the Dead Sea Scrolls and the Khirbet Qumran Site: Present Realities and Future Prospects* (Annals of the New York Academy of Sciences, 722; New York: New York Academy of Sciences, 1994), pp.163-78, esp. p. 175.

11. For the media coverage of this announcement see G. Vermes, 'The Oxford Forum for Qumran Research Seminar on the Rule of War from Cave 4 (4Q285)', *JJS* 43 (1992), pp. 85-86, esp. n. 2. Many of the most recent popular introductions to the scrolls have commented on this text, unanimously arguing that it should be understood that the Prince of the Congregation is doing the killing. A few voices are heard allowing the possibility of Eisenman's approach: e.g. J.D. Tabor, 'A Pierced or Piercing Messiah? The Verdict is Still Out', *BARev* 18 (Nov./Dec. 1992), pp. 58-59.

describing a dying messiah, T.H. Lim addressed the immediate problem of the most suitable reading of 11QMelch and its relation to the Gospel of Luke.[12] Even though Dan. 9.25 seems to be cited in 11QMelch 17-18, it is far less certain that the allusion also intended to include Dan. 9.26 with its anointed one who is cut off, since 11QMelch goes on to say how this figure saves people from Belial. It seems, however, that it is possible that 11QMelch should be viewed as providing much of the exegetical background for Lk. 4.16-21 as has been widely suggested.[13] Lim goes so far as to suggest that 11QMelch provides the exegetical link between Dan. 9.25-26 and Lk. 4.16-21, allowing for the early Christian development of the motif of a dying messiah.[14]

Yet a third recent text has been better appreciated in light of the Third Gospel. The so-called 'Resurrection Text' (4Q521) has received some detailed discussion.[15] In relation to the Gospel of Luke it is 4Q521 frag. 2 2.7-8 and 12-13 that deserve the most detailed consideration:

> For he will glorify the pious on the throne of an eternal kingdom, releasing captives, giving sight to the blind and raising up those who are bo[wed down]... for he will heal the wounded, give life to the dead and preach good news to the poor and he will [sat]isfy the [weak] ones and lead those who have been cast out and enrich the hungry.[16]

In Q 7.22 there is a pre-Synoptic tradition which is almost word for word in both Matthew and Luke. The disciples of John the Baptist are

---

12. T.H. Lim, '11QMelch, Luke 4 and the Dying Messiah', *JJS* 43 (1992), pp. 390-92.
13. See, e.g., G.J. Brooke, *Exegesis at Qumran: 4QFlorilegium in its Jewish Context* (JSOTSup, 29; Sheffield: JSOT Press, 1985), pp. 319-23.
14. '11QMelch, Luke 4 and the Dying Messiah', p. 92.
15. R.H. Eisenman, 'A Messianic Vision', *BARev* 17 (Nov./Dec. 1991), p. 65; E. Puech, 'Une apocalypse messianique (4Q521)', *RevQ* 15 (1992), pp. 475-522; R. Eisenman and M. Wise, *The Dead Sea Scrolls Uncovered* (Shaftesbury: Element Press, 1992), pp. 19-23; G. Vermes, 'Qumran Forum Miscellanea I', *JSS* 43 (1992), pp. 303-304; J.D. Tabor and M.O. Wise, '4Q521 "On Resurrection" and the Synoptic Gospel Tradition: A Preliminary Study', *JSP* 10 (1992), pp. 149-62; H. Stegemann, *Die Essener, Qumran, Johannes der Täufer und Jesus* (Freiburg: Herder, 1993), pp. 49-51, 290-91; E. Puech, *La croyance des Esséniens et la vie future*, II, pp. 627-92; J.J. Collins, 'The Works of the Messiah', *Dead Sea Discoveries* 1 (1994), pp. 98-112; O. Betz and R. Riesner, *Jesus, Qumran and the Vatican* (London: SCM Press, 1994), pp. 90-93; L.H. Schiffman, *Reclaiming the Dead Sea Scrolls* (Philadelphia: Jewish Publication Society, 1994), pp. 347-50.
16. Trans. J.J. Collins, 'The Works of the Messiah', p. 99.

told by Jesus to relate to John what they have seen and heard, 'the blind receive their sight, the lame walk, the lepers are cleansed, the deaf hear, the dead are raised, the poor have good news brought to them' (Lk. 7.22 NRSV). As is widely acknowledged, the first three elements of Q 7.22 are based on Isa. 35.5-6, the fifth on Isa. 61.1. Furthermore the actual phrasing of the first is a direct quotation from the LXX of Isa. 61.1b. The same rendering is used by Luke in Lk. 4.18. It is this link to Luke 4 which gives the Third Gospel preeminence in helping determine the better understanding of 4Q521. Most notably this seems to rest in the way in which it is not necessary to assume that the anointed one referred to in 4Q521 frag. 2 2.1 is a royal messiah. In light of Luke's concern with prophetic elements in Jesus' ministry, particularly as he distinctively in Luke raises the widow of Nain's son,[17] the anointed one in 4Q521 might just as well refer to the eschatological prophet. At the least it can hardly be coincidental that in going beyond the biblical passages both 4Q521 and Q 7.22 refer to the raising of the dead: 'It is quite possible that the author of the Sayings source knew 4Q521; at the least he drew on a common tradition'.[18] More precisely, 'Although it is unlikely that Luke knew the Qumran text directly, it seems that he shares with its author a common set of messianic expectations'.[19]

A fourth example can be seen in the Song of Miriam (4Q365, frag. 6, 2.1-7).[20] This poorly preserved new song appears in this Reworked Pentateuch immediately before Exod. 15.22-26.[21] It is addressed to God

---

17. Lk. 7.11-17. The acclamation of the crowd is 'A great prophet has arisen among us' (Lk. 7.16). This incident immediately precedes the enquiry of John's disciples. The prophetic background can be seen in 1 Kgs 17.17-24 and 2 Kgs 4.32-37.

18. J.J. Collins, 'The Works of the Messiah', p. 107.

19. J. Tabor and M.O. Wise, '4Q521 and the Synoptic Gospel Tradition', p. 161. They highlight Luke's interest in using Isa. 61: the unique cleansing of the lepers story (Lk. 17.11-19), the raising of the widow of Nain's son (Lk. 7.11-19), and the story of the woman bent double (Lk. 13.11-16).

20. First published by S.A. White in '4Q364 and 365: A Preliminary Report', in J. Trebolle Barrera and L. Vegas Montaner (eds.), *The Madrid Qumran Congress* (STDJ, 11; Leiden: Brill; Madrid: Editorial Complutense, 1992), pp. 222-24.

21. The song reads,

    1. you despised/you plundered...
    2. for the triumph of (cf. Exod. 15.1)...
    3. You are great, a saviour...

as saviour; together with the triumphant recollection of the military victory, there is the dramatic portrayal of a complete reversal. With 'you despised' perhaps God is portrayed as deriding the enemies of Israel; by contrast he is great. This greatness seems to be echoed in the exaltation of a feminine figure: 'and he exalted her to their heights'.[22] We may fairly presume that God is being extolled for elevating somebody of lowly status, giving her a sense of triumph.[23] The closest parallel to such phrasing can be found in the victory song of Judith but some consideration should also be given to the Magnificat. In Lk. 1.46-55 there is similarly the magnification of God as saviour and the exaltation of the lowly in the place of the powerful and rich. While it has been commonly proposed that the Magnificat may well be a slightly edited Jewish hymn,[24] perhaps from the Maccabean period, what becomes all the more striking is that the Song of Miriam, the victory song of Judith, and the Magnificat are all sung by women, commonly thought to have been a group of particular concern to Luke of all the evangelists.

All this recent activity in relation to Luke is suggestive, not only of how the New Testament has become part of the evidence for better understanding early Palestinian Judaism in all its diversity, but also for highlighting the place of Luke in preserving, in its special material and in its author's handling of inherited traditions, the viewpoint of a strand of Judaism which can be found in some fragmentary scroll texts, albeit that such traditions are reoriented in light of the death and resurrection of

    4. the hope of the enemy perishes and he is...
    5. they perished in the mighty waters (cf Exod. 15.10), the enemy...
    6. and he exalted (cf. Exod. 15.2) her to their heights...you gave...
    7. wor]king a triumph (cf. Exod. 15.1).

Some of these words and phrases are closely related to the song which Moses and the Israelites sing, but the poem is not simply a restatement of the Song of the Sea.

22. The reference to a female figure in the third person need be no problem, if the song was sung antiphonally by Miriam and the women with her. This phrase would then possibly belong to the part sung by the women.

23. For further comments on the significance of this song for women and for the New Testament, see G.J. Brooke, 'Power to the Powerless: A Long-Lost Song of Miriam', *BARev* 20/3 (1994), pp. 62-65.

24. Most notably Paul Winter suggested in 1954 that both the Magnificat and the Benedictus (Lk. 1.68-79) were Maccabean psalms: 'Magnificat and Benedictus—Maccabean Psalms', *BJRL* 37 (1954), pp. 328-43. See also D. Flusser, 'The Magnificat, the Benedictus and the War Scroll', *Judaism and the Origins of Christianity* (Jerusalem: Magnes Press, 1988), pp. 126-49.

Jesus and their meaning for everyday thought and practice in the Lukan communities.

It is intriguing to note that the two significant parallels from the early years of comparison of the scrolls with Luke–Acts both fall in Lukan contexts concerning behaviour in the community, more particularly with behaviour involving money and in the case of Luke 16 also Jesus' teaching on divorce; the more recent parallels highlight overlaps in exegesis and theology rather than ethics. But, as far as what characterizes Judaism in the late second temple period, it is matters of behaviour, daily living, halakhah which are at the root of the distinctiveness of the various groups and subgroups of the time. So, as part of the overall rejuvenation of interest in the way the New Testament and the scrolls might be used for their better mutual understanding, the rest of this study will draw out some of the similarities and differences between Luke–Acts and the halakhic text known as Miqṣat Ma'aśe Ha-Torah (= MMT) which has recently been officially published.[25]

E. Qimron has observed with some justification that 4QMMT should be seen as a pivotal text in understanding the reasons why groups distinguished themselves from one another in the two and a half centuries before the fall of the temple. He notes that MMT describes the opinions of three groups ('We', 'You', 'They') and that in many respects the views of these three groups might not be inappropriately linked with Essenes, Sadducces and Pharisees, in some form.[26] For Qimron MMT stands at the centre of how early Judaism should be defined. For him three matters of halakhah stand at the centre of the self-definition of the various group opinions: the calendar, purity, and marriage practice. As a text with such possibilities concerning group self-definition in the late second temple period, it is worth juxtaposing with Luke–Acts to see to

---

25. E. Qimron and J. Strugnell in consultation with Y. Sussmann and with contributions by Y. Sussmann and A. Yardeni, *Qumran Cave 4. V. Miqṣat Ma'aśe Ha-Torah* (DJD, 10; Oxford: Clarendon Press, 1994). The composite text and English translation is reprinted in 'For This You Waited 35 Years', *BARev* 20 (Nov./Dec. 1994), pp. 56-61. An alternative English translation is available in F. García Martínez, *The Dead Sea Scrolls Translated: The Qumran Texts in English* (Leiden: Brill, 1994), pp. 77-85. See also B.W.W. Dombrowski, *An Annotated Translation of Miqṣāt Ma'aśēh ha-Tôrâ 4QMMT* (Weenzen, 1992; Weenzen/Kraków: Enigma Press, 2nd edn, 1993); B.W.W. Dombrowski, 'Miqṣāt Ma'aśēh ha-Tôrâ (4QMMT) in English', *The Qumran Chronicle* 4.1/2 (1994), pp. 28-36.

26. The same tripartite differentiation is of course found in Josephus, but is also implied in the ciphers of Judah, Ephraim and Manasseh in 4QpNah.

what extent some of the concerns of Luke–Acts may be brought into focus by it. It must be underlined that this is not an attempt to argue that there is any literary dependence, but rather that some of the same issues may be argued through in both writings, sometimes in a similar manner. In this way it is hoped that the literary achievement of Luke in his two volume work will be clarified from yet one further direction.

2. *Miqṣat Ma'aśe Ha-Torah*

MMT exists in six fragmentary copies, the oldest 'from about 75 BCE, and the youngest from about 50 CE'.[27] Enough remains to enable the reconstruction of a single composite text. As presented by Qimron and Strugnell this composite text has three parts, though they acknowledge that there may well have been other material at the start of the text.[28] In the first extant section, preserved only in 4Q394 (= 4QMMT[a]), there is a calendar. It lists the sabbaths and the festivals for the year: dates for the period from the second to the sixth month are preserved in five columns on two fragments, then dates for the twelfth month, together with a summary formula, are preserved at the start of 4Q394. It is true that the other manuscript which preserves the start of the second section, 4Q395 (= 4QMMT[b]), has a blank space at its opening and that on this basis Strugnell has dissociated himself from his coeditor's opinion about the overall makeup of the text, but Strugnell argues his position on the basis that the calendrical material contains no polemic as is found in the second section. It could be maintained, however, that the polemic is implicit in the presentation of a calendar of 364 days in which none of the principal days of the festivals fall on a Sabbath and which mentions festivals (New Wine, New Oil) which are only found in the Temple Scroll.

The second section of the composite text contains 82 lines as reconstructed. After an overall brief introduction which recalls the opening words of Deuteronomy, there is discussion of 17 halakhic topics. Though there are allusions to biblical passages in many of these halakhic discussions, the order of the topics does not depend on that of the Bible: the first eight concern sacrifices and related matters of purity (B 3-38), the other nine include six which concern the purity of Jerusalem and the temple (B 39-62; 64-74) with three short supplements, two on gifts for

---

27. *Miqṣat Ma'aśe Ha-Torah*, p. 108.
28. *Miqṣat Ma'aśe Ha-Torah*, p. 109.

priests (B 62-64) and one on priestly marriage practice.

The third section is exhortatory. The language changes somewhat from the matter-of-fact presentation of the halakhot in the second section. However, just as that section opened with an echo of Deuteronomy, so the third section recalls the covenantal framework of Deuteronomy as it suggests that some of the blessings and curses of the Book of Moses have already been fulfilled in the days of Solomon and from the days of Jeroboam until the exile respectively (C 17-21). The third section is addressed by a first person plural group to an individual and 'your (s.) people' (C 27[29]).

3. *Luke–Acts and MMT*

a. *Form: The Confirmatory Instructional Treatise*
The first methodological factor to take into consideration is the way elements of a common form are used in both texts. Though the documents end up looking very different, MMT was first presented to the world as a letter and, as is well known, both Luke and Acts are addressed in their prefaces to Theophilus. Neither MMT nor Luke–Acts are letters, but both are treatises of some kind.

Though still commonly talked about as a letter,[30] both of MMT's principal editors have distanced themselves from their earlier definition by insisting that MMT was clearly never intended as a personal letter, but rather as some kind of formal epistle or treatise, 'though formal descriptions of these genres are hard to make'.[31] In an Appendix to the publication of the *editio princeps* of MMT Strugnell distances himself from what was written in the earlier part of the volume: 'The treatise is, at least in Hellenistic literature, a very ill-defined genre, and such a distribution of the personal pronouns [as in MMT] could be expected in many other literary contexts too. So the suggestion...that this was a treatise rather than a letter, should be withdrawn.'[32] The problem, as

---

29. The phrase 'your (s.) people' is missing from 4QMMT^f, but the term Israel is preserved at the very end of the text.
30. See, e.g., the extensive description of MMT as the 'Halakhic Letter' in L.H. Schiffman, *Reclaiming the Dead Sea Scrolls*, pp. 83-89.
31. *Miqṣat Ma'aśe Ha-Torah*, p. 113.
32. *Miqṣat Ma'aśe Ha-Torah*, p. 204; Strugnell expresses the same reservations in 'MMT: Second Thoughts on a Forthcoming Edition', in E. Ulrich and J. VanderKam (eds.), *The Community of the Renewed Covenant: The Notre Dame Symposium on the Dead Sea Scrolls* (Christianity and Judaism in Antiquity Series,

Strugnell perceives it, is threefold: first, the calendrical material of the first section of MMT is only present in one of the two manuscripts which preserve the part of the opening of the second section of text, thus making it possible that calendrical issues were not an integral part of the polemic of the body of the text.[33] Secondly, a reconstruction of the manuscript which does contain the calendrical material does not seem to allow for enough room at the start for a significant prologue to introduce the whole text. Thirdly, the few words which preface the halakhic second section are not sufficient for introducing a treatise, but look more like an imitation of the opening of the Book of Deuteronomy which has been geared specifically to an odd collection of assorted purity rules.

For all that there are formal problems with the start of the text, the third section continues the second person address and concludes with a phrase, לטוב לך ולישראל ('for your own welfare and that of Israel'), which is not unlike the closing formula of one of the Bar Kokhba letters, אהוה שלום וכל בית ישראל ('May there be peace (to you) and to all the House of Israel').[34] Since the second and third sections of MMT almost certainly belong together,[35] the legal material does indeed seem to have circulated in a text which had an exhortatory close with an epistolary formal element at its very end.

Since MMT exists, even today, in six copies, it is clear that it was always intended as an open circular, designed to be heard by a wide audience who might identify themselves with the 'you' of the addressee. The author speaks consistently in the first person plural. It is probably wrong to search for an individual author behind such a stylistic feature; whoever it is writes on behalf of a group to an audience with whom he shares much in common. His general purpose is to confirm that the two

---

10; Notre Dame: University of Notre Dame Press, 1994), p. 63.

33. Schiffman describes B1-3 as the beginning of the letter (*Reclaiming the Dead Sea Scrolls*, p. 83).

34. Mur 42.7; see *Miqṣat Ma'aśe Ha-Torah*, p. 113. For detailed discussion of the formulae used in letters of the time, see P.S. Alexander, 'Epistolary Literature', in M.E. Stone (ed.), *Jewish Writings of the Second Temple Period* (CRINT, 2.2; Assen: van Gorcum; Philadelphia: Fortress Press, 1984), pp. 579-96, esp. pp. 588-92.

35. The theory of R. Eisenman and M. Wise (*The Dead Sea Scrolls Uncovered*, p. 196), that sections A + B and C are two separate letters, has been substantially refuted by F. García Martínez, 'Dos notas sobre 4QMMT', *RevQ* 16/62 (1993), pp. 295-97.

groups are much in agreement. For the particular addressee in C 28-29, this confirmation will come about through considering 'all these things', 'for we have seen that you have wisdom and knowledge of the Torah'.

Luke, distinctively among the Gospels, provides his two-part work with a prologue or preface which is echoed in the introduction of the second part. Though addressed to a particular reader, his labours are not intended for private consumption alone. Nor is his work to be considered as a letter, but more properly as a treatise of some kind directed at a certain audience. The preface to the Gospel in particular has been the subject of very extensive study, since it is widely held that to understand it would be to understand the overall purpose of the author. Some scholars have preferred to leave the generic significance of Lk. 1.1-4 on a quite general level. So, for example, J.A. Fitzmyer merely underlines that the key to the prologue rests in its final phrase: 'Luke writes for Theophilus, a catechumen or neophyte, in order to give him assurance about the initial instruction that he has received'.[36] For Fitzmyer the assurance contained in the Gospel and Acts is doctrinal and didactic and does not depend on a particular understanding of what genre of preface Luke may be attempting to imitate. More recently L.C.A. Alexander has addressed the issue of the preface most searchingly and concluded that it is to be seen in the context of 'scientific' works of the hellenistic schools, thus suggesting that Luke–Acts should be read similarly.[37]

Now it is clear that MMT and Luke–Acts are rather different kinds of work, but both might be classed generically as treatises with a didactic element. More significantly, both appear to have been written to confirm, strengthen and assure the reader that the position they have been taught or now hold is indeed the correct or appropriate one. Both MMT and Luke–Acts are confirmatory instruction.

Beyond the overall similarity between MMT and Luke–Acts it is interesting to note that what is planned after the meeting in Jerusalem described in Acts 15 is the writing of a letter informing the recipients of the decisions made; perhaps MMT is best understood not as a letter authored by an individual (the 'Teacher of Righteousness') but rather as

---

36. *The Gospel according to Luke I–IX* (AB, 28; Garden City: Doubleday, 2nd edn, 1983), p. 301.

37. *The Preface to Luke's Gospel: Literary Convention and Social Context in Luke 1.1-4 and Acts 1.1* (SNTSMS, 78; Cambridge: Cambridge University Press, 1993).

the reporting of decisions perhaps taken in a council session, not unlike that in Acts 15. This would make better sense of the first person plural pronoun used in MMT.[38]

All this has broader implications. In a previous scholarly generation it would be deemed appropriate to tease out this parallel in literary method in terms of supposing either that the author of MMT should be accounted among his literary peers in the hellenistic world or that the outward literary form of Luke's two volumes should be considered within the parameters of Palestinian Judaism. Nowadays, such divisions are seen to be increasingly inappropriate and the real situation far more complex. This parallel in literary method should rather be seen as yet another example of how universal was the literary culture of the ancient Mediterranean world.

b. *Content: The Centre of the Law*
Since the overall perspective of exclusivity and rigorist interpretation of the Law is clear to see in MMT, there is little point in attempting to work through each of the halakhic statements in MMT looking for detailed parallels in Luke–Acts. However, on a general level in terms of content, three intricately related matters come to the fore in Luke–Acts through laying it side by side with MMT: the place of Jerusalem, the role of the Temple, and the issue of who may worship there. This commonality is all the more surprising when it is remembered that MMT was written when the Temple was very much a live institution, whereas Luke–Acts was written after the Temple's demise.

In Luke–Acts Jerusalem plays a special role. 'The overarching geographical perspective in Luke–Acts can be seen in the author's preoccupation with Jerusalem as the city of destiny for Jesus and the pivot for the salvation of mankind', says Fitzmyer.[39] The Gospel begins and ends in Jerusalem and the city of Jerusalem may be seen as controlling individual incidents in the Gospel, such as the order of the temptations in the

---

38. This seems preferable to pushing the Teacher of Righteousness as the possible author of MMT on the basis of 4QpPs[a] 3-10 iv 7-9 which describes how the Wicked Priest spied on the Teacher of Righteousness and tried to put him to death because of the precepts (חוק) and the law (תורה) which he had sent him. This identification is pursued in the principal edition, *Miqṣat Maʿaśe Ha-Torah*, pp. 119-20.

39. *Luke I–IX*, p. 164; Fitzmyer devotes 10 pages to discussing the geographical aspects of the Gospel, especially the central role of Jerusalem.

temptation narrative which reach their climax in Luke with the reference to Jerusalem, or such as the complete lack of any resurrection appearances except those in the vicinity of Jerusalem; Jerusalem also controls whole sequences in the Gospel, such as the distinctive journey narrative (9.51–19.27) when Jesus sets his face to go to Jerusalem. Few would deny this central role to Jerusalem in the Gospel, but the narrative of Acts is commonly thought of as portraying the spread of the gospel from Jerusalem to Rome. However, even in Acts, Jerusalem remains pivotal; not only does the narrative of Acts start in Jerusalem, but the central narrative moment of the 'Council' is held there (Acts 15) and Paul repeatedly gravitates back to Jerusalem (Acts 18.22; 21.15-26). In fact, the name Jerusalem features 60 times in Acts, half in chs. 1–14, and half spread through the remainder of the work.

Within Jerusalem it is the Temple that is the focus of attention, what it signifies in itself and how worship there is rightly ordered and practised. For Jesus it is the place of instruction: in the infancy narrative he is found there among the teachers, listening to them and asking questions (Lk 2.46-49), as a foreshadowing of his later teaching ministry in the Temple (Lk. 19.47). Immediately upon entering Jerusalem the Lukan Jesus goes to the Temple not just to look around but to purge it.[40] In Acts the same characterizes the ministry of the apostles: Peter and John in the court of the Gentiles (Acts 3.11),[41] and the apostles generally (Acts 5.20-21, 42). In addition the Temple is, of course, the focus of prayer and worship (e.g. Lk. 19.45-48; Acts 3.1), the place where ritual obligations are met, particularly those involving matters of purity, whether at the time of purification (Lk. 2.22-24), after the lepers had been healed (Lk. 17.14), or at the discharge of a vow (Acts 21.15-26).

A further matter concerning the depiction of the Temple and its worship in Luke–Acts concerns the issue of who may worship there. For example, both Jesus' parents bring him to be presented at the Temple (Lk. 2.22); by implication the Samaritan knows more about the significance of ritual than either the Priest or the Levite (Lk. 10.29-37); the Samaritan leper, though bidden to tell the priests what had happened, is the one who returns to Jesus and prostrates himself before him

---

40. Fitzmyer notes how this echoes Mal. 3.1 with its motif of 'coming', (*Luke I–IX*, p. 168).

41. Josephus locates the portico in the eastern outer wall, in the court of the Gentiles (*War* 5.185; *Ant.* 20.221).

(Lk. 17.11-19); the Ethiopian eunuch[42] has come to Jerusalem to worship (Acts 8.27); and Paul is falsely accused of introducing Greeks into the Temple (Acts 21.28-29). It is almost as if Luke is interested in women, Samaritans, the lepers,[43] the Gentiles, not because they were marginalized socially by Jews and, by implication, by some Jewish Christians, but because they were religiously marginalized. Luke seems to insist that all should have their proper place in the worship of God.

However, there is a further implication that comparison of Luke–Acts with MMT highlights. Luke–Acts is not concerned with social and religious inclusiveness for its own sake. Such inclusiveness is according to the Law. This is shown chiefly in the way in which the charges against Paul for profaning the Temple are repeatedly rehearsed. This concern with the Law is summed up by D. Juel: for Luke the 'Torah served as a pointer to the one true God in a world full of idols; it identified those who lived by it as worshippers of that God', and so Luke's 'narrative assumes that if there is a people of God, they will live by the law'.[44] Juel goes on to show how Paul's attitude to the Law is of special concern: Paul never did anything 'against the people or the customs of our fathers' (Acts 21.21), and the Jerusalem elders know that Paul has lived in observance of the Law (Acts 21.24).[45]

MMT presents a rigorist and exclusivist interpretation of the Law. The sacrificial offerings of Gentiles are prohibited, the Ammonite, the Moabite and the sexually deformed or mutilated are to be excluded from entering the congregation and from intermarriage, the blind and the deaf are legislated against, the leper cannot be readmitted until after sunset on the eighth day. The rules concerning these groups are stringent because of the holiness of Jerusalem: 'Jerusalem is the camp of holiness, and is the place which He has chosen from among all the tribes of Israel. For Jerusalem is the capital of the camps of Israel' (MMT B 60-62).

In addition to this range of sacrificial and purity regulations, we noted earlier in this study that Qimron also considered marriage rules to lie at the heart of the legal self-definition of any group in late second temple

---

42. Sexually mutilated; such are legislated against in MMT B 39-40.
43. Lepers are legislated for in MMT B 64-72.
44. D. Juel, *Luke–Acts* (London: SCM Press, 1984), p. 108.
45. Not all scholars read the place of the Law in Luke–Acts in this way. For a summary of various views see J.A. Fitzmyer, 'The Jewish People and the Mosaic Law in Luke–Acts', *Luke the Theologian: Aspects of his Teaching* (London: Chapman, 1989), pp. 175-202.

Judaism. Apart from Lk. 16.18 on divorce, which was discussed briefly above as pertinent to how the Law should be upheld in matters of property and marriage, it is noteworthy that the other reference to marriage law comes by implication in association with purity regulations (just as in MMT) in the decree of the apostles in Acts 15.20 which is repeated in Acts 21.25. The apostles determine to write to Gentiles who are turning to God, instructing them 'to abstain only from things polluted by idols and from fornication and from whatever has been strangled and from blood'.

The term for fornication, πορνεία, corresponds with זנות (or זונה or their verbal counterpart זנה), technical terminology which is variously used four times in MMT. In B 9 some aspect of the offering of Gentiles is 'like a woman who whored with him'. In B 75 (with a minor variant in MMT^d) Qimron and Strugnell translate the term as 'illegal marriage', with Qimron considering that MMT condemns intermarriage between priests and laity.[46] In B 82 this same ruling is repeated; this time the preferred translation for זונות is 'women whom they are forbidden to marry'. In the very broken context of C 5 there seems to be a general statement in the context of further marriage law which argues that 'because of] malice (חמס) and the fornication (הזנות) [some] places were destroyed'. While some have seen πορνεία in Acts 15.20 as merely concerning the kinds of unchastity mentioned in Lev. 18.6-30,[47] it seems clear from MMT that other matters in marriage practice may be involved.[48] What these may be in the case of Acts 15 requires further research.

If MMT's particular concerns in matters of cultic and marriage practice are indeed the focus for the self-definition of the group which the text represents in its first person plural pronoun, then to discover a similar combination of cultic purity rules together with mention of πορνεία in Acts 15 may be very significant for how Luke considered the early Christian community to be defining itself in continuity with the precepts

46. *Miqṣat Ma'aśe Ha-Torah*, p. 55.
47. E.g. H. Conzelmann, *Acts of the Apostles* (Hermeneia; Philadelphia: Fortress Press, 1987), p. 119.
48. Other newly released texts from Qumran also use זנות and זנה in a range of contexts. For a recent discussion of some of these, but in relation to the Matthaean divorce pericope, see J. Kampen, 'The Matthean Divorce Texts Re-Examined', in G.J. Brooke with F. García Martínez (eds.), *New Qumran Texts and Studies: Proceedings of the First Meeting of the International Organization for Qumran Studies, Paris 1992* (STDJ, 15; Leiden: Brill, 1994), pp. 149-67.

of the Law which it was seeking to uphold, without insisting that the whole Law had to be kept by all the Gentile converts. What is taking place in MMT for the groups it is defining is also taking place in Acts 15 for the way Luke is trying to define the new heirs of the promises of God in the Law.

c. *Method: The Argument from Scripture*
Discussion of the place of the Law in MMT and Luke–Acts leads us to the third area in which the juxtaposition of MMT and Luke–Acts helps us to see more clearly what is taking place in each text without insisting that there is any literary relationship between the two. In terms of the place of the Law and Scripture more broadly, it is remarkable that of all the texts in the late second temple period and just beyond which define the extent of the authoritative scriptural base with which one must grapple and from which one can argue a point, it is Luke and MMT that share a definition. In MMT C 10 the partially damaged text can be suitably restored to read 'so that you may study (carefully) the book of Moses and the books of the Prophets and (the writings of) David'. This corresponds most closely of contemporary literature with Lk. 24.44: 'everything written about me in the law of Moses, the prophets, and the psalms must be fulfilled'.[49]

The place of Scripture in Luke–Acts has commonly been understood in terms of the model of the fulfilment of prophecy, with the prophets and psalms playing an obvious role in the two works. On this basis it is argued that Luke presents the ministry, death and resurrection of Jesus as the fulfilment of prophecy so that with him or after him there is a new period of history. We have already noted above that Luke does not seem to propose that what is new is discontinuous with the past, so the periodization of history with Jesus as the middle of Lukan time should not be pressed too far. The apostolic decree in Acts shows that what is happening, at least in the scheme of Luke–Acts, is not something entirely new. Furthermore we should note that the Law still has a part to play, even if for most Gentile Christians that is rather minimal. Thus it is not entirely appropriate for the entire use of Scripture in Luke–Acts to be subsumed in the prophecy–fulfilment model. For Luke Jesus is, among other things, a law-abiding, Jerusalem oriented prophet; he is

---

49. J.C. VanderKam (*The Dead Sea Scrolls Today* [London: SPCK, 1994], pp. 142-57) has provided the most comprehensive collection of references in relation to up to date information on the extent and character of the 'canon' at Qumran.

concerned with restoration rather than innovation.

If for Luke–Acts an awareness of the three divisions of the canon mentioned explicitly in Lk 24.44 enables the modern reader to appreciate the continuing significance of the Law in the Lukan scheme, it is pertinent to ask conversely of MMT where the place of prophets and of David lies. For the individual halakhot in section B the reference point is predominantly matters in the Torah, especially Leviticus, Numbers (chs. 15 and 19) and Deuteronomy (ch. 23); there is little, if any, appeal to the prophets[50] or to the psalms. However, in section C (with the help of some restoration) it is clear that the author links adherence to the particular interpretation of the Law which is advocated in MMT B to historical experiences as these are narrated in the former prophets: '[the blessings have (already) befallen in...] in the days of Solomon the son of David. And the curses [that] have (already) befallen from the days of Jeroboam the son of Nebat and up to when Jerusalem and Zedekiah King of Judah went into captivity' (C 18-19). The exhortation of MMT is grounded in the recollection of the past which demonstrates that some of the blessings and curses presented in the Torah have already been fulfilled. Thus simply articulating the Law is not sufficient; its particular application has to be justified from as broad a perspective as possible. Part of that perspective is the example of David, known not just from the histories but also from his psalms; he is the example of the righteous man who was delivered and, most importantly, forgiven (C 25-26). The interpretation of Law in MMT, like the Law itself, is thus offered as a gift, not a threat.

Within Scripture itself this justification for adhering to a particular interpretation of the Law is presented most explicitly in the so-called Deuteronomistic History. The precepts of Deuteronomic theology are the criteria applied to each ruler in turn. It is not surprising, then, that Strugnell should have noted in particular the place of Deuteronomy in the overall structure of MMT B and C. As MMT B is introduced with words which echo Deut. 1.1, so C focuses on how blessing and curse (echoing Deut. 27–28) are to be fulfilled especially as the end time is upon the reader. In a less explicit fashion parts of Deuteronomy have been seen to be instructive for appreciating some of the compositional

---

50. Qimron and Strugnell (*Miqṣat Maʿaśe Ha-Torah*, p. 55) prefer to see the words from Jer. 2.3 in MMT B 76 as a general reference to Scripture as a whole which declares Israel to be holy. Since there is an introductory formula, it may be preferable to see it as an explicit citation.

elements in Luke, especially Lk. 9.51–18.14, which is entirely made up of non-Markan material,[51] or even ideas behind the composition of the whole of Luke–Acts.[52] In these ways the book of Deuteronomy appears schematically influential in both works, as in several others of the time.

A final point can be made which is not distinctive of what MMT and Luke–Acts may share, but is common to the scrolls and the New Testament in general. The attitude to Scripture is displayed through the formulae which introduce quotations of it. In MMT there are several such formulae: שא כתוב (B 27 introducing a form of Lev. 17.3), אף כתוב (B 66 introducing a paraphrase of Lev. 14.8), כת[וב ש- (B 70 introducing a paraphrase of Num. 15.30), כשכתוב (B 76 probably introducing Jer. 2.3), כתוב ש- (B 77 introducing a paraphrase of Lev. 19.19), כת[ו]ב בספר מושה ש- (C 6 introducing a paraphrase of Deut 7.26), בספר כתוב (C 11 with no further text preserved), כתוב ש- (C 12 introducing a paraphrase of Deut 31.29), כת[וב (C 12 introducing a paraphrase of Deut 30.1-3), [כתוב בספר] מושה ובס[פרי הנביא]ם ש- (C 17 with little text extant), שכתוב בס[פר מו]שה (C 21 closing a general statement). The formulae all concern writing, probably because formulae with terms for speaking are used to represent the opinions of the author and his group. In MMT there is no instance of an introductory formula not introducing a scriptural text or paraphrase, though specific books are only mentioned in the exhortatory section. There thus appears a clear demarcation between Scripture and the author's own or his group's own interpretations, which is also the case for Luke–Acts and the whole New Testament.

4. Conclusion

There can be little question of any literary dependence of Luke–Acts on a text like MMT, but by putting the two texts side by side in this brief fashion several aspects of each have been highlighted. Both have some

---

51. See, e.g., C.F. Evans, *Saint Luke* (TPI New Testament Commentaries; London: SCM Press; Philadelphia: Trinity Press International, 1990), pp. 34-37.

52. So, e.g., R. Morgenthaler has described the composition of the whole of Luke–Acts in terms of the 'law of duality', the literary pattern of the two-volume work being the working out of the principle that true testimony must be established by the mouth of at least two witnesses (Deut. 19.15): *Die lukanische Geschichtsschreibung als Zeugnis: Gestalt und Gehalt der Kunst des Lukas* (2 vols.; Zürich: Zwingli Verlag, 1949), II, p. 8.

generic features in common as being treatises with the aim of instruction that confirms views with which the recipient is already sympathetically familiar. Both place considerable importance on Jerusalem and the Temple as the locus for defining their own stances on issues; such definitions involve matters of purity, particularly as these may concern who may participate in the appropriate way in the worship of God. Sexual laws or marriage practice is also a community marker, though again the two texts take very different lines. Both texts argue on a similar scriptural basis, a seemingly trite observation which is of value in seeing that MMT is not just legal prescription for its own sake and Luke–Acts is not tied exclusively to the prophecy–fulfilment model of the use of Scripture, but has a continuing place for the Law. With many of the issues in common, it is nevertheless all the easier to see that the answers proposed by each writing are poles apart. While the author of MMT looks for the day when Temple practice will be pure, Luke comes to realize that it not only can be but has to be done without, though its significance abides. Whereas MMT is rigidly exclusivist, Luke–Acts is inclusivist. In light of a newly published text like MMT the literary achievement of the author of Luke–Acts may be seen a little more clearly; at the least we can see that his literary concerns cannot be entirely divorced from the issues around in the Palestinian Judaism of his day.

THEOPHILUS'S FIRST READING OF LUKE–ACTS

F. Gerald Downing

Theophilus, the Performance and the Audience

Theophilus

Theophilus may well have been the real name for a real person. Loveday Alexander tells us it was a favourite name among Hellenistic Jews, and she assures us that there is very little evidence, if any, for dedications to imaginary people.[1] Whether he was a patron of superior status, or a friend of similar standing to the author's we cannot tell, and still less whether he would have been expected to finance the further 'publication', the wider circulation of the two-volume work. We do not know for sure whether he was a committed Christian, and of course it has been argued that Luke was writing a defence of the Christian movement, directed to an important pagan Roman official. However, Dr Alexander also argues that the Preface to the Gospel strongly suggests that the work which follows is intended as a reminder for people already well aware of much of the contents. It is not an introduction for outsiders.[2] If Christian Luke has Theophilus as a friend or patron (or friendly patron), he is most likely at least a sympathizer, more likely a member of the group.

Reading—Aloud

I want us to imagine his first reading. I have to allow that someone else may have done this imagining already—and more competently. But recent studies in Luke–Acts have not pointed me to any such recent reconstruction,[3] and attempting such in this essay also allows me to

---

1. L. Alexander, *The Preface to Luke's Gospel* (SNTSMS, 78; Cambridge: Cambridge University Press, 1993), pp. 73-75, 133, 188.
2. L. Alexander, *Preface*, pp. 142, 188-193.
3. There are a number of 'reader-response' analyses available. J.B. Tyson, 'The Implied Reader in Luke Acts', in his *Images of Judaism in Luke–Acts* (Columbia:

survey together some recent monographs and collections, as well as to air again one or two orginal studies of my own.

We may take it that the reading would almost certainly have been aloud.[4] Perhaps the author himself would have read his work, or some other competent speaker would have read for him. We have been reminded of late that silent reading was less uncommon in the ancient Mediterranean world than is sometimes supposed, but Frank Gilliard's 1993 study nonetheless accepts there is no reason to question 'the predominance of orality'.[5] Of course, not only is performance oral, composition is, too. Almost certainly some of Luke's friends—if not Theophilus himself—would have been invited to discuss his early drafts of the work with him while it was in progress.[6]

The Wider Audience (a)
The reading would have taken one or two sittings, and it would probably have been in company. In some circles, of course, men and women would have been segregated. When Pliny junior gave a reading of his own work, his wife Calpurnia sat behind a screen to listen (*Letters* 4.9). However, I have suggested that Luke's and Theophilus's circle will have been Christian, and all the Pauline and later deutero-Pauline letters suggest Christian men and women met together, albeit, after the earliest days, on very clearly unequal terms. Luke himself suggests much the same conclusion (Lk. 10.39; 11.27; Acts 1.14; 12.12; 16.13-14, etc.), and

University of South Carolina Press, 1992), pp.17-41, attempts to profile the implied reader in the appropriate cultural setting; and see the useful survey in F.S. Spencer, 'Acts and Modern Literary Approaches', in B.W. Winter and A.D. Clarke (eds.), *The Book of Acts in its First Century Setting*. I. *The Book of Acts in its Ancient Literary Setting* (Grand Rapids: Eerdmans, 1993; Exeter: Paternoster Press, 1994), pp. 381-414. The sketch that follows does not seem to have been anticipated.

4. Cf. P. Gempf, 'Public Speaking and Published Accounts', in B.W. Winter and A.D. Clarke (eds.) *The Book of Acts*, I, pp. 259-304, but esp. pp. 260-62; F.G. Downing, 'A bas les Aristos', *NovT* 30 (1988), pp. 212-30; L. Alexander, 'The Living Voice', in D.J.A. Clines *et al.* (eds.), *The Bible in Three Dimensions* (JSOTSup, 87; Sheffield: JSOT Press, 1990), pp. 221-47; *per contra*: P.F. Esler, *Community and Gospel in Luke–Acts* (SNTSMS, 58; Cambridge: Cambridge University Press, 1987), p. 7.

5. F. Gilliard, 'More Silent Reading in Antiquity', *JBL* 112 (1993), pp. 689-94, quoting from p. 694.

6. Cf. F.G. Downing, 'Ears to Hear', in A.E. Harvey (ed.), *Alternative Approaches to New Testament Study* (London: SPCK, 1985), p. 98; and my 'Word-Processing in the First Century' (forthcoming).

perhaps the amount of apparently sympathetic attention given to women in the Gospel supports this view. Dr Alexander has argued for an adult 'school' setting for the reading of Luke–Acts.[7] We may note Luke's account of Paul in Tyrannus's lecture-hall (Acts 19.9). If we accepted that conclusion, then I do not think we would expect children to have been present. I do not think we have any accounts of children being included in meetings of adults for study, even among Christians. However, households that had been baptized together would doubtless have included any children in festival meals, and so, presumably, in the supper of the Lord Jesus, and I shall argue that relaxed mealtime is a yet more likely occasion for the 'performance' of Luke–Acts. But at this, as at every point, further evidence of any sort would be very welcome.

Social Composition

We are assured these days of a kind of consensus among New Testament historians, to the effect that the early urban Christians mostly if not universally will have included in their number relatively prosperous fellow-townspeople, able to act as patrons to local congregations, at least to the extent of affording hospitality for meetings (and perhaps bed and board for visiting missionaries).[8] *Kratistos*, 'most excellent' Theophilus will presumably have been such a person. Certainly recent studies by H. Moxnes and by J.C. Lentz both indicate that the ideal hearer would share the attitudes of those from whom patronage would be expected.[9] The Pauline writings would also lead us to expect that a number of less wealthy people would also be present at Theophilus's invitation, and Luke's own highlighting of *some* wealthier and more influential converts suggests that he had a similar expectation (Acts 17.12, 34).

---

7. L. Alexander, 'Acts and Ancient Intellectual Biography', in Winter and Clarke (eds.), *The Book of Acts*, I, pp. 31-64, expanding the suggestion in *eadem*, *The Preface*, pp. 202-205.
8. E.g. W. Meeks, *The First Urban Christians* (New Haven: Yale University Press, 1983), ch. 2, pp. 51-73; B. Holmberg, *Sociology and the New Testament* (Minneapolis: Fortress Press, 1990), pp. 59-60.
9. H. Moxnes, *The Economy of the Kingdom: Social Conflict and Economic Interaction in Luke's Gospel* (Philadelphia: Fortress Press, 1988), and 'Patron–Client Relations and the New Community in Luke–Acts', in J.H. Neyrey (ed.), *The Social World of Luke–Acts* (Peabody: Hendrickson, 1991), pp. 241-68; J.C. Lentz, *Luke's Portrait of Paul* (SNTSMS, 77; Cambridge: Cambridge University Press, 1994).

The Setting: Public Open Space, Lecture Hall, Symposium?
As to the precise kind of occasion, as already noted, it is difficult to decide. Quite a lot of teaching in both the Gospel and in Acts takes place in the open where crowds happen to gather. People did read their works in the open, for any who would collect to hear, 'crowds of wretched sophists around Poseidon's temple, and their disciples, as they are called, fighting with one another, many writers reading aloud their stupid works, many poets reciting their poems while others applauded them', is how Dio in the late first century imagined the Isthmian Games in the late fourth (*Discourse* 8.9; cf. 27.5-6); but he describes contemporary Alexandria and Tarsus in his own day very similarly (32.9-12; 33.1-7). And he himself delivered some public orations of around the same length as the Gospel or Acts (around 20,000 words). I do not think we can imagine the reading taking place in a synagogue, though our hearers could have gathered in someone's lecture hall. However, there seem to be strong indications both in his narrative and in his ethos that Luke's own preference would have been for a decorous symposium (though of course a 'school' might very well share a symposium). A large number of the occasions for teaching in the narrative are in a convivial setting (Lk. 5.29; 7.34, 36-50; 9.4; 10.7, 38-42; 11.37-52; 13.26; 14.1-24; 22.14-38; 24.13-35(?) and Acts 2.42; 6.1-6; 20.7-12).[10] Very engaging is Dio's description of a symposium:

> Some attend for the sake of drinking, and devote themselves to that...saying and doing indecorous things...the naturally loquacious, feeling they've got their table companions for an audience, recite stupid and tedious speeches, while others are singing in tune and out of it— almost more annoying than the quarrelsome and abusive...others bore

10. Lk. 14.1-24 is the subject of a useful discussion by W. Braun, *The Use of Mediterranean Banquet Traditions in Luke 14.1-24* (SNTSMS; Cambridge: Cambridge University Press, forthcoming); there are some apposite references collected in C.A. Bobertz, 'The Role of the Patron in the *Cena Dominica* of Hippolytus' Apostolic Tradition', *JTS* (NS) 44 (1993), pp. 170-84; and a fine if not flawless discussion in K.E. Corley, *Private Women, Public Meals* (Peabody: Hendrickson, 1993): 'the primary setting of early Christian dialogue and worship was a formal public meal' (p. 24; 'formal' should not be over-stressed in the light of much of the evidence Corley herself collates!). There is further relevant matter in D. Aune, '*Septem Sapientem Convivium*', in H.D. Betz (ed.), *Plutarch's Ethical Writings and Early Christian Literature* (Leiden: Brill, 1978), pp. 51-105; see also D.E. Smith, 'Table Fellowship as a Literary Motif in the Gospel of Luke', *JBL* 106 (1987), pp. 613-38.

people to death by their uncongenial manner, refusing to share a drink or the conversation (Dio, *Discourse* 27.2-3).

There are also plenty more accounts of rowdy suppers (Lucian, *The Carousel*; Petronius, *Satyricon*), with which to compare Paul's account of goings on in Corinth. Pliny, however, had expected a rather less unruly occasion when a friend let him down: 'You would have heard a comic play, a reader, or a singer—or all three if I had felt generous...a feast of fun, laughter and learning' (*Letters* 1.15; cf. 9.17.3). The character of Luke's writing would fit this setting well, if it be agreed that he affords 'serious entertainment'—as I shall urge at a little more length below (following R.I. Pervo).[11]

The Audience (b)
Here we might expect our most mixed audience, free and freed men and women—and children and male and female slaves. The wider evidence for their respective roles (as silent or vocal participants) is not unambiguous. Juvenal in Rome expects women and scholarly conversation at parties (and does not like the mixture: Juvenal, *Satire* 6.434-41). Dio's *Discourse* 61, a literary discussion with a well-read woman who holds her own, may well be relevant. Plutarch imagines the Dinner of the Seven Wise men to have included Eumetis, the young daughter (*paidos*) of Cleobulos, admired for her intelligence. She sits for the meal, while an older woman, Melissa, reclines with her partner. Here, too, of course, there are slave attendants. Eumetis is engaged in conversation initially, but none of these join in the conversation, once the serious talking—and drinking—have begun (*Sept. sap. conviv.* 148C-150B). Diogenes Laertius (or his source) finds it noteworthy that the Cynic Hipparchia went to dinners with her man Crates, and joined in the cut and thrust of debate (6.97-98). Epicureans will probably have included women in their symposia. In other accounts, there are free women present, as well as the servants, flute-girls and actresses, but none of these take part in the discussions.

In Luke's narrative, Mary is there as supper is prepared, but there to listen (Lk. 10.38-42).[12] Luke at 7.37 seems to evince surprise that a woman should dare to be the focus of attention, and certainly no women

11. R. Pervo, *Profit with Delight* (Philadelphia: Fortress Press, 1987).
12. On which see L. Alexander, 'Sisters in Adversity: Retelling Martha's Story', in G.J. Brooke (ed.), *Women in the Biblical Tradition* (Lewiston: Edwin Mellen, 1992), pp. 167-86; Corley, *Private Women, Public Meals*, pp.133-44.

are recorded at Jesus' last meal (Lk. 22.14-38, again). Yet the indications given above, and the Pauline and deutero-Pauline evidence, suggest Luke would have expected mixed company at Christian symposia, women for sure,[13] but also quite possibly children (though Eutychus, Acts 20.9, is a young man, *neanias*, not a child); also Jews and sympathizers with Judaism become Christian, as well as converts from 'paganism'.[14] There is, then, plausibly, quite a wide ranging audience along with Theophilus, while only the adult males are likely to feel free to comment at the time on Luke's work. However, anyone might applaud.

The Script

The Preface—As for a Technical Treatise?
We take it that the reading starts with the preface as we find it in our texts. Dr Alexander shows that this preface most closely resembles in style and in length the prefaces of surviving technical works on medicine, astronomy, engineering and architecture. Historians' prefaces, even when covering similar themes and using similar key words, are longer, usually very much longer, and (for instance) where dedicated do not use a second person address. The rest of Luke's work rarely even approaches the high style adopted by those historians whose writings have come down to us.[15]

Yet the company assembled round Theophilus would hardly have come expecting to hear a technical treatise; and even if the first sentence had them revising their expectations, the second would have immediately re-directed them. As Dr Alexander herself admits, '...may it not be asked, is not our hypothetical informed reader still going to be disappointed, or at the very least, puzzled, when the narrative which unfolds proves to be so very unlike the mathematical or medical treatises which begin with prefaces like this?'[16] She canvasses two main possible responses: 'biography...within the school traditions' (but most philosophical biographies are rather different, series of didactic anecdotes),[17] and a presentation of the *content* of the school's tradition (but that fits Acts much less well than Luke).[18]

13. Aune, '*Septem Sapientem Convivium*', p. 77.
14. Esler, *Community*, pp. 71-109.
15. Alexander, *The Preface*.
16. Alexander, *The Preface*, p. 202.
17. Cf. Alexander, 'Acts and Ancient Intellectual Biography'.
18. Alexander, *The Preface*, pp. 202-205, again.

'Non-Professional' History-Writing

It would seem worth going back a little to consider more generally the kinds of expectations Theophilus and his Christian friends might have brought with them. They are likely to have had some awareness of the distinction of *genres, Gattungen*.[19] But even if they had some knowledge of rhetorical theory, they would have realized that in practice *genres* tended to overlap (as the theorists themselves acknowledged).[20] Accepting Dr Alexander's main contention—the preface to Luke most nearly resembles prefaces to technical works—Luke is unlikely to have been the first writer whose main familiarity was with works of that kind, but who had also undertaken to write a Life or a History—or both. Only one example happens to come to mind, and that is the military surgeon of whose history Lucian writes,

> he has compiled a bare record of the events and set it down on paper, completely prosaic and ordinary, such as a soldier or artisan or pedlar following the army might have put together a diary of daily events. However, this non-professional (*idiōtēs*) was not that bad—it was quite obvious at the beginning what he was, and his work has cleared the ground for some future historian of taste and ability...

Some further criticisms of the style of this 'Callimorphus, surgeon of the Fifth Lancers' follow, and then Lucian concludes, 'and, after beginning in Ionic, for some reason I cannot fathom, he suddenly changed to the vernacular...taking the rest from the language of everyday, most of it street-corner talk' (*De Historia conscribendi* 16). The coincidence with the tradition of 'Luke the beloved physician' is not to be pressed, but it does seem unlikely that Luke and Callimorphus were the only two amateur writers of histories or biographies in the ancient Mediterranean world whose styles may have been influenced by technical treatises—and Callimorphus does not appear to have been writing for the use of a 'school'. Furthermore, as Dr Alexander herself notes, and as I have myself pointed out elsewhere,[21] much of the language of Luke's preface *is* found in the (albeit much longer) prefaces of Josephus to his history of the Jewish War, his *Antiquities*, and his *Against Apion*, and much of it

---

19. Cf. R.A. Burridge, *What are the Gospels?* (SNTSMS, 70; Cambridge: Cambridge University Press, 1992), pp. 26-81.
20. Burridge, *Gospels*, e.g. pp. 68-69; and F.G. Downing, 'A Genre for Q and a Socio-Cultural Context for Q', *JSNT* 55 (1994) (forthcoming).
21. F.G. Downing, 'Redaction Criticism: Josephus' *Antiquities* and the Synoptic Gospels', I, II, *JSNT* 8 (1980), pp. 46-65, and 9 (1980), pp. 29-48.

also appears in the more straightfowardly historical *Roman Antiquities* of Dionysius of Halicarnassus. Lucian would surely have been even more dismissive of Luke–Acts than he was of Callimorphus. But I do not think our gathering would have been all that surprised or puzzled by the kind of material that followed the preface: that preface would not have channelled their expectations all that precisely (though they would have realized they were not then likely to hear a poem, a letter or a speech).

Septuagintal and Commonplace Greek

They might well have been not all that shocked when Luke did not maintain the somewhat pretentious language of his first sentence. But it does leave me with a question for which I have not found a satisfactory answer (and do not feel well equipped to attempt one). The narrative that follows is not even in the 'street corner' talk that Lucian disparaged; it is, as everyone notes, in the archaic 'dialect' of the Septuagint. There seems to be little if anything in any way analogous to this mixture. Lucian himself writes his *de dea syriae* in what we are told is dialect, and other writers sometimes quote brief utterances in local speech. One can only assume (with E. Plümacher)[22] that Luke's Septuagintal archaism would be expected to reinforce the anchorage of the narrative in a Jewish antiquity known to the hearers, and accepted by them as a validating ancient tradition (on which more again, later).

A Bios?

It has taken us much longer to get past the preface than it would Theophilus's first reader. We now need to move on a little, and rather faster. It is worth asking again what sort of genre appraisal might be forming in people's minds as they listened. According to the recent study by Richard Burridge, the Gospel would clearly—and swiftly—emerge as a *bios*, a character portrait (a 'character-sketch' might seem as suitable). *Bioi*, Lives, share together in varying degrees a large number of features, and this sharing is strong enough to afford a 'family resemblance' (L. Wittgenstein) which is different from simple identity, but still genuinely recognizable.[23] The most important common feature

---

22. E. Plümacher, *Lukas als hellenistischer Schriftsteller* (Göttingen: Vandenhoeck & Ruprecht, 1972), pp. 72-74.

23. Burridge, *Gospels*, p. 39 *et passim*; L. Wittgenstein, *Philosophical Investigations* (Oxford: Blackwell, 1953), pp. 31-32, for 'family resemblance'.

Burridge discovers may seem on reflection rather obvious. In works classified as Lives a single named person predominates among references in the nominative, as the subject of verbs, and as the utterer of verbs in speech. Even leading figures in histories do not figure as prominently.[24] I shall not try to summarize the remainder of Burridge's criteria for an ancient Life, but would note that I am not alone among reviewers in finding his case overall convincing.

Apologetic Historiography?
Some of Burridge's own conclusions, however, would lead us to expect that Theophilus would then be somewhat surprised later on when he heard Acts read, now clearly linked by its preface as the sequel in a two-part work. Another recent monograph, Gregory E. Sterling's *Historiography and Self-Definition*, discerns a genre for the two volumes taken together: that of 'apologetic history' in the tradition of (though not directly influenced by) Josephus' *Antiquities*, and works by Berossus, Manetho, Eupolemos and others.[25] Perhaps the distinction between 'genre' and 'mode' which Burridge takes from A. Fowler is also relevant here: Luke–Acts shares many of the features of an apologetic 'mode', even if the evidence does not warrant the positing of a distinctive genre or sub-genre.[26] It would seem still more appropriate, however, to stress the flexibility of and overlap between all the genres we or the ancients discern.[27] Loveday Alexander finds in Acts' outline of Paul's life and character elements of a narrative pattern that has much in common with sketches of eminent philosophers (as in Diogenes Laertius).[28] In fact Plutarch in his *Parallel Lives* treats such characters as Romulus, Numa, Publicola and Camillus in a manner very similar to their treatment by Dionysius in his *Roman Antiquities*; and we may compare Joseph and Moses in Philo and in Josephus, respectively. Josephus himself refers us to his *Jewish War* for his own *Vita*'s continuation (*Vita* 413). Thus we can read Luke's Gospel on its own as a Life

24. Burridge, *Gospels*, pp. 134-38, 195-97.
25. G.E. Sterling, *Historiography and Self-Definition: Josephus, Luke–Acts and Apologetic Historiography* (Leiden: Brill, 1991).
26. Burridge, *Gospels*, pp. 41-42, referring to A. Fowler, 'The Life and Death of Literary Forms', in R. Cohen (ed.), *New Directions in Literary History* (London: Routledge & Kegan Paul, 1974), pp. 77-94.
27. Cf. D.W. Palmer, 'Acts and the Historical Monograph', in Winter and Clark (eds.), *The Book of Acts*, I, pp. 1-29; Downing, 'A Genre for Q'.
28. Alexander, 'Acts and Ancient Intellectual Biography'.

of Jesus, or Luke–Acts as a two-part apologetic history of the Christian people and their movement and their leaders; but we can also read them for much the same kind of entertainment as we might gain from a romance, as I shall further argue, shortly (with R.I. Pervo).

So, Theophilus and his party soon realize they are hearing the content of the tradition they have learned here presented—performed—as a Life, a character-sketch, of Jesus. Yet when, later—maybe a lot later—they then hear Acts, or if they hear both volumes read together, it is still quite easy for them to take the whole as an effective reaffirmation of the validity of their lived tradition within the Greco-Roman world, apologetic historiography in that sense.

Sacred Tradition and Divine Ordering

Luke begins his narrative not only in a 'hieratic' language, but in an ancient and sacred enclosure, where tradition is respected, and where humans are most open to divine intervention (and it is often noted how emphatically the ongoing story returns to the Jerusalem and the Temple). There is to be no arbitrary human interruption of the safe providential ordering of things; if anything new or startling happens, it will be by divine necessity. This latter motif is amply illustrated from pagan and from Jewish sources by J.T. Squires, *The Plan of God in Luke–Acts*:

> epiphanies of divine messengers and their oracular pronouncements indicate that God is to be at work in the events which follow, while a hint of the necessity of ensuing events is also given.
>
> The interrelation of providence, fate and the various means of divination (portents, dreams and oracles) is evident in the hellenistic historians, while Josephus demonstrates how this hellenistic perspective is congenial with the scriptural perspective of the Hebrew people. Luke's interweaving of the strands thus makes sense because they were already understood to be related to one another, as our survey of other hellenistic literature has shown.[29]

Order and Law

What needs to be added to Squires's case here is a note of the close connection between this strand and issues of custom, law, law-abiding, and the avoidance of 'innovation', any threat of anarchy. There has seemed to many to be a puzzling tension in Luke between instances (as

---

29. J.T. Squires, *The Plan of God in Luke–Acts* (SNTSMS, 76; Cambridge: Cambridge University Press, 1993), pp. 188-89.

here, in the early chapters of the Gospel) where sacred tradition is (at least in the intention of the text) faithfully observed, and others (as in Peter's vision in Acts 10) where sacred tradition is decisively abrogated. Discussions in the eighties tended to ignore contemporary Hellenistic debates about law, custom and tradition, and so (I would argue) failed to recognize the fairly conventional stance Luke is affirming. I quote a conclusion for which I have argued elsewhere

> The observance of the actual ancestral practices themselves (whether codified or not, whether written or not) was commended on all sides, save only for any that could clearly be shown to harm human flourishing, *eudaimonia*... The observance of ancestral custom is part of a concern for cosmic order, but also for civic order.[30]

And so, for instance, Jesus' parents are very soon shown complying at some cost with (supposed) Roman taxation law. What Luke will go on to reassert, to Theophilus's and his friends renewed relief, is that God himself has insisted that the most obnoxious and exclusive and notorious Jewish customs do not have to be imposed on non-Jews: male circumcision, the most troublesome food laws, and any strict Sabbatarianism. Yet other roots in ancient Jewish piety remain—the Christian movement is no arbitrary innovation, and so presents no threat of social disruption.[31] As we listen we can say, this tells our story: we are an interesting, admirable, patient and law-abiding group who maintain an inheritance of ancient piety with pleasure and joy, while by divinely commanded selectivity we avoid any demeaning or craven ('superstitious') restrictions. (This previously argued conclusion of mine then tallies well with the analysis of 'apologetic historiography' presented since then by Sterling.)

Revolt or Propriety?
Just how law-abiding in other respects does the Christian movement appear in Luke's narrative? Mary's song sounds quite revolutionary, and even the two mission-charges propose clothing that would have betokened a Cynic assault on convention if adopted in Corinth or

---

30. F.G. Downing, 'Law and Custom: Luke–Acts and Late Hellenism', in B. Lindars (ed.), *Law and Religion* (Cambridge: J. Clarke, 1988), p. 152; *per contra*: Esler, *Community and Gospel*, pp. 110-30; though compare his pp. 214-17 on 'ancestral tradition'.

31. It is of course entirely plausible that Luke is *also* trying to reassure both present and potential Jewish Christians: see D. Marguerat, 'Juifs et chrétiens selon Luc–Actes. Surmonter le conflit des lectures', *Bib* 75 (1994), pp. 126-46.

Athens. I have argued in various places that much of the 'Q' material Luke uses would on its own sound startlingly Cynic (as it did to many later Christian commentators).[32] But at 22.35-36 Luke has Jesus make it quite clear that the Cynic-sounding period is over, 'now' things are different, purses and satchels and swords, even, are the order of the day.[33] Even the realized ideal of 'friends having all in common' (Acts 2.44; 4.32) happens only at the start, in the holy city; there is no suggestion of its recurring later.[34] And though Paul does voluntarily work for a living, he is clearly presented as someone entirely acceptable to many people of middle eminence and good will. Christianity as it spreads is led by a decent man who can appeal to decent people who retain their social propriety.[35]

Entertainment: Romance and Emotion

Those in the first-century Mediterranean world who put words together for others to listen to seem to have been well aware of the need to work hard to hold their hearers' attention.[36] You had to give them a lot of what they wanted—they were, in a very real sense, your masters. You had to feed back to them, attractively, convictions they already held, and that could be difficult enough (though sometimes financially very rewarding). And even if you wanted people to change at some point, your proposal had to be shown to be consistent with their most deeply held convictions. And all the time, you had to entertain.

It is no coincidence that there is considerable overlap, not only in such works as Philostratus' *Life of Apollonius*[37] but also in high-brow

---

32. Most recently, F.G. Downing, *Cynics and Christian Origins* (Edinburgh: T. & T. Clark, 1992), esp. ch. 5, pp. 115-42, in the light of the second half of the book; but also *Christ and the Cynics* (Sheffield: JSOT Press, 1982), pp. 9-87.

33. That this marked a change from Cynic-style poverty is noted by John Chrysostom, *Homily on 1 Corinthians* 9.

34. Cf. A.C. Mitchell, 'The Social Function of Friendship in Acts 2.44-47 and 4.32-37', *JBL* 111 (1992), pp. 255-72.

35. Cf. J.H. Neyrey and B. Malina, 'Conflict in Luke–Acts', in Neyrey (ed.), *The Social World of Luke–Acts*, pp. 97-122.

36. Cf. D. Litfin, *St Paul's Theology of Proclamation: 1 Corinthians 1–4 and Greco-Roman Rhetoric* (SNTSMS, 79; Cambridge: Cambridge University Press, 1994), pp. 105-106; Palmer, 'Acts and the Ancient Historical Monograph'; Pervo, *Profit with Delight*; and Dionysius of Halicarnassus, *Roman Antiquities* 1.8.3.

37. Cf. R. Bauckham, 'The *Acts of Paul* as a Sequel to Acts', in Winter and Clarke (eds.), *The Book of Acts*, pp. 105-52.

historians, between history and romance.[38] There seems to be still more in common with contemporary romances in Luke–Acts, as demonstrated by Richard Pervo.[39] In particular we should note the prominence of the travel motif, as discussed by Loveday Alexander.[40] It hardly figures at all in histories (or in most Lives, save the later *Life of Apollonius of Tyana*) but provides the basic structure for ancient novels. Its importance in Acts is obvious, and in Luke 9–19. But earlier still in the Gospel Jesus is already a travelling man. Jesus travels to a trial and death presumably already well-known to the hearers, and the journey does not need extra perils to maintain interest (and, anyway, the main incidents are also already known). But Paul's journeys through prisons and lynchings and shipwreck in particular are very much the stuff of the novels, even if (as Richard Bauckham points out)[41] the mission in mind is clearly different—the spread of the gospel, not the ultimate reunion of fraught lovers.

Of course Luke–Acts does not have a prominent heroine to share the story-line (and provide more or less explicit erotic interest—only in the picaresque satires are men on their own sex-objects!); that development among Christians has to wait for the writing of *The Acts of Paul and Thecla*. But the histories certainly give space to female characters—as erotic figures, and as tragic pleaders and victims; and just occasionally as taking some unexpected initiative. Josephus responds to these motifs in models such as Dionysius *Roman Antiquities* by imaginative elaborations of incidents in the Jewish Scriptures. Luke, as is often noted, gives more space than do either Mark or Matthew to women in the story, with the prologue centering on Mary. Luke's sinful woman wiping Jesus' feet with her hair is subtly but powerfully erotic in a first-century context; Martha's sister Mary is the ideal 'docile' disciple.[42] Priscilla and Lydia display more enterprizing initiative.

Hints of sexuality connect with other emotional issues, obviously present in the romances, but also in the histories. Josephus adds notes of joy, exaltation, sorrow; and Luke has similar notes where none such appear in Mark (cf. D. Marguerat's discussion of the pathos of Luke's

---

38. As acknowledged by, e.g., Palmer, 'Acts and the Ancient Historical Monograph', p. 29.
39. Pervo, *Profit with Delight*.
40. L. Alexander, 'Voyaging in Luke–Acts', pp. 17-49 in this volume.
41. Bauckham, 'The *Acts of Paul* as a Sequel to Acts', p. 137.
42. See n. 12 above.

dramatic narrative, Acts 5.1-11).[43] It is also clear that repentance (with overtones of contrition) is a dominant theme in Luke's theology. Dionysius remarks on the efficacy of the acknowledgment of fault and the craving of pardon, and assures his hearers that the gods are disposed to forgive, and are easily reconciled (*eudialaktos*, *R.A.* 11.12.3 and 8.50.4). Josephus quotes the latter assertion at *War* 5.416, and stresses in a number of the speeches he composes both repentance and the availability of forgiveness. The drama of someone changing from one entrenched commitment to another makes for good listening—and so the 'conversions' of Peter and of Paul are each repeated three times in Acts.[44] In the romances characters are constantly having to change their attitudes and confess and be reconciled. The ass tales of Lucius of Patras, Lucian (possibly) and Apuleius in particular celebrate conversion.

Yet another gripping motif, as we know from our own television screens, is the courtroom drama. Some of the novels include such scenes, and they are given considerable space by Josephus and by Dionysius before him. In the histories they allow issues to be debated, and especially do they allow awkward charges to be voiced and answered, rather than risking seeming to gloss over them. So Luke has obviously false charges levelled against Jesus (23.2; the charges have been rebutted in advance, and Pilate rejects them), and against the Jerusalem Christians, and Paul. The Christians around Theophilus are reassured, whatever the rumours and popular gossip, no one can validly suspect them of being a threat to society—but neither are they boring.

However, the critics of Pervo are almost certainly right when they insist that the presence of romantic features does not constitute Acts or Luke–Acts as 'a romance' as such.[45] It is *bios*-cum-history in apologetic and romantic mode.

The Social World: The Village and the Town
Once again we return to the start of the performance. We have been entertained as we would have been by Josephus or by Dionysius with

---

43. Cf. D. Marguerat, 'La mort d'Ananias et Saphira (Ac 5.1-11) dans la stratégie narrative de Luc', *NTS* 39 (1993), p. 209.

44. On which see D. Marguerat, 'Saul's Conversion (Acts 9, 22, 26) and the Multiplication of Narrative in Acts', pp. 120-48 in this volume.

45. E.g. Palmer, 'Acts and the Ancient Historical Monograph', pp. 3 and 29; Baukham, 'The *Acts of Paul*', pp. 140-41.

scenes from an enchanted world full of holy people and divine powers and wondrous births and a precocious child for whom much is promised. And then we are brought up sharp in the 'real world' of Tiberius, Pilate, Herod and the rest. And it now becomes a world with which we are much more familiar, as Harold Moxnes has explained for us. It is not exactly 'our' world, because 'we' are the townspeople found in Acts. But it is the world of the villages around us, with which we have more or less friendly links. It is a world of top-heavy power structures, centred in the towns, and weighing heavily on the village people. Among themselves villagers can usually expect solidarity—their slightly less impoverished neighbours recognize their 'patronal' responsibilities, both to share their wealth for festivities, and to act as 'brokers' between the village community and the absentee urban landlords and administrators. 'Thus Luke describes the world of Jesus in Palestine, but in such a way that his readers would recognise it. It was partly an unfamilar world, but partly also a familiar one. Luke's redactional comments serve to make this world more relevant and familiar.'[46] Moxnes notes some of the differences between the social setting of the followers of Jesus in the Gospel from the setting suggested in Acts. Pressing the evidence rather further than he chooses to, I would urge again that the idealized village ethos of the Gospel is abandonned for a much more conventional patronal ethos in Acts. No one in Acts imitates the birds or the flowers, as Jesus bade in the Gospel. Friends share all in common only in Jerusalem.[47] Paul works for a living or relies on patrons, but his patrons do not take on clients wholesale into their households or for indefinite support. There are no penitent and extravagantly generous tax-collectors. Theophilus can breathe easy. However, he is not entirely let off the hook, if Richard Rohrbaugh is right in suggesting that the city has invaded the countryside in Luke ch. 14's version of the Great Supper, becoming contaminated, to some degree, by its ethos. The host is shamed by those he considered his equals, and must now expect guests only from among those he considers his inferiors, drawn from among the poorest inhabitants and the outcasts on the fringes.[48] Perhaps this actually *is* Theophilus, together with his new friends, listening to the first performance of the Gospel?

46. Moxnes, *The Economy of the Kingdom*, pp. 62, 74 and 162.
47. Mitchell, 'The Social Function of Friendship in Acts'.
48. R.I. Rohrbaugh, 'The Pre-Industrial City in Luke–Acts', in Neyrey (ed.), *The Social World of Luke–Acts*, pp. 125-49.

Some aspects of a first-century Mediterranean ethos are, we thus see, more pervasive throughout both books—especially concerns for honour and shame. Roman soldiers are worthy in both (and one acknowledges that Jesus was *dikaios*). The shame of Jesus' crucifixion is reversed by his ascended glory (and it had all been a mistake); the shame of Paul's flogging is reversed by the humble apologies of the magistrates, and so on.[49] For all the stress on repentance and change, and emotion, Luke sees people socially, and in terms of status rather than of personal relationships.[50] You convert to a new group and its ethos and beliefs; any effect on your personality is ignored.

The remainder of this essay is a sketch of how the overtly announced ideas, the theology-ideology of Luke, especially as set out in the speeches in Acts, might have appeared to Theophilus and his friends.

A Recipe for a Deliberative Speech in Dionysius, Josephus and Luke[51]
In my 'Ethical Pagan Theism and the Speeches in Acts' I adduced evidence that seemed to indicate a fairly general common 'recipe' employed by all three writers in composing speeches. Many of the speeches I suppose might well have been categorized as 'deliberative', as long as that does not suggest any strict or exclusive adherence to formula. In broadest outline the recipe runs:

> A—God is powerful
> B—We must therefore be virtuous, keeping the ancient rules
> C—We shall then enjoy the good life
> D—And avoid the unpleasant alternatives.

The speeches can, however, be analysed in much more detail, to support many more common sub-headings (in Dionysius 'God' may be *theos, theioi* or *to theion*).

---

49. B.J. Malina and J.H. Neyrey, 'Honour and Shame in Luke–Acts: Pivotal Values of the Mediterranean World', in Neyrey (ed.), *The Social World of Luke–Acts*, pp. 25-65.

50. B.J. Malina and J.H. Neyrey, 'First Century Personality: Dyadic, not Individualistic', in Neyrey (ed.), *The Social World of Luke–Acts*, pp. 67-96.

51. The following section summarizes F.G. Downing, 'Ethical Pagan Theism and the Speeches in Acts', *NTS* 27 (1981), pp. 544-63. On this issue see now also E. Plümacher, 'Der Missionreden der Apostelgeschichte und Dionys von Halikarnass', *NTS* 39 (1993), pp. 161-77.

A (a) God has and exercises foresight, as all-seeing, present, powerful, righteous.
  (b) God shares this foresight in prophecy and omens; his presence may be felt.
  (c) God also makes known his regular demands: there is law.
  (d) God is gracious, and kind to the good, forgiving to the penitent.
B (a) We must respond with virtue, piety, righteousness, be worthy (or penitent).
  (b) We must bear in mind the divine commands given in law, custom, conscience.
  (c) We must put them into practice
     (i) in cultic ritual properly understood
     (ii) in submission to hierarchic authority
     (iii) in maintaining family and tribal custom; in solidarity with 'our' people
     (iv) in natural human kindliness, forgiveness, magnanimity.
C (a) The Good Life will be our reward, now
  (b) We can have confidence, be hopeful
  (c) We shall be remembered; we shall live with God after death.
D (a) Failures (small ones) will be forgiven those who repent.
  (b) Serious and terminal failure is a real possibility, we must be aware.
  (c) And punishment is bound to follow; bad conscience, illness, destruction, slavery, contumely and eternal loss.

Taking for an example Acts 13.16-47 as a single speech (like Josephus, Luke often breaks his speeches into two uneven parts), we find it is a *logos parakleseos*. The opening address leads into a narrative (vv. 17-25) that prepares for the statement of the thesis (26), 'to us has been sent the message of this salvation'. The narrative is resumed (27-31) and the thesis restated (32). Proofs from Scripture (33-37) follow, and the conclusion is stated (38-39). There is then a negative exhortation with a further proof (40-41), followed by a peroration (the brief second part of the speech, 46-47). It certainly has enough of the look of a deliberative speech to have been recognized as such by Theophilus and his dinner-party guests.

Yet the content would also be recognizable to anyone used to the kind of things that historians put in the mouths of their protagonists—and presumably to those used to the kinds of appeals to publicly approved sentiments that would be trotted out in popular assemblies. We Christians, Luke is reminding his hearers, have a very creditable variant of the beliefs and attitudes that are approved by the best and most prestigious writers and speakers in our society—not only the best of Judaism, but the best of non-Jewish ideas and attitudes.[52] Reading Acts

---

52. Marguerat, 'Juifs et chrétiens', p. 146, notes Luke's concern to preserve 'ce

today we may take it Luke will have been convinced that it was not just a good variant, but the best—and true. But it was important that its validity could be demonstrated in terms of the beliefs and attitudes of 'enlightened' contemporaries.

Here is a sketch of the detail of our chosen example, the speech of Acts 13, in context:

A (a) God...chose...led...brought...raised.
  (b) prophet...testified...promise fulfilled...prophets...
  (c) law of Moses...'a man who will do my will'.
  (d) God bore with the wilderness generation...salvation...[grace of God (v. 43)].[53]
B (a) 'you that fear God'; David, 'a man after my own heart'; worthy/unworthy; [the devout (v. 43, again)].
  (b) the whole passage is a reminder; the utterances of the prophets read every Sabbath...
  (c) (i) baptism, sepulchral burial, synagogue liturgy.
      (ii) The introductory narrative sketch is about divinely delegated authority (Josephus takes the Saul–David sequence as a signal example of this theme).
           John acknowledges Jesus' authority; rulers acted in ignorance, not malice.
      (iii) the people...fathers...sons of the family of Abraham...us their children.
      (iv) David is a man after God's heart; rulers' ignorance, not malice (again); [those already devout (v. 43, again)].
C (a) Canaan as inheritance; saviour, salvation, announcement of good news.
  (b) promised fulfilled to us; every believer is justified/forgiven; Paul and Barnabas speak out boldly.
  (c) God raised Jesus [v. 48, eternal life is made explicit].
D (a) God bore with the fathers; baptism of repentance; forgiveness of sins.
  (b) Saul rejected (implicit); condemnation under Mosaic law; 'beware', 'you judge yourselves unworthy'.
  (c) Destruction of the Canaanites; 'corruption'; 'perish'; 'unworthy of eternal life'.

Verse 39 imports a Pauline-sounding word (in a non-Pauline sense), and the whole contains a lot of explicit and also implicit Septuagintal allusion, to which trait we have already referred above. But the themes, the

que le judaïsme a de meilleur'; but this is also (as in Josephus) very closely akin to 'the best of "paganism"'.

53. A (a) and (b) are now massively supported by Squires's monograph, *The Plan of God in Luke–Acts*, in which he acknowledges my essay, p. 63 n. 136.

motifs, are from the familiar stock common to Dionysius and Josephus.

The sequel to the article just summarized is entitled 'Common Ground with Paganism in Luke and in Josephus', and discusses the 'prayer' at Acts 4.24-30, the speech at Lystra, Acts 14.8-18 and that before the Areopagus, Acts 17.22-31.[54] I would actually draw a slightly different conclusion now: I would take as a more important motive for Luke's writing, that of reassuring the hearers of the intellectual and moral—and social—respectability of their group and its beliefs and ethos; and, while still affirming the concern to entertain, I would not now suppose Luke expected to have his work bought by or read to complete outsiders. He is entertaining and reassuring Theophilus and his Christian friends, not least reassuring them that their faith is both entertaining and eminently respectable.

His friends may well have found Theophilus' dinner party enjoyable and comforting—and, very likely, encouraging.

54. F.G. Downing, 'Common Ground with Paganism in Luke and in Josephus', *NTS* 28 (1982), pp. 546-59.

LUKE–ACTS AND THE PASTORAL EPISTLES: THE THESIS OF A COMMON AUTHORSHIP

Jean-Daniel Kaestli

Introduction: The Debate about the Pseudepigraphy of the Pastorals

What is the relationship between the Pastoral Epistles and the Lukan writings (Luke–Acts)? This question can be approached in different ways and stated in different terms, depending on the views one has about the origins of both literary works.

As long as the Pastorals' authenticity was self-evident, the main question was to correlate the events they mention with the narrative of Acts. Ever since antiquity, there have been attempts to reconcile the unexpected end of the book of Acts (Paul is under house arrest in Rome, a condition which allows him to preach freely), and the situation depicted in 2 Timothy (Paul is a prisoner in Rome, forsaken by almost all his companions, and aware of his impending condemnation and death). The solution given to this problem by Eusebius has been widely accepted: at the end of two years of captivity (Acts 28), the apostle was released and resumed his missionary activity. He was arrested and imprisoned a second time in Rome, where he wrote 2 Timothy and died as a martyr.[1]

---

1. 'Luke also, who commited the Acts of the Apostles to writing, finished his narrative at this point by the statement that Paul spent two whole years in Rome in freedom, and preached the word of God without hindrance. Tradition has it that after defending himself the apostle was again sent on the ministry of preaching, and coming a second time to the same city suffered martyrdom. During this imprisonment he wrote the second Epistle to Timothy, indicating at the same time that his first defence had taken place and that his martyrdom was at hand. Notice his testimony on this point: "At my first defence", he says, "no man was with me, but all deserted me (may it not be laid to their charge). But the Lord stood by me and strengthened me that the preaching might be fulfilled by me and all the Gentiles might hear, and I was delivered from the lion's mouth" [quotation of 2 Tim. 4.16-17]. He clearly proves by this that on the first occasion, in order that the preaching which took place through him might be fulfilled, he was delivered from the lion's mouth, apparently referring

Thanks to this theory of Paul's double Roman captivity, it becomes possible to explain why the Pastorals—and especially 2 Tim. 4.9-21—contain various personal and geographical data which cannot fit in with the narrative framework of the book of Acts: these data refer to a new period in Paul's missionary work in the East, taking place after the imprisonment of Acts 28.

Since the beginning of the nineteenth century, the Pauline authenticity of the Pastoral Epistles has been questioned. Today, a considerable number of scholars, including Catholic ones, consider the Pastorals as pseudepigraphical letters, written in the post-apostolic period. My personal view is that the pseudepigraphy thesis is supported by strong and decisive arguments. The Pastorals differ in several respects from the other genuine Pauline letters.[2]

However, this thesis has constantly met with objections and opposition. From a theological point of view, many people consider that admitting the presence in the New Testament of letters which falsely claim to be written by Paul casts doubt on the biblical canon and undermines the authority of Scripture as the Word of God. In the case of the Pastorals, this theological resistance to pseudepigraphy is strengthened by a literary feature which seems difficult to understand: the presence of personal sections, where the apostle gives very concrete details on his and his collaborators' situation. The objection is that such precise and life-like details cannot have been invented by an epigone writing in the name of the apostle.

Various solutions have been put forward in order to overcome these difficulties and to vindicate the Pastorals as genuine Pauline letters, despite their differences with the apostle's other writings. There is on

---

to Nero thus for his ferocity. He does not go on to add any such words as 'he will deliver me from the lion's mouth', for he saw in the spirit that his death was all but at hand' (Eusebius, *Ecclesiastical History* 2.22.1-4, trans. K. Lake [LCL, 153; Cambridge, MA: Harvard University Press; London: Heinemann, repr. 1965], I, pp. 165-67).

2. Language and style show considerable differences in comparison with those of the genuine Pauline letters; what the Pastorals say about Paul's itinerary and destiny does not fit in with the reconstruction of his biography based on the other sources; the situation of the Church and the role of the various ministers do not correspond with those of the Pauline communities and belong to a later stage in the development of ecclesiastical organization; the way of dealing with doctrinal errors in the Pastorals is very different from that of Paul (there is no theological argumentation); with respect to theology and ethics, the Pastorals diverge considerably from Paul.

one side the theory of the fragments. This theory, while admitting that the Pastorals are not Pauline, seeks to account for the presence of the personal sections: the author of the pseudepigraph would have blended his own composition with biographical elements belonging to some genuine Pauline letters or some genuine fragments.[3] There is another type of solution which maintains the Pauline authorship of the Pastorals: the redaction of the letters is attributed to a secretary, who would have composed them in his own way, but according to the apostle's instructions.[4]

The Thesis of the Lukan Authorship of the Pastorals and its Relation to the Pseudepigraphy Debate

It is in the context of this debate on pseudepigraphy, and of these attempts to refute it or to limit its consequences, that the question of the relationship between the Pastorals and the Lukan writings has been given a new impulse. Several authors have tried to prove that Luke or the author of Luke–Acts wrote also the Pastoral Epistles. My purpose in this paper is to examine and evaluate this thesis. Let us first consider in which perspective it has been put forward, and what kind of arguments it has adduced.

To clarify the discussion, it is necessary to distinguish two different approaches among the advocates of the Lukan authorship. For some authors, such as C.F.D. Moule, A. Strobel or A. Feuillet, Luke is identified with Paul's secretary: he wrote the Pastorals following Paul's instructions, and during Paul's lifetime.[5] Other scholars, like S.G. Wilson

---

3. This theory has been developed at length by P.N. Harrison, *The Problem of the Pastoral Epistles* (London, 1921).

4. One of the main advocates of this hypothesis is O. Roller, *Das Formular der paulinischen Briefe: Ein Beitrag zur Lehre vom antiken Brief* (BWANT, 58; Stuttgart, 1933). According to Roller, what holds for the Pastorals holds for all the other letters of Paul: the apostle neither wrote nor dictated them, but entrusted their writing to a secretary, and later corrected them and signed them with his own hand (see Gal. 6.11).

5. C.F.D. Moule, 'The Problem of the Pastoral Epistles: A Reappraisal', *BJRL* 47 (1965), pp. 430-52; A. Strobel, 'Schreiben des Lukas? Zum sprachlichen Problem der Pastoralbriefe', *NTS* 15 (1969), pp. 191-210; A. Feuillet, 'La doctrine des Epîtres Pastorales et leurs affinités avec l'oeuvre lucanienne', *RevThom* 78 (1978), pp. 181-225. See also, in the same perspective, the huge monograph of S. de Lestapis, *L'énigme des Pastorales de Saint Paul* (Paris, 1976), approvingly quoted by Feuillet ('La doctrine', pp. 219-20).

and J.D. Quinn, also consider that 'Luke', the author of Luke–Acts, has written the Pastorals, and they date his literary activity in the last decades of the first century.[6] It is clear that the thesis of the Lukan authorship does not have the same significance in both perspectives. The first one establishes a close link between the Pastorals and the historical figure of Paul, and thus maintains their genuineness, at least partially. The second perspective, allowing pseudonymity, places the Pastorals at a greater distance from Paul; but it casts the pseudonymity in a favourable light, because in some way the canonical legitimacy of Luke–Acts falls upon the Pastorals.[7]

6. S.G. Wilson, *Luke and the Pastoral Epistles* (London, 1979); J.D. Quinn, 'The Last Volume of Luke: The Relation of Luke–Acts to the Pastoral Epistles', in C.H. Talbert (ed.), *Perspectives on Luke–Acts* (Edinburgh, 1978), pp. 62-75. According to Wilson, Luke wrote the Pastorals around 90–95, some time after having written Luke–Acts (which he dates back to 85–90), and with the aim of answering new needs (defending Paul's genuine tradition against the claims of gnostic teachers). As indicated by the title of his article, J.D. Quinn holds that Luke, an author belonging to the second Christian generation (between 70 and 100), published a work in three volumes, conceived from the outset as a unity; the two scrolls of Luke and Acts were followed by a third one, containing the Pastoral Epistles in this order: Titus, 1 Timothy, 2 Timothy. In his 1978 article, Quinn announced that he would argue his thesis more fully in a commentary which he was preparing for the Doubleday Anchor Bible; I do not know why this commentary has not been published.

7. I see several indications of this 'indirect legitimization'. I find it significant that Wilson accepts the theory of the genuine fragments (especially for 2 Tim. 4.9-21) and that he sees Luke more as a historian concerned with collecting and transmitting traditions of various provenance than as a theologian with his own original thinking (see especially Wilson's conclusion, *Luke and the Pastoral Epistles*, pp. 138-43). A similar concern shows itself in this concluding remark of Quinn: 'A review of the whole question of what is meant by the pseudonymity of the PE [Pastoral Epistles] is called for' ('The Last Volume of Luke', p. 75). H. von Campenhausen, who sees the Pastorals as a work of Polycarp of Smyrna composed in the middle of the second century to oppose Marcionism, has an interesting note about the legitimacy of pseudepigraphy: this device would be much easier to justify if the Pastoral Episltes were attributed to Luke: 'Es gäbe nur eine Möglichkeit, den Verfasser dieser unechten Paulusbriefe von jedem Vorwurf zu schützen: das wäre die Annahme, Lukas habe sie geschrieben' (H. von Campenhausen, 'Polycarp von Smyrna und die Pastoralbriefe', in *Aus der Frühzeit des Christentums: Studien zur Kirchengeschichte des ersten und zweiten Jahrhunderts* [Tübingen, 1963 (first published in 1951)], p. 245 n. 207). Campenhausen himself deems this solution to be impossible (see the end of the same note); but it is possible that his remark has stimulated some of the later studies advocating Lukan authorship.

What are the arguments adduced in favour of the Lukan authorship? The above mentioned scholars have noticed similarities between the Lukan writings and the Pastorals at various levels: language and style, theological ideas, knowledge about Paul and his missionary activity. The way they use these similarities in their argumentation is partly the same, but with significant differences in emphasis. Given the the limits of this essay, I will focus on two representative studies: that of C.F.D. Moule, who relies principally on linguistic considerations, and that of S.G. Wilson, who gives greater importance to the theological aspect.

C.F.D. Moule: An Attempt to Explain the Personal Sections of the Pastorals

I have chosen to examine the contribution of C.F.D. Moule for several reasons. Moule is the first to have supported the Lukan authorship of the Pastorals with a solid argumentation. The way in which he develops his theory also deserves to be noticed for it is a model of scientific rigour and modesty. Moreover, this choice is commanded by the history of the University of Manchester: the article published in 1965 in the *Bulletin of the John Rylands Library* was first presented thirty years ago as a Manson Memorial Lecture. Remembering his contribution is a way to pay homage to an eminent representative of British scholarship and to the academic institution which welcomed him.

Moule starts from what he calls an impasse in the interpretation of the Pastorals. On the one hand, he aknowledges the difficulty of accepting them as wholly Pauline, considering their differences of vocabulary, style and mentality from the other letters of Paul.[8] On the other hand, he deems it just as difficult to reconcile the concrete biographical data of the Pastorals (for example 2 Tim. 4.13, the cloak left by Paul in Troas) with the idea of pseudonymity, even if it considered as well-intentioned.[9]

---

8. He illustrates this 'change of mentality' by quoting 1 Tim. 1.8-9 ('We all know that the law is an excellent thing, provided we treat it as law, recognizing that it is not aimed at good citizens, but at the lawless and unruly, the impious and sinful...') and he makes the following comment: 'The law, meant to be "lawfully" (νομίμως) used, as a restraint, to prevent excessive sin! In what a different world of thought this stands from the noble Pauline conception of the law as the revelation of God's will and character, liable to abuse precisely when it is used "lawfully"!' (Moule, 'The Problem of the Pastoral Epistles', p. 432).

9. 'But even so, the problem remains: How explain the circumstancial references in the Pastorals to the apostle's movements and plans? Critics who rightly or

After discarding the so-called fragments-theory as unlikely, he offers his own solution in terms which are worth quoting:

> It seems to me, therefore—and here I come to my own desperate effort to suggest a way through the impasse—that we are driven to a theory of free composition (in the case of I Timothy, very free composition) by an amanuensis during the apostle's lifetime. In this case, we have to resort, once more, to the postulate—as old as Eusebius (H.E. ii.22.2)—that Paul was released from prison and did the travelling implied by the Pastorals (...) My suggestion is, then, that Luke wrote all three Pastoral epistles. But he wrote them during Paul's lifetime, at Paul's behest, and, in part (but only in part) at Paul's dictation.[10]

As we see, Moule's hypothesis originates from the need to overcome the difficulty in understanding the biographical sections in the Pastorals from the perspective of pseudepigraphy. This difficulty remains indeed a serious one, as long as these sections are explained by the will of the post-Pauline author to give his fictitious letter an appearance of genuineness.[11] However, I consider that this difficulty can now be solved. The solution is provided by recent research on the pseudepigraphical letters in the Greco-Roman world, whose characteristics are better known than at the time of Moule's study. The parallels supplied by the fictitious letters of antiquity show that many personal and concrete details in the Pastorals can be understood as expressing a literary and theological intention of the author.[12]

To illustrate this new perspective, let us take the example of 2 Tim. 4.13: 'When you come, bring the cloak that I left with Carpus at Troas, and my scrolls, especially the parchments'. As many others scholars, Moule considers that this realistic detail cannot be accounted for in terms of pseudepigraphy: 'But what would a posthumous epigraph want with

---

wrongly defend the naturalness and the honesty of pseudonymity in general, too often ignore this particular problem' (p. 433).

10. Moule, 'The Problem of the Pastoral Epistles', p. 434. Further on, Moule distances himself, with a good deal of humour, from his own hypothesis: 'At very best it is a sorry attempt to make the best of a bad job, and I shall not be surprised if I carry no one—perhaps not even the whole of myself—along with the argument' (pp. 436-37).

11. For an example of this kind of explanation, see H. von Campenhausen, 'Polycarp von Smyrna und die Pastoralbriefe', p. 201.

12. See N. Brox, 'Zu den persönlichen Notizen der Pastoralbriefe', *BZ* 13 (1969), pp. 76-94: L.R. Donelson, *Pseudepigraphy and Ethical Argument in the Pastoral Epistles* (HUT, 22; Tübingen, 1986), in particular pp. 23-43.

the cloak left at Troas...?' (p. 433). In fact, referring to concrete data and personal details is part of the common literary techniques in the Greco-Roman pseudepigraphical letters. Frugality and simple clothing habits are typical of the philosophical way of life, and such features are often illustrated by some practical advice or personal detail which the philosopher gives to the addressee of his letter. In the collections of Cynic Epistles and of Socratic Epistles, several passages aim at showing that the true philosopher is content with a single and very simple cloak.[13] Thus the request that Timothy should bring back the cloak left in Troas takes on a new meaning; it has to be related to the teaching of 1 Timothy 6, about the true riches and the need to be satisfied with what one has: 'But if we have food and clothing, we will be content with that' (1 Tim. 6.8). In 2 Tim. 4.13, the author of the Pastorals illustrates this ideal of soberness in the use of material goods through the personal example of Paul: nearing his death, the apostle recalls his belongings; all he owns and all he needs, is one single cloak.

My conclusion is that we have come out of the 'impasse' which led Moule to suggest Luke as the author of the Pastorals and that this suggestion is no longer necessary. However Moule's great merit is to have drawn up a list of characteristics shared by Luke–Acts and the Pastorals. This list, concerning vocabulary,[14] style and ideas, has paved the way for other studies and remains very useful.

13. See Letter of Crates 30; Letter of Diogenes 46 (to Plato); Letter of Socrates 6.2; Letters of the Socratics 9.2 (Aristippus to Antisthenes); texts edited and translated by A.J. Malherbe, *The Cynic Epistles* (SBLSBS, 12; Missoula, 1977), pp. 80-81; 176-77; 232-33; 246-47.

14. It is interesting to note that Moule is rather wary about arguments drawn from statistics of vocabulary; he is right in thinking that mere vocabulary-counts do not allow one to conclude that Luke wrote the Pastorals. What really matters is the way in which the words are used and the ideas with which they are associated. On the basis of his own statistics, he concludes that there is nothing hindering the Lukan thesis, unless one considers as decisive the following counter-argument : particles, adverbs, prepositions and conjunctions which characterize the Lukan language do not occur in the Pastorals. (See the list drawn up by P.N. Harrison, *The Problem of the Pastoral Epistles*, p. 53, and reproduced by Feuillet, 'La Doctrine', p. 223 n. 69.) Whereas Strobel, some years later, makes an inventory of 36 terms which are used exclusively by Luke and the Pastorals in the New Testament ('Schreiben des Lukas?', pp. 194-95), Moule considers only a few of them as relevant (for example, the words of the root εὐσεβ-, the verbs ζωγρεῖν, ζῳογονεῖν, περιποεῖσθαι, the adjective φιλάργυρος).

S.G. Wilson: A Suggestive and Well Argued but Unconvincing Solution

I come now to S.G. Wilson, who has tried to establish on a broader basis the thesis of the Lukan origin of the Pastorals. In his view, the author of Luke–Acts, who is not to be identified with Luke the physician and the companion of Paul, wrote the three Pastoral letters a few years after the book of Acts was ended. In the intervening time between the two writings, he had got hold of new sources, among which there were some letters of Paul and other documents coming directly from the apostle. On the basis of these 'genuine fragments', he then composed the Pastoral Epistles in a new situation, marked by the rising influence of gnosticism and the need to defend the true heritage of Paul ('the sound doctrine') against the distorsions of the heretics.

Drawing upon the evidence compiled by Moule and Strobel, Wilson begins by reviewing the similarities of vocabulary and style between the Pastorals and Luke–Acts. Given the difference in length and literary genre between them, he considers the number of these similarities to be remarkably high. But at the same time, he admits that they are not sufficient as such to establish common authorship, and they need to be strengthened by theological and historical similarities.[15]

Wilson devotes most of his book to highlighting these similarities. He shows that Luke–Acts and the Pastorals share comparable or even identical points of view on several theological issues. His analysis deals successively with eschatology, salvation, the attitude of the 'Christian citizen' towards State and society, conception of Church and ministry, Christology, the use of Law and Scripture, and the image of Paul.

Let us illustrate on some points the results of Wilson's analysis. As far as eschatology is concerned, Luke and the Pastorals have in common the traditional belief in the parousia, but they do not expect that it will come soon and they consider that the Church is called to settle down in a lasting history. Their understanding of salvation is also similar: they do not emphasize the redeeming significance of Jesus' death and have no special interest in Paul's theology of the cross. They share the same

---

15. Unlike Strobel, who considers philological arguments as decisive ('Schreiben des Lukas?', pp. 193, 209 n. 3). For a thorough criticism of Strobel's article, see N. Brox, 'Lukas als Verfasser der Pastoralbriefe?', *JAC* 13 (1970), pp. 61-77, especially pp. 63-65.

positive attitude towards the State and the same ethical teaching; they underline the necessity of loyalty and responsibility, without, however, excluding the possibility of persecution as a dimension of Christian witness.

Wilson also notices important similarities regarding the church and its officers. Paul's farewell speech to the Ephesian elders (Acts 20.15-35) is especially rich in common points with the Pastorals. These are the only texts in the New Testament which simultaneously mention 'bishops' and 'elders'. These titles (ἐπίσκοπος and πρεσβύτερος) seem to refer to the same group of leaders in the community. There is no detailed description of the duties of these officials, but both texts emphasize the same points: their task is to defend the true teaching of Paul against the deviations of false teachers; they are requested to behave blamelessly in all matters, especially in their attitude towards wealth. Luke–Acts and the Pastorals are also similar with respect to the role of the prophets and the significance of the laying on of hands as a ceremony of consecration of Christian leaders (1 Tim. 1.18; 4.14; 2 Tim. 1.6; Acts 13.1-3).

Wilson has undoubtedly brought to light numerous theological agreements between Luke–Acts and the Pastorals. But he has not left it at that. His argumentation would have remained unconvincing, had it not taken into account the differences which separate and sometimes oppose the two works. Therefore Wilson takes care to examine and try to explain these differences.

The main points he mentions are the following. (1) In Luke, the ethical teaching is less prominent: there are no parallels either to the catalogues of vices and virtues, nor to the explicit connection between the moral behaviour of Christians and the reputation of the Church in society. (2) The Pastorals reflect a more advanced stage in ecclesiastical organization and in defence against heresies. (3) The attitude towards Law and Scripture is fairly different in the two groups of writings. (4) In the book of Acts, there are only a few allusions to Paul's death (Acts 20.24-25, 38; 21.10-14), whereas it is clearly announced in 2 Timothy (4.6-7), which underlines the fact that Paul is facing martyrdom alone, deserted by his close companions (2 Tim. 1.15; 4.10, 15). (5) Luke keeps the title 'apostle' for the Twelve and gives Paul a high but subordinate status, whereas the Pastorals portray him as *the* apostle, as the only source of genuine tradition, and make no mention of his predecessors.[16]

---

16. On these various points, see S.G. Wilson, *Luke and the Pastoral Epistles*, pp. 48-49, 66-67, 102-106, 112-13, 120-24.

In the view of many scholars and in my view too, these differences, especially the last one, are sufficient to disprove the thesis of a common authorship. To support his opinion, Wilson does his best to explain these differences. They are traceable to the fact that Luke–Acts and the Pastorals belong to different literary genres, that their subject-matter is different, and that Luke composed them at some distance in time, in order to answer different problems. According to Wilson, the book of Acts was written for Pauline communities, living in a milieu with a strong Jewish population; the purpose of the book was to defend these communities against external attacks, coming from Jews or Jewish Christians. For these communities, gnosticism was only an incipient threat, which Luke only mentioned by the way (the 'fierce wolves' of Acts 20.29-30). Some years later, when Luke composes the Pastorals, the situation has changed and the danger comes from within: gnostic teachers have infiltrated the Pauline churches and appeal to Paul and his authority to justify their 'false doctrine'. It is thus to preserve the genuine Pauline tradition and to oppose its being used by the gnostics that Luke writes these epistles in Paul's name.

This change in the situation allows one to explain the differences in emphasis between Acts and the Pastorals, especially with respect to the figure of Paul as an apostle. In Acts, facing an anti-Pauline polemic of a Jewish or Jewish Christian character, Luke emphasized Paul's faithfulness to his Jewish heritage and his peaceful relationship with the Jerusalem Church. In the Pastorals, facing people who claimed Paul and his writings as the source of their teaching, Luke had to deal with another problem. What was at stake was no more the relationship of Paul to Judaism or to his predecessors, but the question of the true Pauline tradition: who was the legitimate keeper of the 'good deposit', and how was this deposit to be transmitted to future generations? To answer this question, it was quite natural to focus on Paul alone as 'the apostle', and on his successors.

Wilson's argument is impressive. But it leads me to ask two critical questions. (a) Does the reconstruction of these two polemical backgrounds do justice to the purpose of Acts and of the Pastorals? I find it unlikely that Jewish or Jewish Christian criticism of Paul and his communities would have been the main reason for the writing of Acts. As for the Pastorals, I am quite willing to admit that the false teachers were claiming to be faithful to Paul, but I find difficult to label them plainly as 'gnostics'.

(b) Even if we admit that the reconstruction of these polemical fronts is correct, is it conceivable that one and the same author could have had to face such different conflicts within a distance of a few years? This seems to me all the more doubtful since Wilson has to assume other important changes in the intervening time between Luke–Acts and the Pastorals. One of these assumptions is that Luke, who never mentions Paul's epistolary activity in Acts nor shows any knowledge of his letters, would have come across these letters in the meantime and drawn inspiration from them to write the Pastorals in Paul's name. Moreover, Wilson suggests that Luke would have gained new information and traditions on the activitity of Paul and his companions; he would have used this additional material in the Pastorals, which would explain the discrepancies between the latter and the data of Acts about the 'biography' of the apostle.

These critical obseravtions do not detract from the worth of Wilson's work. He has really made out a good case in favour of the thesis of Lukan authorship. One of his merits is that he has freed this thesis from a fetter: its usual association with the theory of the secretary and with the attribution of the Pastorals to Luke the physician and companion of Paul. Wilson is also the first to have systematically compared the theology of Luke–Acts and that of the Pastorals. His analysis of their common characteristics and differences is useful and suggestive, even if the thesis of a common authorship is not convincing.

Other Possible Explanations for the Similarities between Luke–Acts and the Pastorals

This thesis being dismissed, we have to admit that Luke–Acts and the Pastorals have been written by two different authors. But the question remains: how should we explain the obvious relationship brought to light by Wilson's study? This relationship implies at least that both authors belong to the same historical and theological milieu, that of Christian communities which claim to have their roots in the figure and the teaching of Paul. But we have to take a further step and consider the possibility of a direct filiation between the two writings. Did one of the two authors know of and use the work of the other? Or did they write independently, each of them drawing from a common stock of traditions relating to Paul?

The second of these solutions is certainly easier to accept and to defend. It does correspond to a general trend in present-day research. To account for the affinities between two documents, there is today a sound reluctance to resort primarily to direct literary dependence, and a preference for another type of explanation: the sharing in the same traditional heritage, the dependence on a common stock of written or oral sources.

However, the possibility of direct dependence deserves serious attention in the present case. The linguistic and theological similarities noticed by the defenders of the Lukan thesis are a strong incentive to explore this possibility. In my opinion, if there is a filiation, it can only be in the direction that Luke–Acts influenced the Pastorals. The above-mentioned differences show that the Epistles reflect a later stage in the development of the Pauline theological tradition and of ecclesiastical organization.

My purpose in the last section of this essay is a limited one. I shall ask whether the biographical data of the Pastorals, especially those of 2 Timothy, can have been drawn directly from the narrative of Acts. In certain respects, this amounts to asking the traditional question of the compatibility of the two writings on the chronology of Paul's life: is it possible to harmonize the data of Acts with the information given by the Pastorals about the apostle's career, his relations with his coworkers, and his dealings with the Roman law?

If we accept the theory of the double captivity of Paul in Rome, the answer is clearly yes. But this solution is difficult to reconcile with the idea that the author of the Pastorals drew his inspiration from the book of Acts. One would have to suppose that he devised a new period of Paul's activity in the East, beyond the scope of Acts 28. Such a supposition seems most unlikely. A good reader of Acts cannot ignore the fact that Paul's journey to Rome was a journey from which there is no return, and that his farewell to the elders of Asia implied that he was leaving for good.[17] If the author of the Pastorals knew the book of Acts and wanted to give it a kind of epistolary complement, the situations he alluded to must take place within the narrative framework that ends with the captivity of Acts 28.

But did he really know and use the book of Acts? For the moment I have not settled the question definitively. However, I would like to point out some pieces of evidence that might suggest a positive answer.

17. Cf. Acts 20.25: 'And now, behold, I know that all you among whom I have gone about preaching the kingdom will see my face no more'; see also Acts 20.38; 21.10-14.

1. 2 Tim. 3.10-11: 'But you have followed, step by step, my teaching, my way of life, my purpose, my faith, my patience, my love, my endurance, my persecutions, my sufferings—all that happened to me at Antioch, at Iconium, at Lystra, all the persecutions I endured; and the Lord rescued me from all of them'. Why, among the many cities related to Paul's mission, does the author choose to mention Antioch, Iconium and Lystra? These are the three cities where the major episodes of Paul's first missionary journey take place (Acts 13–14), and where the apostle has to face a persecution set off by Jews.[18] Of course, this coincidence may be explained by the use of an independent tradition. But an argument can also be put forward in favour of a direct knowledge of the book of Acts: Timothy was from Lystra, and it is in this city, at the beginning of his second missionary journey, that Paul met him and decided to take him along (Acts 16.1-3). Having read the story of Acts, the author of the Pastorals may have wanted to recall here persecutions prior to Timothy's association with Paul.

2. 2 Tim. 4.11: 'Only Luke is with me. Take Mark, and bring him with you, because he is very useful to me in the ministry.' Mark, who is mentioned here, is certainly to be identified with the person mentioned among Paul's collaborators in the greetings of Phlm. 24 and Col. 4.10 (in both cases, his name occurs in the same context, along with those of Luke and Demas). In this passage, the author of the Pastorals has probably been inspired by Col. 4.10: 'Aristarchus my fellow prisoner greets you, and Mark the cousin of Barnabas—concerning whom you have received instruction: if he comes to you, receive him'. This text led him to imagine that Mark, who had already been a companion of Paul in prison at the time when Colossians was written, had to leave Asia and come to Rome to assist the apostle during a new period of captivity. But there is another interesting parallel to draw. The person named Mark in the Pauline letters should probably also be identified with 'John whose other name is Mark', who is mentioned several times in the book of Acts. He is at home in Jerusalem, where his mother Mary owns a house which is a meeting-place for the Christians (Acts 12.12); he is taken to Antioch by Saul and Barnabas on their way back from their 'service' in favour of Jerusalem (Acts 12.25). At the beginning of the first missionary journey, he unexpectedly leaves Paul and his companions to return to Jerusalem (Acts 13.13). Later, at the beginning of the second

---

18. Antioch of Pisidia: Acts 13.14-50; cf. 13.50; Iconium: Acts 13.51–14.5; cf. 14.1, 5; Lystra: Acts 14.6-20; cf. 14.19.

missionary journey, this previous desertion of 'John called Mark' gives rise to a disagreement between Paul and Barnabas, which leads them to part: Paul takes Silas with him, whereas Barnabas leaves for Cyprus along with Mark (Acts 15.36-40). If we admit that the author of the Pastorals read the book of Acts, he might very well have wanted to rehabilitate Mark. The very man whom Paul had refused to 'take with' him because of his desertion (Acts 15.38: Παῦλος δὲ ἠξίου (...) μὴ συμπαραλαμβάνειν τοῦτον) has now to be 'taken' and 'brought' by Timothy (Μᾶρκον ἀναλαβὼν ἄγε μετὰ σεαυτοῦ) to assist the apostle in his last moments.

3. 2 Tim. 4.13: 'When you come, bring the cloak that I left with Carpus at Troas, and the books, especially the parchments'. How did the author of the Pastorals come to mention Troas in this context? As in other cases, there are several possible explanations: this mention may be a mere literary invention, or it may be based on an independent tradition, or it may be inspired by other New Testament passages. My hypothesis is that the author usually composes his biographical passages with the help of indications found in Paul's letters or in the book of Acts. In this case, two passages mentioning Troas have to be considered. The first one is 2 Cor. 2.12-13 (about Paul moving from Asia to Macedonia): 'When I came to Troas to preach the gospel of Christ, a door was opened for me in the Lord, I still had no rest (οὐκ ἔσχηκα ἄνεσιν), because I did not find my brother Titus there. So I took leave of them and went off to Macedonia.' It is quite conceivable that this passage could have influenced 2 Tim. 4.13: the author of the Pastorals may have understood the phrase 'a door was opened for me by the Lord' as a reference to hospitality offered once by a person living in Troas, and he may have seen in the phrase 'I had no rest' an allusion to a shortened stay and to a hastened departure—hence the things 'left with Carpus at Troas'. The other passage is Acts 20.5-15 (the second 'we-section' of Acts). Paul stops off at Troas, on his way from Greece to Asia, and then to Jerusalem. Seven of his companions have reached the town a few days before (20.5-6). The stay in Troas is marked by the fatal fall and the resurrection of Eutychus (20.7-12). Paul's fellow travellers ('we') sail for Assos, where they will meet up again with the apostle who will travel by foot: 'But going ahead to the ship, we set sail for Assos, intending to take Paul aboard there; for so he had arranged, intending himself to go by land' (Acts 20.13). There is no explanation for these different ways of travelling. My suggestion is that the peculiarity of this trip by foot led

the author of the Pastorals to the idea that Paul had to leave in Troas some cumbersome objects.

4. 2 Tim. 4.20: 'Erastus remained at Corinth, and I left Trophimus ill at Miletus'. You may wonder why I adduce this verse, for it contains the plainest case of a contradiction between Acts and the biographical data of the Pastorals. What it says about Trophimus cannot fit in with the narrative framework of Acts 20–28.

Let us first consider the case of Erastus, which is easier to deal with. This name occurs twice elsewhere in the New Testament. In Rom. 16.23, Erastus is one of several brothers (including Timothy) who stay with Paul when he writes his letter to the Romans, and he is identified by his social office: 'Gaius, who is host to me and to the whole church, greets you. Erastus, the city treasurer, and our brother Quartus, greet you.' Since Gaius is one of the few Corinthians to have been baptized by Paul (1 Cor. 1.14), Corinth must be the place where the letter to the Romans was written (or at least Rom. 16), and where Erastus fulfilled the function of οἰκονόμος. In Acts 19.22, Erastus and Timothy are sent by Paul from Ephesus to Macedonia to prepare for his coming. 'And having send into Macedonia two of his helpers, Timothy and Erastus, to Macedonia, he himself stayed in Asia for a while.' What became of Erastus afterwards? Unlike Timothy, his name is not mentioned in the list of companions travelling with Paul when he leaves Greece (Acts 20.3-4). Carrying on with my hypothesis, I suggest that the author of the Pastorals, as a careful reader of Acts (and of Romans), noticed that Erastus had disappeared from the party of Paul's fellow travellers, and concluded therefrom that he had remained in Greece, more precisely in Corinth, where he had been active as city treasurer.

Let us now turn to the main difficulty. The information about Trophimus ('I left Trophimus ill at Miletus') cannot be harmonized with the narrative of Acts. In the list of Acts 20.4, Trophimus is mentioned as one of the seven travelling with Paul when he leaves Greece to go to Syria and Jerusalem. Later, his staying in Jerusalem along with Paul triggers off a violent reaction of the Asian Jews: 'For they had previously seen Trophimus the Ephesian with him in the city, and they supposed that Paul had brought him into the temple' (Acts 21.29). Thus the illness and the prolonged stay in Miletus mentioned in 2 Tim. 4.20 cannot take place within the itinerary described in Acts 20.1–21.16: from Ephesus to Jerusalem, passing through Macedonia, Greece (Achaia, see 19.21) and again Macedonia, Troas, Assos, Miletus, Tyre and Caesarea. Paul cannot possibly have left Trophimus ill in Miletus during this journey since they arrived together in Jerusalem. I must admit that this impossibility seems to contradict the hypothesis of an author who would be familiar with Acts and draw from there his biographical data. The difficulty is a serious one, and there have been various attempts to do away with it. But I think that it resists the explanations that have been proposed up to now, however ingenious they may be.[19]

My main purpose in these last pages was to show the necessity to scrutinize the biographical data contained in the Pastoral Epistles. Until now, the origin and the function of these data within the pseudepigraphical fiction have not been studied with sufficient attention. I have raised the question of their possible dependence on the book of Acts. But this is only a partial inquiry. One should also examine their relationship to other ancient Christian documents, especially to the *Acts of Paul*. The debate about the relationship between this apocryphal writing and the Pastorals has many analogies with the question addressed in this paper. Various solutions have been put forward, and they show the same hesitation between direct dependence and relationship through a common tradition.[20]

---

19. For example, the conjecture of Beza on 2 Tim. 4.20, who suggests to read ἐν Μελίτῃ ('in Malta') instead of ἐν Μιλήτῳ ('in Miletus'). See also the explanation proposed by S.G. Wilson, *Luke and the Pastoral Epistles*, pp. 130-31.

20. See the recent and stimulating study by R. Bauckham, 'The Acts of Paul as a Sequel to Acts', in B.W. Winter and A.D. Clarke (eds.), *The Book of Acts in Its Ancient Literary Setting* (Grand Rapids–Carlisle, 1993), pp. 105-52 (esp. 116-30). Bauckham rejects the solution of D. MacDonald (*The Legend and the Apostle: The Battle for Paul in Story and Canon* [Philadelphia, 1983]), who wants to explain the common points between the Pastorals and the *Acts of Paul* on the basis of a common oral tradition, and he defends the thesis of the literary dependence with a new argumentation. The author of the *Acts of Paul* used the Pastorals (especially 2 Timothy) and gave a narrative exegesis of some passages. E.g. he has interpreted 2 Tim. 4.17 as a reference to a real fight of Paul against lions (see the Ephesus episode of the *Acts of Paul*); he has combined the various pairs of apostates mentioned in 2 Tim. 1.15; 2.17 and 4.10, 14 into one pair (see 'Demas and Hermogenes the blacksmith' in the *Acts of Paul and Thecla*). He has thus resorted to hermeneutical procedures that were common in the Jewish exegetical tradition (explaining a given text by means of a narrative; putting together the elements of related passages). The kind of narrative exegesis that Bauckham attributes to the author of the *Acts of Paul* is very close to the reading of passages of the book of Acts and of the Pauline letters which I have tried to detect in some biographical texts of 2 Timothy.

The similarities between Luke–Acts and the Pastorals deserve further research. As to the question of their relationship, my intention was to clear the ground. In any case, the study of the Pastorals and that of the Lukan work have to be firmly linked to each other and will enrich each other. Both writings belong to the Pauline 'trajectory', both are rooted in a movement claiming to Paul's figure and teaching. This evidence compels us to treat them as two members of the same family. Those who advocate the thesis of a common Lukan authorship have made an important contribution in helping us to recognize their many common characteristics and family links. But the weakness of the thesis is that it does not sufficiently respect the individuality of both literary works and leads to the establishment of what I would call, in the language of psychoanalysis, a 'fusional' relationship between them.

SAUL'S CONVERSION (ACTS 9, 22, 26) AND THE MULTIPLICATION OF NARRATIVE IN ACTS

Daniel Marguerat

'The historian's only task is to tell the facts just as they have occurred.'[1] This injunction by the famous second-century rhetor Lucian of Samosata is a pretty good reflection of the requirement of accuracy to which Greco-Roman historiography was subjected. How would Lucian have reacted on reading the three accounts of Saul's conversion at Damascus as presented by the book of Acts? For between the first account of the event in ch. 9 and its twofold resumption in an autobiographical mode in speeches by Paul (Acts 22 and 26), there is considerable variation. Such a combination of repetition and variation remains even today a *crux interpretum* in the Acts research: why three accounts of Saul's conversion, and why such divergence among the three versions?[2]

---

1. *How to Write History* 39. In context, Lucian wants to guarantee the historian's objectivity in view of the risk of pressure or flattery toward the audience.
2. Among the studies devoted to this issue, cf. E. Hirsch, 'Die drei Berichte der Apostelgeschichte über die Bekehrung des Paulus', *ZNW* 28 (1929), pp. 305-12; H. Windisch, 'Die Christusepiphanie vor Damaskus (Act 9, 22 und 26) und ihre religionsgeschichtlichen Parallelen', *ZNW* 31 (1932), pp. 1-23; D.M. Stanley, 'Paul's Conversion in Acts: Why the Three Accounts?', *CBQ* 15 (1953), pp. 315-38; C. Burchard, *Der dreizehnte Zeuge* (FRLANT, 103; Göttingen: Vandenhoeck & Ruprecht, 1970); S. Lundgren, 'Ananias and the Calling of Paul in Acts', *ST* 25 (1971), pp. 117-22; K. Löning, *Die Saulustradition in der Apostelgeschichte* (NTA, 9; Münster: Aschendorff, 1973); V. Stolle, *Der Zeuge als Angeklagter: Untersuchungen zum Paulusbild des Lukas* (BWANT, 102; Stuttgart: Kohlhammer, 1973), pp. 155-212; O.H. Steck, 'Formgeschichtliche Bemerkungen zur Darstellung des Damaskusgeschehens in der Apostelgeschichte', *ZNW* 67 (1976), pp. 20-28; R.F. O'Toole, *Acts 26: The Christological Climax of Paul's Defense* (AnBib 78; Rome: Biblical Institute, 1978); C.W. Hedrick, 'Paul's Conversion/Call: A Comparative Analysis of the Three Reports in Acts', *JBL* 100 (1981), pp. 415-32; N.A. Beck, *The Lukan Writer's Stories about the Call of Paul* (SBLSP, 1983; Chico, CA: Scholars Press, 1983), pp. 213-18; J. Calloud, 'Sur le chemin de

The present contribution aims to revisit this classical question, but from a different perspective provided by narrative criticism. To begin with, I want to specify my way of questioning, for the treatment of the multiplication of narrative reveals how the exegete relates with the text. In the case of Acts 9, 22 and 26, source criticism coped with the excess of narrative by appealing to a multiplicity of documents (Spitta; Wendt; Hirsch).[3] But since the work of Cadbury and Dibelius has drawn attention to Luke's own literary creativity, commentators most commonly identify behind Acts 9 a traditional narrative, of which the narrator then gives two redactional variants in Acts 22 and 26.[4] Some see in this an

---

Damas. Quelques lumières sur l'organisation discursive d'un texte, Actes des apôtres 9,1-19', *SemBi* 37 (1985), pp. 3-29; 38 (1985), pp. 40-53; 40 (1985), pp. 21-42; 42 (1986), pp. 1-19; R.F. Collins, 'Paul's Damascus Experience: Reflections on the Lukan Account', *Louvain Studies* 11 (1986), pp. 99-118; G. Lohfink, *The Conversion of St Paul* (Chicago: Franciscan Herald Press, 1986); S.R. Bechtler, 'The Meaning of Paul's Call and Commissioning in Luke's Story: An Exegetical Study of Acts 9, 22, and 26', *Studia Biblica and Theologica* 15 (1987), pp. 53-77; J.J. Kilgallen, 'Paul before Agrippa (Acts 26,2-23): Some Considerations', *Bib* 69 (1988), pp. 170-95; D. Hamm, 'Paul's Blindness and Its Healing: Clues to Symbolic Intent (Acts 9; 22 and 26)', *Bib* 71 (1990), pp. 63-72. Within a New Literary Criticism perspective: B.R. Gaventa, *From Darkness to Light: Aspects of Conversion in the New Testament* (Philadelphia: Fortress Press, 1986), pp. 52-95; C.J. LaHurd, *The Author's Call to the Audience in the Acts of the Apostles* (Dissertation; Ann Arbor, MI: University Microfilms International, 1987), pp. 182-229; R.W. Funk, *The Poetics of Biblical Narrative* (Sonoma, CA: Polebridge, 1988), pp. 156-61, 204-206; M.-E. Rosenblatt, 'Under Interrogation: Paul as Witness in Juridical Contexts in Acts and the Implied Spirituality of Luke's Commnity' (PhD dissertation, Graduate Theological Union, 1987), pp. 92-123; R.D. Witherup, 'Functional Redundancy in the Acts of the Apostles: A Case Study', *JSNT* 48 (1992), pp. 67-86; W.S. Kurz, *Reading Luke–Acts: Dynamics of Biblical Narrative* (Louisville: Westminster–John Knox, 1993), pp. 26-27, 125-31; S. Reymond, 'L'expérience du chemin de Damas. Approche narrative d'une expérience spirituelle' (Diplôme de spécialisation en sciences bibliques, Université de Lausanne, 1993). The issue of the relationship between Acts 9, 22, 26 and the data from Gal. 1.13-17 remains outside my purview.

3. Status of research in G. Lohfink, *Paulus vor Damaskus* (SBS 4; Stuttgart: KBW, 1965), pp. 36-40.

4. This literary verdict is founded on the redactional origin of the Lukan speeches (and hence of Acts 22 and 26) according to the judgment of M. Dibelius, *Studies in the Acts of the Apostles* (London: SCM Press, 1956), pp. 110, 159-60. The one exception to this consensus has been voiced by T.L. Budesheim, 'Paul's Abschiedsrede in the Acts of the Apostles', *HTR* 69 (1976), pp. 9-30, who ascribes

effect of stylistic variation.[5] Others ascribe to a careless Lukan redaction, as well as to a lack of attention to narrative discrepancies, the fact that sometimes Saul's companions are said to hear the voice but not to see anything (9.7), and sometimes to see the light without hearing anything (22.9); or sometimes they are said to remain standing (9.7) and sometimes to fall to the ground along with Saul (26.14).[6] The merit of redaction criticism lies in having perceived that 'this technique of repetition is one to which Luke always resorts when he wants to impress something specially upon the reader' (E. Haenchen).[7] The unresolved question is: *why* is repetition combined with so much difference ?

To my knowledge, the first who replaced this line of questioning, focused on the genealogy of the text, was David Stanley in his 1953 article, 'Paul's Conversion in Acts: Why the Three Accounts?'[8] His own formulation deserves quoting: 'The triple narrative of that supremely critical hour in a life fraught with crises deserves to be studied from another aspect: the function assigned it in the exposition of his theme by the author of the book of Acts' (p. 315). Anticipating more recent research, Stanley was framing the problem in narratological terms: How does this triple emergence of the narrative actually function within the overall plot of the book of Acts? I broaden the issue: *How one is to evaluate the interplay of repetition and variation among Acts 9, 22 and 26 ? Can one explain from a narrative viewpoint the variations of Acts 22 and 26 compared with Acts 9 ? Luke could not but be aware that the differences between his three narratives were not just a matter of details; unless he was counting on forgetfulness on the part of his reader/hearer, what means did he provide him or her with so that she or he would be enabled to manage such variation?*

Acts 22.1-21 to the tradition and sees in Acts 9 a Hellenized adaptation traceable to the redactor's pen; before that, D.M. Stanley had adopted a similar though less clear-cut position ('Paul's Conversion in Acts', pp. 325-28).

    5. F.F. Bruce, *The Acts of the Apostles* (Grand Rapids: Eerdmans, 3rd edn, 1990), p. 232; A. Weiser, *Die Apostelgeschichte Kap. 1–12* (ÖTKNT, 5.1; Gütersloh: Mohn, 1981), pp. 219-22; C.W. Hedrick, 'Paul's Conversion/Call', pp. 427-32; R. Pesch, *Die Apostelgeschichte (Apg 1–12)* (EKK, 5.1; Zürich: Benziger; Neukirchen: Neukirchener Verlag, 1986), p. 302.

    6. H. Conzelmann, *Die Apostelgeschichte* (HNT, 7; Tübingen: Mohr, 1963), p. 59; G. Schneider, *Die Apostelgeschichte*, II (HTKNT, 5.2; Freiburg: Herder, 1982), p. 22.

    7. *The Acts of the Apostles* (Philadelphia: Westminster Press, 1971), p. 357.

    8. See n. 2.

My present article contains three parts. The first discusses the question of redundancy as narrative criticism treats it. The second part deals with Acts 9, 22 and 26 by looking at them as a whole. The third part will conduct a detailed examination of Acts 9, then Acts 22, then Acts 26. By way of conclusion, I shall return to the significance of the Damascus event within the plot of Luke–Acts.

1. *The Question of Narrative Redundancy*

1.1. *Redundancy in Luke–Acts*

The question of the multiplication of narrative is an interesting one to raise in the work of Luke, because it receives a sharply different treatment depending on whether one deals with the Gospel or with the book of Acts. The redaction of the Gospel of Luke avoids the literary doublets which, in the case of Matthew for example, are caused by the reception of traditions from Mark and Q; for instance, the duplication of the feeding miracle (Mk 6.32-44 and 8.1-9; Mt. 14.13-21 and 15.32-38) is avoided by Luke (9.10-17).[9] Conversely, the book of Acts knows several cases of repetition of a narrative episode. Thus the Ascension account is related in two variant forms (Lk. 24.50-51; Acts 1.9-11). The events surrounding the meeting between Peter and Cornelius are related as many as four times between Acts 10 and 11, and yet again at the occasion of the Jerusalem assembly (15.7-11).[10] The 'apostolic decree' promulgated by this same assembly (15.20), regulating the communion among Christians originating from the Jerusalem and Antioch missions respectively, is duplicated in 15.29 and in 21.25. The account of Saul's conversion is thus not the only one to undergo this multiplication effect.

One can broaden those findings going beyond single episodes and observing that *the reader of Acts frequently sees repetition of narrative patterns*. Chapters 2 to 5 present, three times over, the same structural pattern. The first sequence is identifiable in 3.1–4.4, where an event (3.1-10, miracle of healing) is followed by an interpretative speech by Peter

---

9. R. Morgenthaler has devoted himself to the study of the Lukan doublets, seeing in them (and rightly so) a literary device of the author, yet unfortunately, he does not differentiate between the Gospel and Acts: *Die lukanische Geschichtsschreibung als Zeugnis*, I (ATANT, 14; Zürich: Zwingli Verlag, 1948).

10. Cornelius's vision is told four times (10.1-8, 22, 30-33; 11.11-14), that of Peter is related twice (10.9-16; 11.5-10). See the study by R.D. Witherup, 'Cornelius Over and Over and Over Again: "Functional Redundancy" in the Acts of the Apostles', *JSNT* 49 (1993), pp. 45-66.

(3.11-26), itself followed by a contrasting effect upon the audience, on the one side the opposition of religious leaders, on the other the adherence of the people (4.1-3, 4). The same pattern is renewed in 4.5-31 and 5.17-40 (see already 2.1-41).[11] From ch. 13 on, the Pauline mission is governed by the following well-known scheme: Paul preaches in the synagogue, but as he faces violent rejection of his message, he turns to the God-fearers and the Gentiles receptive to the Word as his sole audience (13.42-51; 14.1-6; 17.1-9, 10-13; 18.1-7, etc.). More widely, the modeling effect Peter has upon Paul, which leads the narrator to ascribe to Paul similar performances to those of Peter, but generally more brilliant, partakes of the same device. One could add the carrying over into the book of Acts of patterns having their roots in Luke's Gospel.[12] So to summarize: the repetition of narratives of the same event concretizes a phenomenon of narrative redundancy of which the author of Acts makes a more intense use than any other writer of the New Testament.[13] Robert Tannehill has identified this literary device as *a mode of composition typical of the book of Acts*.[14]

But why this use of redundancy? Do we have to do here with some literary nicety of Luke the writer? Or with the typical twist of the pedagogue who repeats to the point of boredom what his pupils should remember? Or else with a regrettable lack of imagination?

My thesis is that this choice reveals a narrative strategy, and that this strategy serves a theological purpose. The idea that a literary process of repetition should serve a theological purpose is not in itself new as far as Luke–Acts is concerned. It is an established fact in Lukan research that

---

11. I sum up here the findings of my article, 'La mort d'Ananias et Saphira (Actes 5,1-11) dans la stratégie narrative de Luc', *NTS* 39 (1993), pp. 209-26, esp. 211-17.

12. See C.H. Talbert, *Literary Patterns, Theological Themes, and the Genre of Luke–Acts* (Missoula, MT: Scholars Press, 1974).

13. Matthew too is fond of the repetition device, which he uses for didactic purposes, in order to reinforce the adherence of the reader to the ideological point of view unfolded by the narrative. See the article by J.C. Anderson, 'Double and Triple stories, the Implied Reader and Redundancy in Matthew', *Semeia* 31 (1985), pp. 71-89, as well as her monograph, *Matthew's Narrative Web: Over, and Over, and Over Again* (JSNTSup, 91; Sheffield: JSOT Press, 1994); also F.W. Burnett, 'Prolegomenon to Reading Matthew's Eschatological Discourse: Redundancy and the Education of the Reader in Matthew', *Semeia* 31 (1985), pp. 91-109.

14. R.C. Tannehill, *The Composition of Acts 3–5: Narrative Development and Echo Effect* (SBLSP; Chico, CA: Scholars Press, 1984), pp. 217-40, esp. 237-40.

the resumption in Acts of patterns originating in the Gospel aims to set up a theological conformity between the praxis of Jesus and that of the apostles. So it is with the miracle accounts in Acts, of which more than one reproduces the pattern of the miracles of Jesus.[15] And so it is with the itinerary motif, which constitutes the formal structure of the life of the Lukan Jesus as of the life of Paul in Acts: there is the same itinerancy, the same hostility met, the same Passion—and yet, nothing is exactly the same between Jesus and Paul, and the witness is not to be confused with the Master.[16] For repetition—at least in written communication—is never the return of the same.[17] The repetition of narrative, with its play of similarity and dissimilarity, allows one to signify *both* continuity *and* displacement, change *and* identity. Which narrative strategy does Luke institute through such a dialectic of resemblance and difference?

Before setting out to analyse Lukan redundancy, we must step back briefly and inquire about the phenomenon of redundancy within biblical narration.

1.2. *Redundancy within Biblical Narration*

In their respective studies of the poetics of biblical narration, Robert Alter and Meir Sternberg have been sensitive to the phenomenon of redundancy, and their contributions have the advantage of overcoming the negative evaluation given to redundancy by classical literary criticism.[18] The classical view disqualifies redundancy as excess, dispensable

---

15. W. Radl has undertaken this detailed and minute comparison: *Paulus und Jesus im lukanischen Doppelwerk: Untersuchungen zu Parallelmotiven im Lukasevangelium und in der Apostelgeschichte* (EH, 23.49; Bern: Lang, 1975).

16. Stolle's study makes a refined analysis of the christological model that shapes the Lukan figure of Paul: *Der Zeuge als Angeklagter*. See pp. 157-212 for an analysis of the three accounts of the Damascus event.

17. Variation within repetition characterizes written communication over against oral tradition, insofar as orality requires the use of stereotyped formulas for mnemotechnical purposes, so as to favour memorization, either on the part of the story-teller or on the part of the hearers; see W. Ong, *Orality and Literacy* (London: Routledge, 1989), pp. 31ff., esp. 39-41.

18. R. Alter, *The Art of Biblical Narrative* (London: Allen & Unwin, 1981), pp. 88-113; M. Sternberg, *The Poetics of Biblical Narrative: Ideological Literature and the Drama of Reading* (Bloomington: Indiana University Press, 1987), pp. 365-440. See also G.W. Savran, *Telling and Retelling: Quotation in Biblical Narrative* (Bloomington: Indiana University Press, 1988), and S. Bar-Efrat, *Narrative Art in*

insistence, superfluity of rhetorical ornamentation. Form criticism has taught us to speak of redundancy in terms of 'doublet'. Alter and Sternberg treat redundancy on the basis of a communication theory that views it as a means to ensure reception of information by reducing meaning ambiguities as much as possible. Re-telling is indispensable in order to counter the noise, that is, quoting John Lyons, 'any disturbances or defects in the system which interfere with the faithful transmission of signals'.[19] The theoreticians of artificial intelligence have thus paved the way for *a valuing of redundancy as a means to ensure optimal reception of a message*. Such informational redundancy[20] is a communication technique, traces of which are found in folklore as well as in oral rhetoric and in literature.[21]

Meir Sternberg has looked for the various factors making up the strategy of informational redundancy within biblical narration. His findings, drawn from the Hebrew Bible, are applicable to New Testament narration.[22] Besides verbatim repetition (e.g. in the prediction–fulfilment scheme), Sternberg identifies *5 types of variation* within repetition: (1) amplification, (2) suppression, (3) interpolation, (4) grammatical transformation (e.g. turning active into passive), (5) substitution. Among the factors leading to variation, Sternberg mentions change in the source

the Bible (JSOTSup, 70; Sheffield: JSOT Press, 1989), pp. 211-16.

19. J. Lyons, *Semantics*, I (Cambridge: Cambridge University Press, 1977), p. 44. Anderson lists seven functions of redundancy: (1) to highlight attention; (2) to fix in the mind; (3) to emphasize importance; (4) to create expectations; (5) to cause reassessment; (6) to unify disparate elements; (7) to build patterns of attention or draw contrasts (*Matthew's Narrative Web*, p. 44).

20. The formula is from Sternberg, *Poetics*, p. 365. R.D. Witherup prefers the phrase 'functional redundancy', which indicates that the function of redundancy is not just to communicate information ('Functional Redundancy', p. 68 and n. 4).

21. The classic reference for the study of literary redundancy is the article by S.R. Suleiman, 'Redundancy and the "Readable" Text', *Poetics Today* 1.3 (1980), pp. 119-42. About the importance of repetition within ancient rhetoric: H. Lausberg, *Handbuch der literarischen Rhetorik*, I (Munich: Hueber, 2nd edn, 1973), pp. 310-36. About redundancy in the New Testament and Greek rhetoric: E.A. Nida, J.P. Louw, A.H. Snyman and J.V.W. Cronje, *Style and Discourse, with Special Reference to the Greek New Testament* (Cape Town: Bible Society, 1983), pp. 22-23. Concerning oral rhetoric, see P.J. Achtemeier, 'Omne Verbum Sonat: The New Testament and the Oral Environment of Late Western Antiquity', *JBL* 109 (1990), pp. 3-27.

22. I only retain here Sternberg's inventory of modalities of repetition from his whole analysis of the rhetoric of redundancy (*Poetics*, pp. 387-93).

of information, that is, modification of the point of view adopted between the first narration of an event and the following ones; I shall return later to this point, which is important for our case. For now, I wish to apply Sternberg's taxonomy to our three narratives.

Acts 9.1-30	Acts 22.1-21	Acts 26.1-23
I. vv. 1-2: Introduction. Saul, persecutor of Christians	**I. vv. 1-2**: *Captatio* **II. vv. 3-5**: Saul, a Jew and persecutor of Christians	**I. vv. 1-3**: *Captatio* **II. vv. 4-8**: Saul, a Pharisee **III. vv. 9-11**: Saul, persecutor of Christians
II. vv. 3-9: Epiphany of Christ (with dialogue) and the apparition's effects upon Saul **III. vv. 10-16**: Ananias's vision (Saul's calling) **IV. vv. 17-19a**: Mandate to Ananias and baptism of Saul	**III. vv. 6-11**: Epiphany of Christ (with dialogue) **IV. vv. 12-16**: Encounter with Ananias and baptism of Saul **V. vv. 17-21**: Ecstasy in the Jerusalem Temple (Saul's calling)	**IV. vv. 12-18**: Epiphany (Saul's calling)
V. vv. 19b-30: Effect. Saul, witness for Christ, and threatened with death.	(22, 22: death shouts from the crowd)	**V. vv. 19-23**: Effect. Saul, witness for Christ, and persecuted. (27-28: voyage to Rome)

Table 1. *The Structure of the Accounts*

2. *A Series of Three Narratives*

2.1. *The Play of Variations*

Sternberg's taxonomy is verified when one compares the three variant accounts of Paul's conversion. The dialogue between Jesus and Saul is characterized by word-for-word repetition: '"*Saul, Saul, why do you persecute me?" (He said to me:) "I am Jesus (the Nazarene), whom you are persecuting*"' (9.4-5; 22.7-8; 26.14-15). An *invariable kernel*, preserved from one narrative to the next, thus crystallizes upon the identification dialogue that succeeds the shock of encounter.

Variations must be assessed from Acts 9, which is the first account. Comparing the structure of the three accounts will allow us better to grasp the play of displacements (see Table 1, above).

Let us look first at *ch. 9*. After an introduction exposing Saul's persecution plan (9.1-2), the epiphany of Christ (vv. 3-9) is followed by an apparition of the Lord to Ananias (vv. 10-16), and then by the fulfilment of his mandate of healing and baptism (vv. 17-19a). The effect is unexpected: Saul, the persecutor, becomes the persecuted witness of Christ at Damascus and Jerusalem (vv. 19b-30). Saul's reversal from persecutor to persecuted concretizes the overturning of his identity at Damascus; this is why commentators are wrong when they break off the narrative at v. 19b rather than going on to v. 30.[23]

A synoptic comparison of the Acts 9 narrative with its autobiographical resumptions in chs. 22 and 26 reveals a series of structural modifications.

The *suppression* factor applies to the role of Ananias, whose vision is suppressed in ch. 22, and who disappears totally from ch. 26. The persecution falling on Saul (9.19b-30) has no equivalent in ch. 22. As for *amplifications*, they touch on several motifs. Saul's Pharisaic past is introduced in 26.4-8. His activity as a persecutor of Christians is amplified and aggravated in 22.3-5 and 26.9-11. The speech in ch. 22 culminates in a scene of ecstasy in the Jerusalem Temple (22.17-21), unknown to the reader of Acts 9; such a scene serves as a *substitution* for the persecution narrative in 9.19b-30. Within the speech in ch. 26, an *interpolation* causes Saul himself to announce his calling, in the course

---

23. The narrative caesura in 9.19a is still being defended by L.T. Johnson, *The Acts of the Apostles* (Sacra Pagina; Collegeville: Liturgical Press, 1992), p. 161; the only thing that speaks for it is a slight break between 9.19a and 19b (ἐγένετο δέ), whereas 9.31 represents a much clearer break, through the insertion of a narrative summary and the disappearance of the character Saul from the narrative until 11.25. But especially, the sequence 9.1-30 is clearly identifiable by the inclusion effect orchestrated by the narrator between 9.1-2 and 9.26-30: (a) the journey from Jerusalem to Damascus (9.1) reverses into a flight from Damascus to Jerusalem (9.26); (b) Saul the persecutor (9.1) becomes Saul the persecuted one (9.29); (c) the enemy of the Way (9.2) speaks in the name of the Lord (9.27-28); (d) the murderous desire toward Christians (9.1) is reversed into a brotherly relationship (9.30). Besides, a parallelism of motifs is to be detected between 9.19b-25 and 26-30, which function like twin narratives, rather than between 9.13-25 and 26-30 (contrary opinion in D. Gill, 'The Structure of Acts 9', *Bib* 55 [1974], pp. 346-48).

of the epiphany (26.16-18), whereas ch. 9 communicates it only to Ananias, after the shock on the Damascus road (9.15-16). A comparison of 9.6 (λαληθήσεται) with 22.10 (εἶπον) allows us to see a *transformation* of a *grammatical* order, where Saul moves from a passive role ('you will be told') to an active one ('and I said').[24]

The figure of Saul's travelling companions concentrates all the changes. Suppression: they lose their importance progressively from Acts 9 to Acts 26 (compare 9.16-17 with 26.14a). Interpolation: the narrative mentions them sometimes after the dialogue (9.7-8; 22.9-10), sometimes before (26.14). Transformation: in ch. 9 they hear the voice without seeing anybody (9.7), while in ch. 22 they see without hearing (22.9); as the christophany occurs, sometimes they stand speechless (9.7, εἱστήκεισαν ἐνεοί), sometimes they fall to the ground (26.14: πάντων τε καταπεσόντων ἡμῶν εἰς τὴν γῆν).

How is one to interpret this interplay of variations? Which narrative constraints does it answer? What design does it reveal? Before setting out to analyse each account individually, it is appropriate to discuss the status and function of the three accounts within the narration of Luke–Acts.

2.2. *The Status of the Three Narratives*
Among the factors of variation within redundancy, Sternberg mentions change in the source of information involving a change of point of view.[25] That is exactly what is going on here: Acts 9 emanates from the narrator who tells the story in the third person; Acts 22 and Acts 26 are instances of autobiographical discourse, where Paul is speaking about himself, using 'I'. From this observation W. Kurz has derived a key for understanding the relationship between the three accounts of Saul's conversion: variations from one account to the next may be explained by the 'influence of variant narrators'.[26] While emanating from the same author, the three narratives are not provided with the same status within the narration of Acts. Or to put it in Genette's terms,[27] the three

---

24. Over against Witherup ('Functional Redundancy', p. 70), who does not perceive any grammatical transformation between the three narratives, I do see in this mutation of the λαληθήσεται (9.6) into εἶπον (22.10) a modification of this type, consciously playing on the two synonymous terms.
25. *Poetics*, pp. 380-82.
26. *Reading Luke–Acts*, p. 125.
27. G. Genette, *Figures*, III (Paris: Seuil, 1972), pp. 225-67.

variants emanate from the same 'voice' (the narrator), but the enunciator within the narrative varies. Acts 9 is the direct product of the omniscient narrator's action; the telling in the third person confers on the text a status of objectivity that the 'I' discourse of Paul does not have. Acts 9 does not just come first within narrative chronology; it is primary within the hierarchy of narrative instances[28]—to continue with Genette's vocabulary—since the enunciator of Acts 9 is extradiegetic (the narrator), whereas the enunciator of Acts 22 and 26 is intradiegetic (Paul, a figure who is internal to the narrative). Acts 22 and 26 thus set themselves forth as retrospective readings of the Damascus road event that emanate from its main character.

This attention given to the differentiation of enunciators throws a new light on the concurrence of the three narratives. As far as its informative value within the narrative is concerned, Acts 9 as emanating from the ominiscient narrator towers above Acts 22 and Acts 26. The three accounts do not work together according to the principle of a 'coinciding of narrative points of view',[29] but according to the principle of a differentiation of points of view, since the narrative apparatus distinguishes the objective and earlier point of view of the omniscient narrator (Acts 9) from the subjective and later point of view of the speaker Paul in Acts 22 and 26. Three consequences may be drawn from this.
1. Having been forewarned about the difference among the enunciators, the reader will not be surprised when the successive reports of the Damascus road event present divergences among themselves (such was the case between 10.9-16 and 11.5-10, when Peter tells about his ecstasy). 2. Being placed, after Acts 9, in front of two speeches using 'I', the reader will not be surprised at the gradual disappearance of secondary characters (Ananias and the travelling companions) in favour of an increased focus on the character Paul which reaches its peak in the

---

28. According to S. Chatman, in the case of a conflict between the ideology of the narrator and that of a character, the narrator's point of view (unless he is unreliable) 'tends to override the character's' (*Story and Discourse* [Ithaca, NY: Cornell University Press, 1978], p. 156). Such a supremacy of the narrator's version in cases of discrepancies is confirmed by Sternberg, *Poetics*, pp. 75-76, 130, 245-46, 380-82, 389-91, 413-18, 432-33, and Savran, *Telling and Retelling*, pp. 13-15.

29. I quote the formula by Witherup ('Functional Redundancy', p. 74 n. 19; cf also pp. 84-85), who in my view seems to err by overemphasizing the coincidence of the three narratives, while their concurrence precisely brings out their profound divergences.

speech before Agrippa.[30] 3. The supremacy of of the narrator's account (Acts 9) over the retrospective speeches of Paul must be theologically assessed: only after the divine intervention has overturned the life of Saul the Pharisee does a personal rereading of the event become possible (Acts 22 and 26); in other words, the narrative supremacy of the narrator serves here as a literary mediation for the theological precedence of God's intervention in history over the subjective appropriations of the same event (the same thing can be said when one compares 10.1-23 with the autobiographical discourse of both Cornelius and Peter in 10.24-33; 11.4-17).

In the final analysis, it appears that the author of Acts was not content with juxtaposing three competing versions of the Damascus road event. The differentiation of narrative instances which he provided for makes plausible to the reader the reception of three versions of one and the same event which diverge so much among themselves. Refashioning a story from one character's particular point of view constituted a well-known exercise among the rhetorical schools of Antiquity, namely *prosopopeia*, which demanded on the part of students the composition of a speech borrowing the voice of a historical or mythical figure, while adapting it to a specific audience.[31] That Luke had become a master in

30. Of the intervention of the travelling companions and of Ananias, which occupies 12 verses in ch. 9 (9.7-8, 10 19), there remains in ch. 26 only a half-verse (26.14a). The progressive disappearance of secondary characters between the first and the third narrative, and the concomitant rise in prominence of the figure of Saul, have been well noted by Witherup ('Functional Redundancy', pp. 77-80), who speaks of 'literary rheostat' in order to describe this dialectical regulation of the narrative. The focalization on the figure of Paul in Acts 22 and 26 has been analyzed by Kurz, *Reading Luke–Acts*, pp. 129-30. The principle of focalization as a position relative to the story, i.e. external or internal to the story, is described by S. Rimmon-Kenan, *Narrative Fiction: Contemporary Poetics* (New York: Methuen, 1983), pp. 74-77; in the case of the opposite valorization of secondary characters and of Saul, that author would speak of a movement of narrative 'acceleration and deceleration' (*Narrative Fiction*, p. 56). These categories have been well used by Rosenblatt, 'Under Interrogation', pp. 92-123, especially pp. 102-109.

31. Quintilian describes the practice of *prosopopeia* in the *Institutio Oratoria* 3.8.49 and 9.2.29-32, insisting on its usefulness for both orators and historians: 'Ideoque longe mihi difficillimae videntur prosopopoeiae...Utilissima vero haec exercitatio, vel quod duplicis est operis, vel quod poetis *quoque aut historiarum futuris scriptoribus* plurimum confert' (3.8.49, emphasis mine). Lucian of Samosata applies the figure to historiographical writing: 'If you must introduce at a certain point a character who makes a speech, let his language before all things be adapted to

this exercise of a fictitious rhetorical performance is vividly shown by a linguistic comparison of Peter's (semitizing) speech at Jerusalem in Acts 2 and Paul's (atticizing) speech at Athens in Acts 17. The composition of the speeches in Acts 22 and 26 are an additional proof.

Let me conclude. The three narratives are not to be compared on the same plane. The logic of the presentation of the event derives each time from the point of view of the person expressing himself therein. Yet this logic is also bound up with another factor, not yet mentioned: the function of each narrative within the plot of the book of Acts. The examination of the narrative context for each one should give us the clues.

2.3. *The Function of the Three Narratives*

Acts 9 must not be considered in isolation. The conversion of Saul on the Damascus road is part of a sequence that opened at ch. 8 with the persecution against the Jerusalem church following the martyrdom of Stephen (8.1-3). The movement of the Christian diaspora into Samaria (Acts 8) extends as far as the conversion of Cornelius (Acts 10) which inaugurates the access of non-Jews to salvation. Acts 9 intervenes at the peak of a series of conversions (Simon, then the Ethiopian eunuch, then Saul) by which it is shown how God widens the circle of the elect; the decisive step will be made in the encounter of Peter and Cornelius (cf. 10.34-36).[32] The theme that dominates the plot is not the exemplary nature of the converts' faith (neither Simon nor Saul are exemplary).[33] The common theme is the surprising initiative taken by God in the choice of converts: Simon the greedy magician, the mutilated Ethiopian,

---

his personality (εἰκότα τῷ προσώπῳ) and to his object' (*How to Write History* 58). Other references in W.S. Kurz, 'Hellenistic Rhetoric in the Christological Proof of Luke–Acts', *CBQ* 42 (1980), p. 186, and D.E. Aune, *The New Testament in its Literary Environment* (Philadelphia: Fortress Press, 1987), pp. 125-28.

32. The plot structure in Acts 8–9 has been analyzed in detail in the study of S. Reymond, to which I am partially indebted; it shows how Saul's conversion both continues and overshadows the conversions in ch. 8 ('L'expérience du chemin de Damas', pp. 18-86). A similar attention to narrative progression from Acts 8 to Acts 11, as far as conversion is concerned, characterizes the research done by Gaventa, *From Darkness to Light*, pp. 52-129. The greatest merit of these two studies is to break the narrative isolation to which most commentators subject Acts 9 by comparing it with Acts 22 and 26.

33. I agree on this point with R.D. Witherup, 'Functional Redundancy', p. 73; and yet the Lukan insistence on the theme of conversion cannot exclude a paradigmatic connotation underlying the narrative.

excluded from the covenant, Saul the persecutor, Cornelius the unclean one. Each episode within Acts 8–11 relates the divine initiative (8.4-8; 8.26; 9.3-12; 10.1-23) and the believers' reactions, which go from prophetic lucidity (8.20-23) to obedience (8.27a), while also involving embarrassment (9.13-14, 26; 10.17). *Acts 9 is thus inserted within a context that articulates God's initiatives in enlarging the community and the believers' reactions.*

In Acts 22 and Acts 26, the reframing of the Damascus event occurs within a speech; here the important step is to ascertain which rhetorical aim the narrative ascribes to the speech.

Acts 22 is Paul's final speech to the people of Jerusalem, after a Jewish plot has brought him out of the Temple and closed its gates (21.30: see the symbolic importance of this closing of the Temple!); saved from lynching by the Roman police (21.31-36), Paul carries out his ἀπολογία (22.1). The result will be a death shout from the crowd (αἶρε τὸν τοιοῦτον, 22.22), where one hears resonating something of an echo of the shout of the people against Jesus (αἶρε τοῦτον, Lk. 23.18). *The rhetorical function of Paul's speech is to defend himself against the charge of breaking with 'the people and the Law and this place'*.[34] Springing from this charge, Paul's autobiography dramatically addresses his 'brothers and fathers' (22.1) in order to convince them 'in the Hebrew language' of the apostle's Jewishness.

Whereas Acts 22 defends Paul in front of his fellow Jews, *Acts 26* justifies him in front of the other pole of the book of Acts: Greco-Roman culture. In the presence of king Agrippa and his court (25.23), Paul reinterprets the event of his conversion in order that it may be grasped by a literate audience; such a meticulous care for inculturation will bring the narrator to the paradox of v. 14, where Jesus addresses Saul 'in the Hebrew language' (Luke historicizes) and yet utters a proverb that is known solely from Hellenistic literature: 'It is hard for you to kick against the goad' (Luke actualizes). One must be attentive to the status conferred by the exordium of the speech to Agrippa: 'You are especially cognizant of of all the customs of the Jews and of their controversies' (πάντων τῶν κατὰ Ἰουδαίους ἐθῶν τε καὶ ζητημάτων)

---

34. Except for the accusation concerning Temple profanation, which has already been refuted by an explicit comment of the narrator in 21.29, the speech utilizes the biographical material in order to refute the charges levelled against Paul. See the analysis by F. Veltman, 'The Defense Speeches of Paul in Acts', in C.H. Talbert (ed.), *Perspectives on Luke–Acts* (Edinburgh: T. & T. Clark, 1978), pp. 253-54.

(26.3). *The rhetorical aim of the speech is determined: Jewish hostility toward the apostle (26.19-21) will be presented as a matter of internal controversy, a ζήτημα, in which Paul is being unjustly prosecuted.*[35]

Let me summarize. Luke has justified in two ways, for his readers, the variations he introduces within the three versions of the Damascus road event. On the one hand, he varies the enunciators between Acts 9 and Acts 22–26. On the other hand, he explicitly pinpoints the Pauline speeches as apologies (22.1; 26.1), thus determining for them a rhetorical aim which authorizes the speaker, within the canons of Greco-Roman rhetoric, to bend the facts in favour of the thesis he defends. By setting up an ἀπολογία twice, Luke the writer thus authorizes the Paul he is describing to invest his own rhetorical subjectivity in the argumentative use of his life story.

I have thus specified the status and the function of each account within the narration of Acts. It is important now to examine the specific interpretation that the Damascus event receives in each version. This is aim in my third and last part.

3. *What is Specific to each Narrative?*

3.1. *Acts 9: The Ecclesial Mediation*

The narrative of Acts 9.1-30, at least when considered in the extent I have indicated, that is, down to v. 30, is dominated by *the reversal of Saul's identity*. From being the persecutor with schemes of death (9.1-2), Saul becomes the persecuted one, threatened with death (9.23-29). From being a foe to the disciples (9.1), he becomes a master of disciples (9.25, οἱ μαθηταὶ αὐτοῦ). From being a denier of Christ (9.1), Saul becomes a preacher of the Messiah (9.22; 9.20). How does this reversal operate?

The christophany on the Damascus road (9.3-9) has the effect of *reducing Saul to nothingness*. Whereas vv. 1 and 2 set forth Saul as an active subject (Σαῦλος is subject of virtually all verbs: ἐμπνέων,

---

35. Gaventa is right when she refuses to include the *captatio benevolentiae* in 26.3a (the appeal to Agrippa's knowledge as to ἔθη καὶ ζητήματα) within the register of flattery, but sees there the formulation of the *status causae* as Paul wants to define it: 'Paul is about to present a defense of himself as the victim of an intramural quarrel regarding resurrection from the dead, and thus the appeal to Agrippa's knowledge serves to introduce the lines of Paul's defense' (*From Darkness to Light*, pp. 78-79).

προσελθών, ᾐτήσατο, εὕρῃ, ἀγάγῃ), the shock dispossesses him of his power: the light that encircles him (περιαστράπτω) makes him fall to the ground (vv. 3-4); from then on, the verbs characterizing him are in the passive (ἀνάστηθι, v. 6; λαληθήσεται, v. 6; ἠγέρθη, v. 8), or when they are in the active voice, they denote either an action undergone by him (ἤκουσεν, v. 4;[36] εἴσελθε, v. 6; δεῖ ποιεῖν, v. 6; χειραγωγοῦντες, v. 8) or an absence of action (οὐδὲν ἔβλεπεν, v. 8; μὴ βλέπων καὶ οὐκ ἔφαγεν οὐδὲ ἔπιεν, v. 9). The significant accumulation of three negatives in v. 9 (neither seeing, nor eating, nor drinking) draws the final statement out of this experience of shock, not through an image of fasting, but through a figure of nothingness and death.[37] Saul, having been powerfully stopped by the Lord, is broken down in the carrying out of his plan.

From now on the narrative is going to work out the reconstruction of Saul as subject. *The Damascus road event here manifests itself as a destruction of his persecution plan and a refashioning of his identity.* The new identity is not one that he acquires for himself (9.1-2), but a received identity; such an identity is signified by the Lord in v. 15: 'This one is an instrument of election to me to carry my Name before the Gentiles and kings and the sons of Israel'. Now, this declaration of identity takes place in a dialogue between Christ and Ananias, located within the visionary register ('The Lord said to him in a vision', v. 10). Ananias is here representative of the Christian community at Damascus (τις μαθητής, v. 10). This visionary dialogue with the Lord constitutes the originality of Acts 9, later abandoned by the autobiographical speeches. It sets the figure of Ananias on front stage, and such insistence is all the more striking since the encounter with Christ has isolated Saul from his companions in order to make him the sole recipient of the word of Jesus: the companions do perceive a voice, but are unable to grasp its

36. Saul is less the subject of the act of seeing than the recipient of an aural phenomenon which he is given to perceive.
37. The enigmatic mention in 9.9 has given rise to multiple interpretations: effect of the psychological shock (Bruce, *The Acts of the Apostles*, p. 323); preparation for the reception of revelation according to Exod. 34.28; Deut. 9.9; Dan. 9.3; *2 Bar.* 9.2, etc. (L.T. Johnson, *The Acts of the Apostles* [Sacra Pagina; Collegeville: Liturgical Press, 1992], p. 164); pre-baptismal fast in the sense of *Did.* 7.4; Justin, *Ap.* 1.61 (Conzelmann, *Die Apostelgeschichte*, p. 58). We see that interpretative models are constantly being sought outside the text, while the text itself seeks primarily to pinpoint the negativity of that time when Saul's identity is being suspended before it is refashioned. Image of a re-creation *ex nihilo*?

origin (v. 7).[38] On the contrary, the dialogue with Ananias confers on this last character a decisive role in the revelation process. This calls for four remarks.

(i) The dialogue with Ananias is a prophetic call account.[39] It obeys the typical structure of the call account as it comes out of Old Testament narratives according to Norman Habel's study.[40] Habel identifies six motifs that make up the structure of a prophetic call account: 1. divine confrontation; 2. introductory word; 3. commission; 4. objection; 5. reassurance; 6. sign. The dialogue with Ananias satisfies the first five motifs (1, v. 10a; 2, v. 10b; 3, vv. 11-12; 4, vv. 13-14; 5, vv. 15-16); the sixth element is lacking. One should especially note that whereas Saul receives a purely passive role in this operation, Ananias on the contrary is instituted as a *mediator* in the refashioning of Pauline identity. His initial readiness for this role is signified by his response to the divine calling: ἰδοὺ ἐγώ = הִנֵּנִי (v. 10).[41]

(ii) Verses 10-16 do not set forth a vision, but the vision of a vision. What is revealed to Ananias in a vision is that Saul himself has had a vision (εἶδεν, v. 12), and that vision has for its object...Ananias coming

---

38. Rather than saying that Saul's companions benefit from hearing but are deprived of sight (9.7), it is preferable to register the fact that the companions are made unable to identify the voice; therefore revelation eludes them. Bechtler has been sensitive to the privilege reserved to Saul: 'The limited participation in the event by Saul's companions as described in 9:7 guarantees the objective nature of the event itself, but this event was revelatory only for Saul' ('The Meaning of Paul's Call', p. 56).

39. In his Ezekiel commentary, W. Zimmerli (*Ezechiel 1–24* [BK, 13.1; Neukirchen: Neukirchener Verlag, 1969], pp. 16-21) had shown the connection between Acts 9.3-9 and the prophetic call narratives, while recognizing that the OT presents two distinct types of the genre: the one is structured by the scheme divine calling–mandate–objection–overruling of the objection and sending out (Jer. 1.4-10; Exod. 3; Judg. 6; 1 Sam. 9–10; Ezek. 1–2); the other includes a theophanic vision (Isa. 6; 1 Kgs 22.19-22). Steck has objected that the first type was in fact identifiable, but in 9.10-16, while the constitutive elements of the second type are lacking here ('Formgeschichtliche Bemerkungen').

40. N. Habel, 'The Form and Significance of the Call Narratives', *ZAW* 77 (1965), pp. 297-323. A more recent study by W. Vogels, 'Les récits de vocation des prophètes', *NRT* 95 (1973), pp. 1-24, confirms his findings, even though Vogels ascribes the six motifs a slightly different appellation. I owe these references to the article by Collins, 'Paul's Damascus Experience', pp. 115-16.

41. The scheme is well known in the Hebrew Bible: Gen. 22.1-2, 11-12; 1 Sam. 3.4-14; *Jub.* 44.5; *4 Ezra* 12.2-13; etc.

to restore his sight. Ananias's mediatorial function is now signified to him by the invitation to a healing gesture whose symbolical dimension shines through:[42] the blinding/recovery sequence in the vision stands for a theological illumination; the 'vision' (v. 12) Saul has in prayer anticipates this already. But one should be attentive to this device of embedded visions; it is unknown in Jewish literature with the exception of Josephus (*Ant.* 11.8.4-5), and within Greco-Roman literature it marks the divine programming of events.[43] The device of double vision represents a strong irruption of the divine into the course of events since not only a prediction is made, but its fulfilment is anticipated and visualized. The reader is therefore not surprised to see Ananias balk at such a *theological forcing of history*. Within the scenario of the prophetic call, this is the typical moment for the objection.

(iii) Ananias's objection bears neither on his own capabilities, nor on the mandate proposed to him; its bearing is upon Saul's identity: 'Lord, I have heard from many about this man, how much evil he has done to thy saints at Jerusalem; and here he has authority from the chief priests to bind all who call upon thy Name' (vv. 13-14). How can we understand this objection? How can we understand that Ananias is still situating Saul as the enemy, while this enemy has just been crushed down by the christophany on the Damascus road? As I see it, to think of a reminder of Saul's past evildoing just in order to underline the importance of his conversion amounts to reducing the narrator's job to the spinning of flat commonplaces. The narrator uses here a narrative device which consists in ascribing to the reader a superior position to one character within the narrative.[44] In this case, Ananias trails behind

---

42. Interpreting the passage from blindness to light symbolically as the granting of a revelation is a common feature of both New Testament tradition and Hellenistic Judaism (Philo, *Virt.* 179; *Jos. Asen.* 8.10; 15.13; *Odes Sol.* 14.18-19); it is also frequent in Luke–Acts (Lk. 2.30; 4.18; 24.16, 31; Acts 9.8, 18, 40; 13.11; 26.18; 28.27). The symbolical value here has been well perceived by Hamm ('Paul's Blindness'), who connects it with the metaphorical vocabulary of Isaiah (6.9-10; 40.3-5; 42.16; 49.6; 59.9-10). One shall nevertheless note that this dimension remains covert in this case, and is unfolded by the narrator according to its full value only in 26.18.

43. We owe the classical inventory of the attestations of double visions in ancient literature to A. Wikenhauser, 'Doppelträume', *Bib* 29 (1948), pp. 100-11. One should add here the references to fictional literature gathered by R.I. Pervo, *Profit with Delight* (Philadelphia: Fortress Press, 1987), pp. 73 and 164 n. 85.

44. Calloud had well noticed this effect of the narrative when he commented,

the reader in his level of information: his reaction takes no account of the Damascus road event (9.3-9). Ananias ignores the action of Christ, and this ignorance confers on his objection the status of a *resistance* to the action of Christ. Otherwise stated, Ananias's reaction manifests on the one hand that Christ has preceded his own in his intervention upon Saul; on the other hand, it casts the disciple into the role of the opponent[45] whose objection the Lord must overcome.

(iv) Christ overcomes the resistance of Ananias by unveiling the new identity he confers upon Saul. We already noted v. 15: Saul will have to bear his Name,[46] and such a formula refers to public testimony before a universal audience (Gentiles, kings and sons of Israel).[47] But now, and this is a new surprise in the narrative, Ananias's intervention with Saul is therapeutic and baptismal (9.18). No mention is made of the mandate to the person chiefly concerned: Saul. This silence of the narrative brings out once more the *precedence* of Christ over his Church: 'I will show him how much he must suffer for the sake of my Name'. The 'doing' for which Saul is being enrolled (9.6: ὅ τί σε δεῖ ποιεῖν) is to be a 'suffering' (9.16: ὅσα δεῖ αὐτὸν...παθεῖν). It belongs to Christ to have this discovered by Saul, and within Luke's strategy it falls to the

---

'Ananias est en retard sur le cours du récit' ('Sur le chemin de Damas', p. 13). The narrative mechanism has been described by Sternberg, who distinguishes three positions of the reader in relation to the characters in the narrative; from the viewpoint of the knowledge communicated to him or her, the reader may be ascribed by the narrator a position that is superior, equal or inferior to the character (*Poetics*, pp. 163-72). Here, a superiority in knowledge in relation to Ananias is clearly being built; this narrative stratagem draws the attention, not on Saul's past as a persecutor (the reader does not ignore this), but on the consequences of the delaying effect as applied to the representative of the Damascus disciples.

45. The term of opponent is here being used in the sense of the actantial model of A.J. Greimas, *Sémantique structurale* (Paris: Presses Universitaires de France, 1986), pp. 172-91, especially p. 180. Greimas distributes among five positions the constitutive functions of a narrative performance: sender–addressee–object–helper–opponent. The opponent is the one who attempts to hinder the realization of the narrative performance.

46. The confessional and missionary dimension of this expression has been shown by G. Lohfink, 'Meinen Namen zu tragen...(Apg 9,15)', in *Studien zum Neuen Testament* (SBAB, 5; Stuttgart: KBW, 1990), pp. 213-21.

47. As Hedrick notices, Acts 1.8 and 9.15 mention both Jewish and Gentile missions, but in reverse order (*Paul's Conversion/Call*, pp. 420-21). The sequence of 9.15 (Gentiles–kings–Sons of Israel) anticipates the development of the plot of Acts with the emphasize on Paul's witness before the pagan world (cf. 28.28!).

narrative progressively to unfold this necessity of the Passion of Saul.[48]
Let me gather up the results gained from these four remarks.

Does the Damascus road event as exposed by Acts 9 set forth 'the overthrow of an enemy'[49] as an effect of God's power? This topic of the overthrown enemy is indisputably a connotation of the narrative; however, it seems to me to correspond more with the tradition used by Luke than with his own reading of the event, since the way he manages his narrative stresses the initiative taken by God in history and the resistance put forward by the community of disciples (in addition to Ananias, see vv. 26-27). While Christ triumphs over the enemy without any difficulty, how much trouble he has persuading his own!

This topic fits quite well with the sequel of the narration of Acts in chs. 10 and 11, where God will have to break resistance in order to extend the benefit of salvation to non-Jews; yet this resistance will not come from Cornelius, it will come from Peter and from the Jerusalem Church who stumble on the time-honoured division of clean and unclean (10.14-16, 28-29, 34-36; 11.1-3). Luke illustrates God's difficulty in implementing this new turn of salvation history by setting up around Peter and Cornelius a cascade of supernatural interventions: an apparition to Cornelius (10.3-6), then an ecstasy of Peter (10.10-16), then a revelation of the Spirit to Peter (10.19-20), and finally a second Pentecost in the house of Cornelius (10.45-46). Such a concentration of the marvellous is without equal in the book of Acts; it signals the importance of the new turn that is the recognition of God's universality (10.34).[50] Yet the topic of the divine forcing of history, catching the Church unawares and at cross purposes, is already being prepared in

---

48. The prolepsis consisting in the statement of Saul's missionary call is destined 'au lecteur qui est conduit par là même à poursuivre sa lecture pour en vérifier la réalisation' (Reymond, 'L'expérience du chemin de Damas', p. 71). This narrative prolepsis takes up a previous prolepsis, which is the itinerary of the apostolic witness stated by the promise of the Risen One in 1.8; it receives from there a first confirmation, though in anticipation. J.-N. Aletti notices an identical function for the proleptic statements in Lk. 1–4: 'Les prolepses formulées par les voix angéliques ont donc pour fonction de donner, dès le départ, au récit lucanien, son caractère gnoséologique' (*L'art de raconter Jésus Christ* [Paris: Seuil, 1989], p. 72). The narrative institutes then, in its very writing, the revelatory function it means to exercise.

49. Gaventa, *From Darkness to Light*, p. 66.

50. Concerning the importance of chs. 10–11 within the plot of the book of Acts, let me refer to my article: 'Juifs et chrétiens selon Luc–Actes. Surmonter le conflit des lectures', *Bib* 75 (1994), pp. 126-46, esp. 139-40.

Acts 9, as we have just seen. In other words, Saul's conversion in Acts 9 is interpreted as the mighty work of Christ who turns his own enemy about, but who must also convert his own Church to Saul's new identity, he whom he is going to make the agent of his universal mission. *The strategy of the narrative in Acts 9 then points up as its dominant theme the establishing of an ecclesial mediation in the transformation of Saul.*[51]

But what becomes of the Damascus road event at the time when Paul operates its autobiographical rereading ? We are going to discover that through a rapid survey of chs. 22 and 26.

3.2. Acts 22: The Affirmation of Jewishness

I have already signalled (§2.3) the narrative situation of the speech before the people of Jerusalem: the accusation to which Paul falls victim (21.28), the eviction from the Temple, the lynching from which the Roman police save him (21.32).

Luke accumulates the signs of Paul's Jewishness: he speaks in Hebrew (21.40), near the Temple, and addresses his own 'brothers and fathers' (22.1). The formula in v. 3 ἐγώ εἰμι ἀνὴρ Ἰουδαῖος is not just a declaration of his identity; it constitutes rather *the theological thesis of his speech, unfolding Paul's uninterrupted faithfulness to the Jewish tradition*. Everything concurs to impress this faithfulness: his résumé focuses on his training in the school of Gamaliel (v. 3), the legality of the proceedings when he persecuted the Damascus Christians (v. 5), his relationship with the 'brothers' in Damascus (v. 5: not Christians, but

---

51. F. Bovon has well shown the importance of mediations in Luke's theological project (*L'oeuvre de Luc* [LD, 130; Paris: Cerf, 1987], pp. 181-203). Luke does not seek to oppose divine intervention and human mediation against each other, but rather to show in what ways the divine requires human mediation for its manifestation. The narrative of Acts 9 comes fully within this perspective, and therefore it is not right to affirm that the function of Ananias 'was to serve as a witness to the fact that Paul was called without mediation of man' (Lundgren, 'Ananias and the Calling of Paul', p. 122). Even though it is obvious that the Damascus event in Acts functions like an accreditation of Paul, Luke could not endorse the antithesis here being built between divine legitimation and human testimony. The same error of perspective occurs in J. Jervell, who erases the mediation of Ananias: 'Die paulinischen "Akkreditive" kommen nicht aus Jerusalem, sondern aus dem Damaskusgeschehen...Paulus ist nicht von Menschen oder durch Menschen ausgesandt' ('Paulus in der Apostelgeschichte und die Geschichte des Urchristentums', *NTS* 32 [1986], pp. 378-92; I quote from p. 379; see n. 15!).

Jews). Ananias is not presented as a disciple (the reader holds this piece of information from Acts 9),[52] but as 'a devout man according to the Law, well spoken of by all the Jews who lived there' (v. 12); therefore the Σαοὺλ ἀδελφέ by which Ananias greets Paul lends itself to be understood as Jewish brotherhood. This refashioning of Ananias's identity is dictated by the rhetorical purpose of the speech, that is, for Paul to receive his call from the hands of a Jewish dissident would not fit the rhetorical situation of his speech.

Ananias's role is also entirely remodeled since he is not essentially the restorer of Saul's integrity, but the interpreter of his calling: 'The God of our fathers appointed you to know his will, to see the Just One and to hear a voice from his mouth; for you will be a witness for him to all men of what you have seen and heard' (vv. 14-15). One notices here that the christological reservation of ch. 9 ('I will show him...', 9.16) has disappeared, the progression of the narrative having made it superfluous.

But it is especially noticeable that one has moved from a christocentric formulation as set down by Acts 9 (Saul, persecutor of Jesus, called upon to bear his Name) to a theocentric formulation, deeply rooted in the Old Testament.[53] The tricolon through which Saul's call is announced (γνῶναι τὸ θέλημα αὐτοῦ, ἰδεῖν τὸν δίκαιον, ἀκοῦσαι φωνὴν ἐκ τοῦ στόματος αὐτοῦ, 22.14) lines up Septuagintalisms that make Paul's apostolic call into the achieved expression of his Jewish identity. One notices once more Luke's skill in wielding language, but I say again that such a language performance does not merely signal the adaptation of Paul the orator to his Jerusalem audience. *The purpose*

52. When one compares with 9.10-16, the information in ch. 22 concerning Ananias's intervention is reduced to a minimum; the reader knows neither why Ananias pays a visit to Saul (22.13), nor whence he knows about Saul's calling (22.14-15). We have here an obvious sign that Luke in ch. 22 refashioned the event by taking into account the memory of his reader/hearer, and therefore the divergences between the narratives did not escape his notice. I find myself here in agreement with Hedrick, 'Paul's Conversion/Call', p. 426.

53. W. Kurz notices the transition from a christocentric perspective in Acts 9 to theocentric language in Acts 22, but he explains it by the transition from an objective point of view (omniscient narrator) to the subjective point of view of the 'Jewish Paul' unfolded in ch. 22, that point of view being discredited as emanating from an 'unreliable' narrator (*Reading Luke–Acts*, pp. 130 and 129). This is to misunderstand the rhetorical purpose of the speech in Acts 22, whose argumentative strategy aims to *establish* Paul's Jewishness rather than to discredit it in the eyes of the reader.

that permeates the speech is to interpret the Damascus road event as a fulfilment of the apostle's Jewishness.

Bringing this statement of Saul's calling (22.14) together with the autobiographical preamble in v. 3 (πεπαιδευμένος κατὰ ἀκρίβειαν τοῦ πατρῴου νόμου, ζηλωτὴς ὑπάρχων τοῦ θεοῦ) will show how much the orator tends to establish a flawless continuity between his past life and his present situation, as far as zeal for God and the relation to the Torah are concerned.[54] In this sense, Paul's apology does indeed work to refute the charge of anti-judaism levelled at him and which originated the tumult (21.28): the encounter with the Risen One at Damascus does not pit Paul against 'our people, the Law and this place'; it is, on the contrary, the means through which the God of the fathers leads him into the heart of his word.

This Lukan effort to actualize the Damascus event from the communication situation of Paul's speech reaches its final concretization in the scene of the ecstasy in the Temple (22.17-21). One must take full stock of the fact that this scene does not represent a secondary appendix to the encounter on the Damascus road; on the contrary, within the narrative scenario of 22.1-21, the ecstasy in the Temple constitutes the climax of the speech, since it confers on the Pauline call its ultimate confirmation. The choice of the Temple is certainly in line with the foundational theological function devolving upon the holy place in the work of Luke, beginning with the infancy narratives.[55] The fact that Paul is praying there (προσευχομένου μου, 22.17) underlines once more his loyalty toward the Jewish tradition and the piety associated with it.[56] Yet ironically, it is within this Temple from where the Asian Jews have just evicted him (21.30) that Saul in prayer hears Christ enjoining him to leave Jerusalem 'because they will not accept your testimony about me' (22.18). One must take full stock of the *double*

---

54. 'Luke knows no break in Paul's attitude to the law' (Haenchen, *The Acts of the Apostles*, p. 625).

55. M. Bachmann, *Jerusalem und der Tempel: Die geographisch-theologischen Elemente in der lukanischen Sicht des jüdischen Kultzentrums* (BWANT, 109; Stuttgart: Kohlhammer, 1980).

56. O. Betz highlights this interpretation in his article: 'Die Vision des Paulus im Tempel von Jerusalem. Apg 22,17-21 als Beitrag zur Deutung des Damaskuserlebnis', in *Verborum Veritas: Festschrift G. Stählin* (Wuppertal: Brockaus, 1970), pp. 113-23. According to him, an apostolic legitimation located in Damascus rather than in Jerusalem would have been deemed radically insufficient from a Jewish point of view.

provocation that Luke composing this scene aims at Paul's Jerusalem audience. First of all, the κύριος who appears in the Temple is not God, but Jesus (despite a [intended?] syntactical ambiguity);[57] Jesus, whom Paul's interlocutors have rejected, is polemically asserted as the Lord of the Temple, under characteristic traits that assimilate him to God. Secondly, the adjunction of vv. 17-21 transfers from Ananias (9.10-16) to Saul the literary form of the prophetic call account. As a matter of fact, the traditional sequence of commission (v. 18)—objection (vv. 20-21)—reassurance (v. 21) involves now Saul directly.[58] Yet the mission order is paradoxical since it consists in leaving Jerusalem as soon as possible by dint of the refusal which the testimony has met![59] Now this is what is going on presently: at this point of the narrative of Acts, Paul is about to leave Jerusalem in order to go to Rome.

Let me sum up my reading of ch. 22. The theme here is no longer the reversal of Saul's identity and the request for ecclesial mediation in that transformation, but the orthodoxy of Paul's religion. His conversion is being invoked at the symbolic moment of the break with Jerusalem, interpreting this break as a gesture that was not desired by Paul, but especially challenging Jewish criticism by stressing how much the new turn in the apostle's life takes place within a fundamental continuity with his Jewishness. What is the significance of Paul's biography and of his

57. The syntactic connection of αὐτόν in v. 18 is not clear; should we link it with θεός in v. 14a or, by way of the αὐτοῦ in v. 16b, to τὸν δίκαιον in v. 14b? Even though the chain of αὐτός (vv. 14b, 15a, 16b) pleads in favour of the second solution, the ambiguity is not entirely dissipated; could Luke be exploiting it on purpose, within his theocentric perspective?

58. Unlike R.F. Collins ('Paul's Damascus Experience', pp. 115-18), I think that Acts 22, and not Acts 26, fits the structure of a prophetic call narrative according to the criteria of N. Habel as sketched above (under 3.1). Indeed, out of a total of six motifs, Acts 26 includes only the first three. By contrast, Acts 22 presents motif 1 (divine confrontation) in vv. 6-7a; motif 2 (introductory word) in vv. 7b-8; motif 3 (commission) in vv. 14-15, with confirmation in v. 18; motif 4 (objection) in vv. 19-20; motif 5 (reassurance) in v. 21; motif 6 (sign) is to be looked for in v. 16, where the baptism no longer concretizes Saul's healing (9, 18), but becomes the sign testifying to his missionary calling (the immediate succession of vv. 14-15 and 16 provokes this reinterpretation of the baptismal act).

59. J. Roloff puts it well: 'Hier entpuppt sich die scheinbare Selbstverteidigung als Angriff von unerhörter Radikalität: Der von den Juden verworfene Jesus erscheint am heiligen Ort und spricht das Verwerfungsteil über sein Volk aus, das Paulus nun am gleichen heiligen Ort öffentlich verkündigt' (*Die Apostelgeschichte* [NTD, 5; Göttingen: Vandenhoeck & Ruprecht, 1981], p. 320).

reversal in this demonstration? The thesis of the speech (22.19-20) is that all this should be enough to convince the reader that Paul's message does not proceed out of anti-Jewish hatred, but out of an impeccable and fanatical zeal toward the God of the fathers; such zeal has not ceased to inhabit Paul from his youth.

3.3. *Acts 26: The Power of the Risen One*
The apology before Agrippa, just like ch. 22, is governed by *prosopopeia*. The interpretation of Saul's conversion obeys the rules of narrative composition that we have just uncovered in the previous speech. There are five of them altogether: the focus rule, the inculturation rule, the variation rule, the actualization rule, and the rule of narrative situation setting.

First of all, the *focus rule*: the move to autobiographical discourse centred on the apostle's 'I' lays maximum stress on the role of Saul and diminishes secondary roles correspondingly (down to the complete disappearance of Ananias).[60] The focus placed on Saul's commission leads the writer to enlarge the wording of the mandate given by Christ (vv. 16-18)—albeit quoted by Paul—in a way that contrasts absolutely with the absence of any commission addressed to Saul in Acts 9.[61] Unlike Acts 9, here 'Paul's commission derives solely from the heavenly Jesus'.[62] The complete disappearance of any intermediary makes Saul and the Kyrios come to grips with each other directly.

The *inculturation rule*: addressing a Hellenistic audience of a high cultural level, the speech clarifies its meaning (v. 14a) or transposes it into Greco-Roman categories (vv. 14b, 18, 21-23).[63] The non-Semitic

---

60. See above, pp. 138-39, §2.2 and n. 30.

61. Hedrick thinks that the progressive unveiling of Saul's commission results from an effect of narrative suspense: the commission is indicated to Ananias (9.15-16), then alluded to by Barnabas before the apostles (9.27); Saul is informed about it secondhand by Ananias (22.14-15), and the Lord refers to it in 22.17-21. 'It is not until 26:16-18 that the suspense is broken and Luke finally tells his (impatient) reader exactly what the Lord said to Paul on the road to Damascus' ('Paul's Conversion/Call', p. 427).

62. Bechtler, 'The Meaning of Paul's Call', p. 72.

63. Verse 14a specifies that Jesus expresses himself 'in the Hebrew language'. Verse 14b cites a proverb known since Aeschyles (*Ag.* 1624), but only in Hellenistic literature (see 'κέντρον', *TDNT*, III, pp. 663-67). Verse 18 describes Paul's mission in three infinitive statements whose wording corresponds with the vocabulary of Hellenistic Judaism (cf. Col. 1.12-14; 1 Thess. 2.12; 1 Pet. 5.10). Haenchen has

proverb of v. 14b brings out with greater power the futility of the struggle while qualifying Paul's missionary activity retroactively (Acts 13–22) as a divinely-ordained destiny.[64]

The *variation rule*: just as the prophetic call scenario, with its typical motif of the recipient's objection, has been transferred from Ananias (9.10-16) to Saul (22.18-21), the motif of the light has been changed and displaced. The encounter on the Damascus road is no longer this luminous shock throwing Saul to the ground (9.3-4); it is an intense illumination (περιλάμψαν με φῶς, 26.13) preparing Saul to 'open the eyes' of the people of Israel and of Gentiles in order to 'convert' them 'from darkness to light' (ἐπιστρέψαι ἀπὸ σκότους εἰς φῶς, 26.18). This device of extending the φῶς metaphor from the theophanic Temple to the vocabulary of mission (26.18) coincides with the application to Paul of the declaration of Isa. 49.6 as was made by the narrator earlier in 13.47: 'I have set you to be a light for the Gentiles' (τέθεικά σε εἰς φῶς ἐθνῶν).[65] No longer is Saul crushed down by the light: in Acts 26, he is rather rereading this numinous encounter as a prophetic call to become himself a light, that is, a bearer of salvation beyond Israel.[66] The

---

noted the many atticisms that permeate the speech (*The Acts of the Apostles*, pp. 681-88), and J.C. Lentz has shown how Luke in Acts 26 portrays Paul as a 'man of virtue' according to the canons of Greco-Roman culture (*Luke's Portrait of Paul* [SNTSMS, 77; Cambridge: Cambridge University Press, 1993], pp. 83-91).

64. The application of the proverb is debated: does it register the inefficiency of Saul's persecuting activity in the past or the impossibility to retreat from his calling in the future? Most commentators incline toward the second solution. Using psychological categories, Reymond opts for the first solution, seeing here the trace of Saul's struggle against his own violence (26.9-11), which only God's intervention through the appearance of Jesus is able to oppose ('L'expérience du chemin de Damas', p. 126).

65. About this mutation of the theme of light between Acts 9 and Acts 26, see the (already cited) article by Hamm, 'Paul's Blindness and its Healing', pp. 66-67. O'Toole thinks that the new mode of being of the resurrected Jesus has influenced this imagery of the light illuminating Saul with brightness (*Acts 26*, p. 58); the insistence of ch. 26 upon the vision (26.16, 19) might corroborate that viewpoint.

66. 'The primary purpose of this address to Agrippa is to induce him to see in Paul a prophet', as Stanley categorically affirms ('Paul's Conversion in Acts', p. 334). In fact, as demonstrated many times, the statement of Saul's commission in vv. 16-18 evokes together at once Ezekiel's call (reminiscences of Ezek. 1.28; 2.1, 3 in vv. 16 and 17), Jeremiah's commission (verbal similarities between Jer. 1.7-8 and v. 17), and the mission of Isaiah's Servant (Isa. 42.6 is virtually quoted in v. 18); see O'Toole, *Acts 26*, p. 67.

inclusion of his missionary activity within the conversion narrative aims to reinforce the credibility of his testimony before Agrippa.

The *actualization rule*: the end of the speech (26.22-23) provides the connection with Paul's present situation by interpreting his testimony 'to the small one as well as to the great one' (μαρτυρόμενος μικρῷ τε καὶ μεγάλῳ, v. 22) as a concretization of the calling received on the Damascus road. In other words, the very wording of the speech before Agrippa confirms the call that Paul received.

Finally, the *rule of narrative situation setting*. Agrippa, who is the narrative addressee of the speech in Acts 26, has been put forward as a specialist of Jewish customs and controversies (26.3).[67] The speech is going to demonstrate skilfully that Jewish hostility toward Paul is a matter of internal controversy, and furthermore, an unjustified controversy. For the blame that is laid on Paul consists in nothing else but that which makes up the heart of the Jewish hope, that is the resurrection of the dead (26.6-8). The whole speech is governed rhetorically by the promise–fulfilment scheme as signified by the *inclusio* of vv. 6-8 and v. 23:[68] the Jewish hope in the resurrection of the dead (vv. 6-8) finds its fulfilment in the resurrection of the Messiah (v. 23). The encounter on the Damascus road is exhibited accordingly as evidence for the resurrection of the dead, a 'heavenly vision' of the Risen One (26.29) from which Paul could not demur.[69] One cannot help thinking that Luke forces the argument, theologically speaking. Subsuming the Jewish faith as believing in a promise (ἐπ' ἐλπίδι τῆς εἰς τοὺς πατέρας ἡμῶν ἐπαγγελίας, v. 6; cf. already 23.6) may be envisaged; but that this promise should be reduced to the resurrection of the dead (26.8) is acceptable only for Pharisaic piety. Moreover, to construe the Christian kerygma as amounting to resurrection faith is typical of Luke, but the speech assimilates without further ado the Pharisaic belief with the Christian faith in the resurrection (compare 26.8 and 26.23!). From such a standpoint, opposing the Christian proclamation of the Risen One

---

67. See above, pp. 140-41.

68. I agree with this structural observation by Gaventa, *From Darkness to Light*, p. 80. This inclusion concretizes the rhetorical purpose of the apology before Agrippa: Paul's innocence is established by the fact that he preaches nothing else but that which Israel expects.

69. A. Barbi has well seen that within the perspective of Acts 26.23 the universal mission is signalled as a post-resurrection activity of Christ, as already stated by 3.26 and 5.31: 'Il paolinismo degli Atti', *RivB* 48 (1986), pp. 471-518, see p. 506.

amounts for a Jew to putting himself in contradiction with his own tradition. One touches here on Luke's effort, not to put Judaism on trial, but to show how incomprehensible is Judaism's denial of continuity between itself and Christianity.

In sum, the Damascus event acquires in this speech an argumentative function which differs from both Acts 9 and Acts 22. The vision of the Risen One becomes a powerful event to which one cannot show disobedience. This is dramatized through the insistence on Saul's past as a persecutor (26.9-11) coupled with the fact that he offers no resistance (26.19). Nonetheless, on the one hand, the uniqueness of the event is devalued, since it is aligned with other visions promised to Paul (26.16b), and on the other hand, the encounter with the Risen One plays the essential role of justifying a call to evangelize the Gentiles,[70] and that not because of its theophanic dimension (9.3-8), nor by virtue of its conformity with the Law (22.14-16), but because the resurrection of the Messiah fulfils the prophecies (26.23; cf. 26.27).

4. Conclusion

The comparative study of the three narratives of Saul's conversion at Damascus has shown how the author of the book of Acts creates an effect of narrative redundancy. The refashioning of the event in Acts 9, 22 and 26 is part of a logic that depends both on the enunciator of the discourse (the narrator or Paul) and on the rhetorical purpose of the discourse as set within the larger narrative. The question of how each narrative functions within the plot of the book of Acts is also a matter of great importance. Acts 9 points up ecclesial mediation; Acts 22 focuses on Saul's Jewishness; Acts 26 points out how the evangelization of the Gentiles is legitimated.

The redundancy effect signals that the Damascus road event has been considered by Luke to be a major event. For what reason? I discern two reasons, beyond the exaltation of the figure of Paul and of his leading role in the growth of the Christian movement. The first is that this event

70. Saul's identity as established by the Risen One is to be ὑπηρέτης καὶ μάρτυς (v. 16), and within this phrase καί has an epexegetical value. The vision of the Risen One culminates not in the prerogative of a spiritual experience, but in a state of subordination to a word to be told, that will conform Paul to the suffering destiny of his Master (26.21-23). On this theme, I refer the reader to the work of Reymond, 'L'expérience du chemin de Damas', pp. 131-37.

serves to sharpen the profile of the Christian identity in its twofold relation of continuity and difference with Judaism; the call of Saul is not presented to the readers as a model of conversion to be imitated,[71] but as the emblematic illustration of the fact that through this very break the Christian faith recovers a basic faithfulness to the God of the Fathers.[72] The second reason is that the Damascus road event allows the author of Acts to unfold the theological theme that he cherishes beyond everything else; the theme of the power of the Risen One as a transforming force within history. For the common theme of the three variants of Saul's conversion account is to show how Saul was bluntly encountered by the exalted Christ while behaving as his enemy, and how he was called to proclaim the necessary conversion of both Jews and Gentiles.

71. This conclusion remains true, even though one may not exclude that a conversion narrative might echo the religious experience of the readers. In his dissertation, LaHurd has noted the possible 'ritual impact' of such narratives setting forth a rite of passage accessible to the reader (*The Author's Call to the Audience*, pp. 182-229).

72. As I see it, the conclusion of the book of Acts (28.16-31) registers the failure of Christian preaching to convert all Israel and envisions a people made up of converted Jews and Gentiles, while leaving open the question of the final salvation of Israel. On this open-ended conclusion of the book of Acts, see my study, 'The End of Acts (28.16-31) and the Rhetoric of Silence', in S.E. Porter and T.H. Olbricht (eds.), *Rhetoric and the New Testament: Essays from the 1992 Heidelberg Conference* (JSNTSup, 90; Sheffield: JSOT Press, 1993), pp. 74-89.

RELEASE OF THE CAPTIVES*—REFLECTIONS ON ACTS 12

David T.N. Parry

The legendary nature of Luke's account of the miraculous release of Peter from prison may send us scurrying to find whatever historical kernel or tradition it may embody. However, the ancient popularity of such stories[1] would suggest at least one reason why Luke has chosen to include it, and to have taken the trouble to make it such a dramatic and polished story, comparable, say, to Paul's shipwreck, and eliciting from Martin Dibelius[2] the following verdict:

> The story itself... is a special gem among the legends of Acts: for purity of style it is comparable only with the stories of Tabitha and of the eunuch, and it is superior to them in the beautiful way in which it is presented.

Stephen Sheeley[3] draws attention to the entertainment value of the story. We are inclined to laugh at Peter who has to be roughly awakened, and at the maid leaving Peter standing outside. Pervo[4] classifies the story as one of the 'burlesque and rowdy episodes'. Rather than

---

* αἰχμαλώτοις ἄφεσιν, Lk. 4.18; see below p. 159.

1. Frequently cited are Dionysiac miracles of liberation in the *Bacchae* of Euripedes 443ff., 516ff., the freeing of Apollonius of Tyana (Philostr., *Vit. Ap.* 8.30), and the story in Artapanos, *Concerning the Jews* (Eusebius, *Praep. Ev.* 9.27.12), of the miraculous release from imprisonment by the king of Moses when the doors open αὐτομάτως—cf. J. Jeremias 'θύρα', in *TDNT*, III, p. 175.

2. 'Style Criticism of the Book of Acts', from *Eucharisterion für H. Gunkel*, II, pp. 27-49 (Göttingen: Vandenhoeck & Ruprecht, 1923), in *Aufsätze zur Apostelgeschichte* (Göttingen: Vandenhoeck & Ruprecht, 5th edn, 1968), p. 26. English translation: *Studies in the Acts of the Apostles* (London: SCM Press, 1956), p. 22

3. *Narrative Asides in Luke–Acts* (JSNTSup, 72; Sheffield: JSOT Press, 1992), pp. 133-34.

4. R.T. Pervo, *Profit with Delight—The Literary Genre of Acts* (Philadelphia: Fortress Press, 1987), pp. 62-63.

examining its literary qualities, however, I want to ask how the story is made to function in Luke's narrative.

Acts 12 in Context

Peter's release from prison is presented as a sequel to the beheading of 'James the brother of John' (12.2). The chapter is given unity by the person of 'Herod the King', that is, Agrippa I. He beheads James; he arrests Peter; he has the guards executed and Herod the persecutor receives appropriate[5] retribution both because of his treatment of the apostles, and also for accepting the crowd's acclamation of him as a god (contrast 14.14-15). As in the Magnificat, 'he has brought down monarchs from their thrones, and raised on high the lowly' (Lk. 1.52). This is one of Luke's attempts to tie his Christian history into more widely known events (or pseudo-events),[6] (as in Lk. 2.1; 13.1; Acts 5.36-37; 11.28).

The opening events of the chapter are loosely fitted into the famine relief visit to Jerusalem from Antioch of Barnabas and Saul (11.29–12.1), and the chapter forms a literary interlude before they return from Jerusalem to Antioch (12.25[7]). A similar interlude occurs between the sending out of the Twelve and their return between Lk. 9.6 and 9.10 par. Mk 6.12 and 6.30, where the subject matter is again about (another) Herod and a beheading (at much greater length in Mark than Luke), and the spread of the apostolic Word (cf. Acts 12.24). Historically, Luke may not be correct to place Herod's death in 44 CE after the famine in Claudius's reign and the famine relief visit of Barnabas and Saul.[8] The imprisonment and release of Peter, and his going εἰς ἕτερον τόπον

---

5. Cf. the worms of 12.23 and 2 Macc. 9.5-6 of Antiochus IV. W. Radl, 'Befreiung aus dem Gefängnis', *BZ* 27 (1983), pp. 81-96, regards this element as typical of a punishment miracle story, and suggests its *Sitz im Leben* is in polemic against the imperial cult.

6. Josephus, *Ant.* 19.8.2.

7. Assuming that the reading ἐξ Ἰερουσαλήμ is correct, rather than the difficult εἰς of Sinaiticus and Vaticanus, etc., and treating 'ΕΙΣ as a misreading of 'ΕΞ or reading εἰς and understanding it in the force of ἐν 'having completed service in Jerusalem (they returned)...' (R.J. Dillon in *The New Jerome Biblical Commentary* p. 748; J. Dupont, 'La mission de Paul "A Jérusalem" [Actes XII,25]', *NovT* 1 [1956], pp. 275-303).

8. J. Dupont, 'Pierre délivré de prison (Ac 12,1-11)', in *Nouvelles études sur les Actes des Apôtres* (LD, 118; Paris: Cerf, 1984) pp. 329ff.

(12.17) may be thought to fit better as a prelude to the stories of his activity outside Jerusalem in Lydda and Joppa. Peter is in Jerusalem from 11.2, and appears there in 15.6, but ch. 12 provides a fitting final Acts story about Peter (except for 15.6) and prepares us for the leadership of the Jerusalem church passing to James (12.17, the first named reference cf. 1.14), and for the momentum of the mission to move to Antioch—John Mark is introduced (12.12) and returns with Barnabas and Saul (v. 25) and joins them in their mission to Cyprus (13.5). The church in Antioch had begun because of earlier persecution of Hellenists in Jerusalem (11.19ff.); so now the attack on the apostles reinforces that outreach. And the account of the mission becomes more weighted towards Gentiles, a move already started by Peter in his conversion of Cornelius.

The leadership of the mission in Acts is divided roughly into four phases, by the Twelve (2.1–6.7), by the Hellenists (6.8–8.40), by Peter (9.31–11.18) and by (Barnabas and) Paul (13–end). However, the sections interweave with each other, as in the ways mentioned above, and, for example, in Saul's presence at Stephen's martyrdom, and the whole interlude of his conversion (ch. 9). One thing that is striking is that in three of these four phases there occurs a miraculous deliverance from prison. In 5.17-25, the Twelve, the apostles, are imprisoned by the priests, but an angel (cf. 12.7) opens the doors during the night (cf. 12.6), in spite of the guards (cf. 12.6). In the morning the doors are found locked, the guards in position, but the prison empty. The divine/angelic reason for the release is so that the apostolic teaching in the Temple may be resumed, unhindered. The second release, of Peter in ch. 12, may be considered the climax of the 'Peter' phase. Then in 16.22-40 Paul and Silas are flogged by the Roman authorities in Philippi and then imprisoned overnight, with feet secured (cf. 12.7). It is during the night, but Paul and Silas are not asleep, but praying and praising God, and this time, rather than an angel, there is an earthquake which opens the prison doors. Escape is not the consequence this time; rather there is the opportunity to witness to the jailer and fellow-prisoners. So it becomes a night of conversion, of baptism, washing wounds and fellowship meal. In several ways, then, the three imprisonment incidents could be called variations on a theme. For reasons that will emerge below, I think the tradition of the release of Peter is the principal theme on which the others are based.

On the wider canvas of Luke–Acts as a whole, we may detect a

Lukan interest in prisons. Luke, in common with the other Gospels, mentions the imprisonment of John the Baptist (3.20); he alone mentions prison with regard to Barabbas (23.19, 25). At 21.12 he adds καὶ φυλακάς to the persecutions that will befall disciples, anticipating the fulfilments in Acts. Most significantly at 22.33 in Luke's version of Peter's profession of loyalty, and in a context where Jesus has spoken of Peter's being sifted and then turning again, Peter declares his readiness to go with Jesus εἰς φυλακὴν καὶ εἰς θάνατον. We may view the releases from prison described in Acts both as literal fulfilments and as symbols of release from spiritual and metaphorical bondage—part of the programmatic citation of Isa. 61.1-2 in the opening Nazareth sermon of Lk. 4.18: κηρύξαι αἰχμαλώτοις ἄφεσιν (as LXX). Analogously, the following καὶ τυφλοῖς ἀνάβλεψιν is fulfilled both metaphorically and literally (7.21; 18.35-43) in the Gospel.

Peter's Release as a 'Resurrection'

Acts 12 is an interlude; some of its threads interweave with the wider context; some of its motifs offer illustration of recurrent themes of Luke's story. I suggest that Luke's presentation of the tradition of Peter's miraculous release offers the finest expression of a tendency within the story-telling of the church that has left its mark elsewhere in the Gospels. I wish now to look at some of these motifs more closely.

I have already mentioned the cohesive role of Herod for ch. 12. The involvement of (a) Herod in action against Jesus is a distinctive part of Luke's narrative (Lk. 9.9; 13.31-32; 23.6-12; Acts 4.27), and a Herod becomes involved in action against Paul (25.13–26.32) as well as here against James and Peter. The same kind of vacillating attitude of Herod that we find in the Gospel (hostility to the Baptist and Jesus, but then concurrence with Pilate in Jesus' innocence) is found in Acts, between the action against James and Peter, and Agrippa II's verdict on Paul.[9] The Herods being partly Jewish, and Agrippa I indeed historically being of Hasmonean descent and sympathetic to Jewish religion,[10] makes it possible for them to represent Jewish hostility to the Christian mission (12.3, 11). The beheading of 'James, the brother of John' (12.2) is a recapitulation of the beheading by another Herod of another John (Lk. 9.9). Luke's brief reference to this event, and only as part of an

---

9. J.T. Sanders, *The Jews in Luke–Acts* (London: SCM Press, 1987), p. 258.
10. *M. Soṭ.* 7.8.

anticipation of Herod's meeting Jesus at the trial, and his omission of Mark's detailed flash-back to John's beheading, finds parallel in the surprisingly terse account of James's execution (when compared with Stephen's in ch. 7). It serves only as prelude to the arrest of Peter; the beheadings of John/James are forerunners to the arrests of Jesus/Peter.[11]

It is a strong motif in Acts that what the church and its leaders do, and what happens to them, re-enacts the story of the Gospel. So, for example, Peter's healing of Aeneas and raising of Tabitha (Acts 9.32-41) remind us of the Paralytic and Jairus's daughter. The martyred Stephen dies with prayers similar to those of the dying Jesus. Paul makes a final journey to Jerusalem and undergoes three trials, like Jesus. So here in Acts 12, Peter is imprisoned at the festival of Passover and Unleavened Bread,[12] and the intention is that public action should take place after the festival is over (vv. 3-4). This is a detail from the account of Jesus' passion in Mk 14.2, which Luke omits in his parallel, 22.2. A similar case is the omission of the false charge of speaking against the Temple (Mk 14.57-61) in Luke's passion narrative, only for it to appear in the action against Stephen (Acts 6.11-14). It is not fanciful, then, to ask whether Luke intends us to see the Paschal action against Peter and his miraculous deliverance from the prison as a recapitulation, in the experience of the apostle, of the passion and resurrection of Jesus.[13]

The prayer of the church for Peter ἐκτενῶς (v. 5) parallels Jesus' prayer of agony (Lk. 22.44 ἐκτενέστερον[14]). Peter is raised from sleep (cf. death),[15] by a dazzling angel (cf. the angels at the tomb of Jesus); the guards are helpless (cf. the guards in Mt. 28.4)[16] and the door of the

---

11. So R.B. Rackham, *The Acts of the Apostles: An Exposition* (London: Methuen, 1906), pp.176-77.

12. Regarded as synonymous by Luke (see Lk. 22.1).

13. Cf. M.D. Goulder, *Type and History in Acts* (London: SPCK, 1964), pp. 45-46.

14. Following ℵ*,2 ΘL and the great preponderance of early versions and citations for the inclusion of vv. 43-44.

15. Cf. the use of rising from sleep as a type of resurrection from death in the hymnic Eph. 5.14

ἔγειρε, ὁ καθεύδων,
καὶ ἀνάστα ἐκ τῶν νεκρῶν,
καὶ ἐπιφαύσει σοι ὁ Χριστός.

16. The earthquake in Mt. 28.2 has its equivalent at the Philippi prison (Acts 16.26), σεισμὸς ἐγένετο μέγας in both places. W. Radl, 'Befreiung aus dem Gefängnis', *BZ* 27 (1983), p. 83, refers to Matthew's Easter Narrative. For the large

prison (cf. the entrance to the tomb) is opened. The sudden disappearance of the angel (v. 10) perhaps recalls the sudden ending of the resurrection appearances of Jesus. Peter's knocking at the house of Mary, and Rhoda's running to tell others, and her message being disbelieved, or the suggestion that Peter's presence is unreal, and then the church's joy, recast several features of resurrection appearance stories, especially Lk. 24.36-37. They are also suggestive of the 'door' imagery of Lk. 13.25-27 and its reversal, to apply to the risen Christ as the one who knocks, which we find in Rev. 3.20.

Another feature of the deliverance of Peter, the instructions to dress, when combined with the Passover setting, suggests more to August Strobel,[17] namely, the eschatological expectations that had come to be associated with Passover. He draws attention to the girding imagery of the eschatological parable of Lk. 12.35 (cf. 1 Pet. 1.13). He notes verbal parallels between Acts and the LXX of the Exodus 12 Passover law:

	Acts		Exodus
12.6	τῇ νυκτὶ ἐκείνῃ	12.12	ἐν τῇ νυκτὶ ταυτῇ
12.7	ἀνάστα ἐν τάχει	12.11	μετὰ σπουδῆς
12.8	ζῶσαι καὶ ὑπόδησαι	12.11	περιεζωσμέναι καὶ τὰ ὑποδήματα ἐν τοῖς πόσιν

He cites *Exod. R.* 18 (81a) which interprets the Passover night of watching as being the night also in which Hezekiah was delivered, when the three youths were delivered from the furnace and when Daniel was rescued from the lions (Dan. 3.26; 6.23) and when Elijah and the Messiah would come. If Strobel is correct, Acts 12 with the dressing imagery suggests that the deliverance of Peter enacts the meaning of Jesus' resurrection as a realization or inauguration of the eschatological deliverance, of which Isaiah's phrase 'release of the captives' is an appropriate symbol.

The Wider Biblical Context—The Old Testament

In viewing the release of Peter as a type of 'resurrection', we have already begun to look beyond its immediate context for help in interpretation. In this final section of my paper I wish to look further into both

---

number of guards at 12.4, suggestive of an important rather than dangerous prisoner, compare Acts 23.23 and Jn 18.3.

17. 'Passa-Symbolik und Passa-Wunder in Act XII.3ff.', *NTS* 4 (1957–58), pp. 210-15. Also J. Dupont, 'Pierre délivré de prison', pp. 329ff.

Old Testament and New Testament, attempting to show that Acts 12 is an example of a more widespread imaginative tendency among the early Christian writers.

Release from prison is a good picture of salvation, and is found for example in the Psalms and Prophets:

> 'Let the groaning of the captives reach your presence
> and in your great might save those under sentence of
> death' (Ps. 79.11).

> 'he brought them out of the dark, and the shadow of death
> and burst their chains' (Ps. 107.14;[18] cf. also 102.20;
> 142.7; 146.7).

> 'to bring captives out of prison
> out of the dungeon where they lie in darkness' (Isa. 42.7).

The return from Exile could be viewed as such a release, a renewing of the Exodus from the 'house of bondage'. The release of King Jehoiachin (2 Kgs 25.27) enables the deuteronomistic history to conclude on a note of hope. The imprisonments of Jeremiah are typical of the persecution of God's messengers, and Luke may have had in mind Jeremiah's rescue by the Ethiopian eunuch, and his release from chains by Nebuzaradan, after which, like Peter, he goes elsewhere (Jer. 40.4). He certainly had in mind (Acts 7.10) Joseph's release from the prison, where he had proved by wisdom in small things his readiness to govern Egypt.

More significant, I think, are the tales of persecution that we find in Daniel, the Burning Fiery Furnace and the Lions' Den. In Daniel 3, King Nebuchadnezzar sees a fourth being in the furnace who 'looks like a god' (v. 25 [92]) and is interpreted as God's angel sent to save his servants (v. 28 [95]).

Dan. 3.95 (Theodotion)	Acts 12.11
ἀπέστειλεν τὸν ἄγγελον αὐτοῦ	ἐξαπέστειλεν ὁ κύριος
καὶ ἐξείλατο τοὺς παιδὰς αὐτοῦ	τὸν ἄγγελον αὐτοῦ καὶ
	ἐξείλατό με ἐκ χειρός...

In Daniel 6 the King Darius tries to find a way out of sentencing Daniel (cf. Pilate). A stone is placed over the mouth of the lion pit (cf. Jesus'

---

18. Of this psalm's four illustrations of salvation—feeding those wandering in the desert, releasing prisoners, healing the sick and calming the storm—three could be said to find fulfilment in the Gospel, leaving the release of prisoners for Acts.

tomb) and it is sealed (cf. Mt. 27.66); sleep eludes the King (cf. Pilate's wife) and Daniel ascribes his safety to the fact that 'God sent his angel to shut the lions' mouths' (v. 22).

The Wider Biblical Context—The New Testament: Do other 'Peter' Stories Function Like Acts 12?

There are these points of connection between the Danielic stories and Matthew's passion–resurrection narrative, and a connection between Matthew and Acts 12 in the guards at the tomb. Matthew also tells of an earthquake, which opens the tombs of 'the saints who had fallen asleep', at the time of the death of Jesus, and their appearances after Jesus' resurrection (27.51-52). Sometimes, in connection with this, reference is made to the ancient notion of the Descent of Christ into Hell, as part of the drama of salvation, and via this doctrine the link is made with the description in 1 Peter (with its strong paschal themes) of Christ's saving work as going to preach τοῖς ἐν φυλακῇ πνεύμασιν (3.19).[19]

Matthew's Gospel has its own picture of Peter being raised up by Christ, from the depths (rather than prison), in the extension to the account of the walking on the water (14.28-33). The walking on the water has much of the character of a christophany, or resurrection appearance—the ambiguous physicality, the suspicion of a phantom, the divine ἐγώ εἰμι, the worship of the Son of God. The Petrine request to share in this experience is granted, and is successful until he looks not at Jesus but at the storm. Sinking, he cries to Jesus for salvation and is lifted by the hand. Undoubtedly this is meant in part to portray, by way of anticipation, Peter's denials and subsequent restoration to faith and apostleship, but does there lie behind it the same kind of imaginative enactment of 'resurrection' by and with Christ that we find in Acts 12? Both, incidentally, happen deep in the night-time, and φυλακή, in the sense of 'watch', is used in Mt. 14.25.

Perhaps the same is true of the epilogue to the Fourth Gospel (Jn 21). There is a night of unsuccessful fishing, followed by the overwhelming catch at the instruction of the unrecognized Christ in the early morning. When the Beloved Disciple tells them 'It is the Lord', the undressed Peter puts on his clothes (cf. Acts 12.8) and jumps out of the boat into

---

19. For discussion of the ancient connecting of Mt. 27.51-52 and 1 Pet. 3.18-19; 4.6, and reference to modern authors who continue to make the connection, see R.E. Brown, *The Death of the Messiah*, II (London: Chapman, 1994), pp. 1127-28.

the sea to go to Jesus (cf. Mt. 14.29). There follows the fellowship meal and the dialogue between Jesus and Peter in which Peter renews his love and faith and is given charge of Christ's 'sheep'.

Finally, mention might be made of the second-century (?) *Epistula Apostolorum*, which takes the form of a post-resurrection discourse, and in this section presents something of an amalgam of themes that we have found in our text—Passover, Peter's imprisonment and deliverance, and his denial, and the renewing in the disciples of the passion and resurrection of Jesus and the eschatological hope. In the Coptic version it reads,[20]

> '...And you remember my death. If now the passover takes place, then will one of you be thrown into prison for my sake, and he will be in sorrow and care that you celebrate the passover while he is in prison and [far] from you; for he will sorrow that he does not celebrate the passover [with] you. I will send my power in the [form] of the Angel Gabriel, and the doors of the prison will be opened. He will go out and come to you; he will spend a night of watch with [you] and stay with you till the cock crows. But when you complete the remembrance that is for me and the Agape he will again be thrown into prison for a testimony until he comes out from there and preaches what I have delivered to you.' And we said to him, 'O Lord, is it perhaps necessary again that we take the cup and drink?' He said to us, 'Yes, it is necessary until the day when I come with those who were killed for my sake'.

I am not suggesting a dependence of one of our New Testament texts upon another, though some mutual acquaintance there may have been. I am suggesting a tendency within the early Christian community to develop stories, especially about Peter, that show the sufferings and resurrection of Christ were recapitulated in the church's experience of persecution. In Acts 12, Luke has developed this in a masterly way, giving us a rich and multi-layered narrative that forms the fitting climax to the first half of his second book for Theophilus.

---

20. Translated by H. Duensing in E. Hennecke (ed.), *New Testament Apocrypha*, I (London: SCM Press, 1963), pp. 199-200.

LUKE AND THE INTERNAL DIVISIONS IN THE EARLY CHURCH*

Andrianjatovo Rakotoharintsifa

The aim of this paper is to examine critically certain episodes in the Acts of the Apostles which involve internal conflicts within the first Christian communities and which are not mentioned in other New Testament documents. In order to do this, I shall first briefly recall two main problems involved in a historical reading of Acts; secondly I shall offer some exegetical observations on the passages selected, and finally I shall evaluate the historical and theological significance of Luke's narrative.

1. *Problems of Approaching Acts*

1.1. As a literary work, Acts presents great difficulties to exegetes, for it cannot be easily classified in any of the literary genres known from antiquity.[1] In fact there is a little bit of everything in Luke's work: precise historical details (Roman administration, Palestinian social and religious facts), some significant silences (cf. James's taking over the leadership in Jerusalem, the collection, the deaths of Peter and Paul),

---

* I would like to thank Ms Ruth-Hélène Quinche for the English translation.

1. Some go so far as to claim that Acts is quite unique: 'Die Apg kann deshalb in keine sonst nachweisbare literarische Gattung eingereiht werden. Lukas hat dabei kein Vorbild vorgefunden, an das er sich halten konnte. Er hat aber auch in der christlichen Literatur keinen Nachfolger gefunden; denn die Apostelgeschichten des 2. und 3. Jh., die in ganz anderer Weise, als Lukas es getan hat, die Taten und Schicksale je eines bestimmten Apostels erzählen, tun dies in überwiegend romanhafter Weise und sind darum nicht als wirkliche Ergänzungen oder Fortsetzungen des lk Werkes zu bezeichnen' (A. Wikenhauser and J. Schmid, *Einleitung in das Neue Testament* [Freiburg: Herder, 6th edn, 1973], p. 352). Cf. also the recent proposals of E. Plümacher, 'Lukas als griechischer Historiker', in *PW* 14 (1974), cols. 235-64; R.I. Pervo, *Profit with Delight: The Literary Genre of the Acts of the Apostles* (Minneapolis: Fortress Press, 1987); *idem*, *Luke's Story of Paul* (Minneapolis: Fortress Press, 1990).

marvellous and transcendent features (cf. the miracles, the direct intervention of the Holy Spirit), political intrigues and adventure stories, historical and kerygmatic elements, familiar and exotic features (cf. city life, the Ethiopian eunuch). It is difficult to measure the exact proportion of these different aspects in the book of Acts. The book is characterized by a mixture of *Gattungen* and literary motifs, as Martin Dibelius has stressed:

> It was the Acts of the Apostles which first tried to form from traditional material the continuous account of an actual period in history. Many details, however, especially the speeches, will make it clear to the reader that this is not the ultimate object of the book, which aims also to preach and to show what the Christian belief is and what effects it has. This dual aspect of the book has, from the beginning, ever since there has been any critical knowledge of the Bible, compelled those who investigate the Book of Acts to ask what value it has as an historical source.[2]

But the intrinsic connection between history and fiction cannot be ignored, for it is inherent to historiography. A positivist approach to historical sources does not do justice to the historical dimension of fiction and vice versa. The remarks of Paul Ricoeur may be appropriate here:

> What turns great historical works into enduring classics, even though their strict scientific reliability has been eroded away by documentary progress, is precisely the nature of their poetical and rhetorical art in their vision of the past. The same work can be both a great book of history and a superb novel. What is surprising is that this interweaving of fiction and history does not undermine the latter's coherence but serves to fulfil it.[3]

1.2. Apart from this purely literary problem, one must also note the central importance of Luke's theology which determines the plot of the story and the selection of the historical facts which are presented. The crucial issue is then is then to determine and understand this theological key. We shall limit our enquiry to the theme of *conflicts* within primitive Christianity, and shall therefore look briefly at the *Tendenzkritik* of the Tübingen school and the idea of 'early Catholicism' as highlighted by E. Käsemann.

1.3. F.C. Baur and his followers[4] are well known for stressing the

---

2. M. Dibelius, 'The Acts of the Apostles as an Historical Source', in *Studies in the Acts of the Apostles* (ET; London: SCM Press, 1956), p. 102.
3. P. Ricoeur, *Temps et récits* III (Points Essais, 229; Paris: Seuil, 1991), p. 337.
4. See H.H. Wendt, *Die Apostelgeschichte* (KEK, 3; Göttingen: Vandenhoeck

incompatibility between the Paul of the letters and Luke's Paul, and hence for casting radical doubts on the historical reliability of Acts. Among the contradictions between Acts and the Pauline letters we may note the multiple visits to Jerusalem (Acts 9.26-30; 11.30; 15; 18.22 ≠ Gal. 1–2), the description of the meeting of the apostles (Acts 15 ≠ Gal. 2), the judaizing attitude of Paul in relation to the Law (Acts 16.3; 18.18-21; 20.16; 21.23-26; 24.11, 17 ≠ Gal., Phil., Rom.), the priority of Paul's mission to the Jews (Acts 13.5, 14; 14.1; 16.13; 17.2, 10, 17; 18.4; 19.8). Conversely, a lax position in relation to the Law is ascribed to the men from Jerusalem, especially Peter, a fact which does not correspond to what Paul says (Acts 10.28, 34-35; 15.10-19); even the inauguration of the Gentile mission comes from them (Acts 8.26-39; 10.1-11, 18; 15.7-9). H.H. Wendt summarizes the situation as follows:

> In general, the book of Acts gives an idealised and harmonised picture of the beginnings of the Christian church, and does not let us foresee developments and real tensions as they hit us head on in the authentic letters of Paul.[5]

The Tübingen school thought that Luke's aim was to reconcile Jewish Christianity, which was particularist and faithful to the Law, with Pauline Christianity, which was universalist and free in relation to the Law. To further his aim of conciliation, Luke therefore edited his historical data with considerable freedom, and also invented some things off his own bat.[6] Hence the unlikely picture which Acts presents: men from Jerusalem with Paulinizing characteristics and a judaized Paul.[7]

& Ruprecht, 8th edn, 1899), pp. 9-17; E. Haenchen, *Die Apostelgeschichte* (KEK, 3; Göttingen: Vandenhoek & Ruprecht, 10th edn, 1956), pp. 11-20 (ET *The Acts of the Apostles* [Oxford: Blackwell, 1971], pp. 15-24); W.G. Kümmel, *Introduction to the New Testament* (ET; London: SCM Press, 1975), pp. 160-61.

    5. Wendt, *Apostelgeschichte*, p.10.

    6. 'Any person who intentionally suppresses so much and who thereby has already placed the objects in another light, will not scruple, if necessary, to proceed more unhistorically still... It is probable that the author altered the actual history not only in a negative sense, through the suppression of essential facts, but also in a positive sense' (F.C. Baur, *Paulus, der Apostel Jesu Christi* [Leipzig, 2nd edn, 1866–67], pp. 13-14, cited by Haenchen, *Acts*, p. 19).

    7. Stating his position in relation to the Tübingen school, Wendt writes, 'Diese Kritik enthält viel Wahres. Freilich sind die unglaubwürdigen Momente in der Apostelgeschichte von den Vertretern der Tübingen Schule übertrieben und verallgemeinert worden. Um die Apostelgeschichte gerecht zu würdigen, muss man mit Bezug auf viele der angeführten Punkte Einschränkungen machen und daneben

Ever since Rudolph Sohm,[8] Protestant, and then Catholic, exegetes have been interested in how the charismatic church at the start evolved towards a more established and juridical form of existence. Bultmann has described the ins and outs of this much debated question very well in his *Theology*.[9] And from the 1950s, E. Käsemann has published a series of studies concerning the catholicizing tendencies within the New Testament, and has given them the name 'early catholic'.[10] The phenomenon of early catholicism is mainly linked to the process leading to the establishment of fixed ecclesiastical ministries, the start of the idea of apostolic succession, the beginnings of a sacramental priesthood, and the vision of the Church as the institution guaranteeing salvation. Luke has been violently attacked by some theologians because of the so-called early catholic elements in his writings. It will suffice here to refer to the strong language used by S. Schulz in his book on early catholicism.

> Luke's Paul is the rigorist arch-Pharisee and a delegate of the 12 apostles, the pioneer of the Una Sancta Catholica, the preacher of a natural theology without any message on justification or a theology of the cross, the unusual miracle-worker and great speaker, and, as a Roman citizen, the consistent peace-maker between the State and the Christian church. No other post-Pauline figure within New Testament early Catholicism transformed the image, the history and the theology of Paul in a more radical way... According to Luke, the Spirit no longer blows where it will (Jn 3.8), nor is it given freely in the sacrament of baptism, but it is linked

andere bedeutsame Punkte hervorheben, welche die Merkmale innerer Wahrscheinlichkeit und guter Überlieferung an sich tragen' (*Apostelgeschichte*, p. 10).

8. *Kirchenrecht*, I, (1892).

9. R. Bultmann, *Theology of the New Testament*, II (ET; London: SCM Press, 1955), pp. 95-118.

10. See, for example, his 'Paul and Early Catholicism', in *New Testament Questions for Today* (London: SCM Press, 1969), pp. 236-51, esp. p. 240: '[Paul] has been repeatedly and in various ways ecclesiastically domesticated, first as a missionary and martyr, later as dogmatician. This was done already by Luke, his first historian, in such a way that one cannot but admire the skill of his disciple as well as his love for his hero... Paul must be shielded against the suspicion that he was an individualist and Christian freebooter. There is salvation only within the Church, whose history, thanks to divine guidance, shows a continuous progression, and it is precisely into this history that Paul is drawn.' See too Kümmel's response in his *Introduction* (n. 4 above), pp. 172-73; also his 'Luc en accusation dans la théologie contemporaine', in F. Neirynck (ed.), *L'Evangile de Luc: Problèmes littéraires et théologiques* (BETL, 32: Gembloux: Duculot, 1973), pp. 93-109 (2nd edn: Leuven: Leuven University Press and Peeters, 1989, pp. 3-19).

to the twelve first apostles and their successors who remain in the line of apostolic succession, the officials of the Church. The Spirit is only to be found in this apostolically based Church, and is handed on only by the ministerial actions of its officials.[11]

Instead of responding to Schulz or members of the Tübingen school by means of equally general claims, we shall analyse a few text in Acts (Acts 6.1-7; 9.26; 11.1-18; 15.37-40; 20.20-21) to see whether real conflicts between Christians come to light, and whether Luke's work, which alone reports these disputes, has an ecclesiology which is rather different from one that is irenic or early catholic.

2. Evidence of Internal Christian Conflicts in Acts

2.1. The disagreement between Aramaic-Speaking Jewish Christians and Greek-Speaking Jewish Christians (Acts 6.1-7)

The episode proceeds as follows:

a. The problem presented (v. 1): the widows of the Hellenists are left out from the daily meals offered to those in need.
b. The Twelve suggest a solution (vv. 2-4): service of the word remains their responsibility, whilst seven extra people are nominated to serve at table.
c. The group approves (v. 5a).
d. The decision is implemented (vv. 5b-6): the seven are set apart by the Twelve.
e. The positive outcome of the decision (v. 7): the word is preached, the Jerusalem community grows, and numerous priests join the Christian faith.

At first sight, the story seems to be nothing but a pious, rather triumphalist, form of edification. There are certain 'early catholic' features,

---

11. S. Schulz, *Die Mitte der Schrift: Der Frühkatholizismus im Neuen Testament als Herausforderung an den Protestantismus* (Stuttgart: Kreuz, 1976), pp. 122-23, 140. Among various reactions, see especially H. Conzelmann and A. Lindemann, *Grundriss der Theologie des NT* (UTB, 1446; Tübingen: Mohr, 5th edn, 1992), p. 160: 'Katholisch wird [ein Traditionsgedanke] erst dann, wenn die Tradition institutionell, durch Lehramt und kirchliche Ordnungen sowie vor allem durch Amtssukzession, gesichert wird, wenn Geist und Sakrament an die Institution gebunden werden und sich die Kirche also zur rechtlich verfasst Heilsanstalt macht. Lukas kennt das Apostelamt, aber er kennt noch keinen Sukzessionsgedanken; er kennt die Tradition, aber noch keine rechtliche Organisation ihrer Weitergabe.'

such as the inauguration of a new ministry authorized by the Twelve. But in fact the story is more subtle and more complex. The author speaks of a γογγυσμός ('murmuring') by the Hellenists against the Hebrews (v. 1), a term which implies not only unhappiness and dissatisfaction, but rather loss of trust and disobedience.[12] The Hellenists could not rely on the Hebrews any more, and the Twelve had understood the situation very well by allowing their leaders to deal with looking after their forgotten widows. This raises a whole host of questions about the details of the situation: why would the Seven be more effective than the Twelve? Who would then cater for the Hebrews' widows after the apostles had handed over responsibility? Why is there no real link between serving at table and the actual activities of the seven Hellenists? L.T. Johnson summarizes—and solves—the puzzle of the narrative thus:

> The problem of the passage is therefore this: there is no obvious connection between the purported role of the seven and their actual function. They were supposed to be in charge of community possessions but they turn out to be prophetic preachers. There seems to be, in fact, only the most tenuous connection between the account of their placement over community possessions and the description of their actual ministry. The discrepancy disappears when we remember Luke's consistent habit of using authority over material possessions as a symbol for spiritual authority.[13]

But if one analyses the *historical* tradition which Luke has reworked, what is the result? The sequel in the story (opposition against Stephen, Stephen's speech, the flight of the Hellenists from Jerusalem) points to the existence of a deeper rift at the theological level. Stephen's group shows itself to be very critical in relation to both the Temple and the Mosaic Law, and pleads for a new understanding of the mission. This unsettles the majority of Aramaic speaking Jewish Christians:

> The conflict concerned an independent leadership within the community by the Hellenists, in which the Seven are placed alongside the Palestinian Twelve. The most important difference between the two communities, or at least between their leaders, concerned the question of whether the

---

12. γογγύζω occurs 15 times in the LXX, and διαγογγύζω 10 times. Behind the usage stands 'the thought of grumbling based on guilty unbelief and disobedience': G.W. Bromiley, *Theological Dictionary of the New Testament Abridged in One Volume* (Grand Rapids: Eerdmans, 1990), p. 125.

13. L.T. Johnson, *The Acts of the Apostles* (Sacra Pagina, 5; Collegeville, MN: Liturgical Press, 1992), p. 111.

mission in the Jewish Diaspora should be limited to Jews and to the circle of God-fearers, whether Gentiles should also be accepted into the Christian community only after their acceptance into the synagogue, or whether they could be converted and baptized without any preconditions... The two communities, almost rival communities in Jerusalem, came after a theological decision to be two confessions, as it were, with differing dogmas and an ever decreasing level of cooperation.[14]

But we should note that such a reconstruction is only possible thanks to the sparse information in Luke's work, a fact which shows that Luke's ecumenism does not make real conflicts disappear but seeks to manage them in the best possible way.

2.2. *The Ambiguous Relationship between Paul and the Jerusalem Christians (Acts 9.26; 21.15-40): From Reticence to Abandonment*

In Acts 9.26-30, Luke tells of Paul's first visit to Jerusalem some time after his conversion. Certain elements in this passage do not correspond with what Paul himself says in Galatians 1–2:

(a) The stay in Arabia and the three-year interval before going up to Jerusalem (Gal. 1.18) are ignored.

(b) The meeting with Peter, staying fifteen days with him, and the meeting with James (Gal. 1.18-19) are replaced by an unhappy attempt to integrate with the group of disciples in Jerusalem, and the mediation by Barnabas between Paul and the apostles.

(c) The lack of any personal relationship with the Jerusalem community (Gal. 1.22-23) seems to be contradicted by a direct face-to-face meeting.

This collection of clues leads us to the conclusion that the author freely constructs, off his own bat, the details which he needed to correspond to the particular circumstances.[15]

---

14. E. Käsemann, 'Urchristliche Konflikte um die Freiheit der Gemeinde', in *Kirchliche Konflikte*, I (Göttingen: Vandenhoeck & Ruprecht, 1982), pp. 37-45, here from p. 40. See also G. Lüdemann, *Early Christianity according to the Traditions in Acts: A Commentary* (London: SCM Press, 1989), pp. 78-79: 'One could make a reasoned guess at the occasion for the conflict: Aramaic-speaking Christians who were strict observers of the law fell out with Greek-speaking Christians over the question of the law, and the language barrier added a further element to the dispute'.

15. Wendt, *Apostelgeschichte*, p. 194: 'Unser ganzer Abschnitt ist eine deutliche Probe für das schriftstellerische Verfahren des Verfassers der Apostelgeschichte,

For this reason, I suggest that Luke knew an oral tradition according to which the Jerusalem Christians did not approve of Paul's theology or practice, and that he inserts it here in the story of Paul's first meeting with the Jerusalem disciples, adding μὴ πιστεύοντες ὅτι ἐστὶν μαθητής. The story of the last journey to Jerusalem (Acts 21.15-40) confirms the fact that the suspicion on the side of Palestinian Christians towards the apostle of the Gentiles never disappeared. We hear from the mouth of James himself:

> You see, brother, how many thousands of Jews have believed; they are all zealous for the Law. They have been informed that you teach all the Jews who live among the Gentiles to turn away from (the Law of) Moses, telling them not to circumcise their children or live according to the customs (Acts 21.20-21).

What must be clearly stated is that Paul's Jewish Christian brothers had not forgiven Paul the enormity of his theology of the justification of the ungodly, and they had left him in the hands of those in the Temple who were zealous for the Law. L.T. Johnson writes to the point:

> It is striking that apart from the (very private and personal) help given by Paul's nephew (23:16-22) and the single mention in 24:23 of 'Paul's associates' being allowed to attend to him while in prison in Caesarea, Luke says nothing about Paul being supported. And even these aids were offered by a family member and Paul's own co-workers. Nothing is said about any role played by the Jerusalem community itself during the whole period of Paul's troubles, either in Jerusalem or in Caesarea. This passivity is even stranger if we take seriously the emphatic point made by his earlier narrative concerning this community's size and influence among the people (see especially Acts 4–6).[16]

The sequel in the story does not mention the results of the collection which Paul is supposed to have brought to the Jerusalem community as a sign of fellowship from Gentile Christians, although Luke knows about it very well (Acts 24.17). Why has the author shied away from reporting such a crucial event? Maybe it was because Paul's premonition, expressed in Rom. 15.31, came true. The sign of κοινωνία had not happened—a fact that is difficult to integrate into Luke's ecclesiology! Here there is a real falsification of Luke's ecumenical theology, facts which refute the vision of a united Church. In the words of J. Roloff,

dass er das Detail seiner Erzählungen frei von sich aus bildet, so wie er es den besonderen Umständen entsprechend findet'.

16. Johnson, *Acts of the Apostles*, p. 378.

The reason for [Luke's] silence is easy to grasp: the source which he used told of the failure of Paul's project. Evidently, while on his visit, Paul came up against hostile resistance from the majority of the primitive community, and he accepted James' proposal of a compromise in order to show his allegiance to the Law by spending part of the money of the collection to pay for the Nazirite vows of some poor Jewish Christians. As he went to the Temple to do this, he was arrested. At the very least, the community did nothing to rescue him, and they refused to accept the collection. To tell this story would have placed an unbearable question mark for Luke against his vision of the unity of the Church over and above all conflicts, for the collection had enormous significance as a symbol of unity.[17]

Such an interpretation of Luke's narrative seems to be necessary to the extent that elements outside the story (e.g. Galatians) and within it (the hurried mention of the collection) allow us to stand back to a certain extent from Luke's own narrative as he presents it.

2.3. *Peter's Transgression (Acts 11.1-18)*

This story tells of one of the most important points of dispute between Jewish and Gentile Christians in the beginnings of Christianity: the question of eating together without any preceding ritual. 'So when Peter returned to Jerusalem, those of the circumcision criticised him, saying, "You went into the house of uncircumcised men and ate with them"' (Acts 11.2-3). The severe reprimand to Peter shows the deep fear of the Jews in relation to defilement which could be incurred by eating with Gentiles. The disappearance of the ritual boundaries established by the Law endangered the unique identity of the people of God. The narrator does not pull his punches in using the expression οἱ ἐκ περιτομῆς. He wants to underline the point of view, basically a ritualist one, out of which Jewish Christians perceive the relationship with Gentiles. For them, Peter has committed a serious offence which might risk creating a precedent within the movement by virtue of his position as leader, and, further, might risk exposing the small Christian community of Jerusalem to repressive measures from the Sanhedrin.[18]

---

17. J. Roloff, 'Konflikte und Konfliktlösungen nach der Apostelgeschichte', in *Der Treue Gottes trauen: Beiträge zum Werk des Lukas für Gerhard Schneider* (Freiburg: Herder, 1991), pp. 111-26 (123).

18. 'Dépourvue, en effet, comme la plupart des mouvements de renouveau au sein du judaïsme de l'époque, de toute représentation au sein de l'instance officielle que constituait le Sanhédrin, [l'Eglise primitive de Jérusalem] devait se garder, sous

Within the narrative in Acts, the meeting of Peter with Cornelius and the ensuing consequences prepare the reader to understand a crucial point in the background to the debate in Acts 15. Thanks to his vision of unclean animals 'coming down from heaven' (καθιεμένην ἐκ τοῦ οὐρανοῦ), Peter has been able to get over the *earthly* obstacle of ritual purity which separates Jews and Gentiles. This particular act of boldness has cost him a high price: he has had to hand over his role as leader to James, the brother of Jesus. The latter's rise to power is never recorded in Acts, but his sudden appearance in 12.17 (just after 10.1–11.18) and 15.13 (the controversy about ritual observance) suggests that his presence may be due to Peter's loss of prestige following the scandal of the meal at Joppa.[19]

Here again, we see that Luke does not hide the existence of severe tensions within the primitive Christianity of Jerusalem, but he tries to tone them down by highlighting the brotherly side of the debate and its resolution (cf. 11.18 and especially 15.1-29). The sequel to the story shows in veiled form the strength of the opposition by the Jewish Christian group to any abandonment of the Mosaic Law.

2.4. *Paul's Separation from Barnabas (Acts 15.37-40)*

Luke took care to mention earlier the links uniting Paul and Barnabas at the time of Luke's first visit to Jerusalem (Acts 9.27), when Paul took part for the first time in the mission directed by the Antioch community (Acts 11.25-26; 13.1-14, 28), and during the debate in Jerusalem where both defended the work of the mission among the Gentiles (Acts 15.12). Here the author presents a severe disagreement between the two men in relation to John Mark, whom Paul did not want to take with him for the coming mission because he had withdrawn from the earlier mission (i.e. apostatised: ἀποστάντα ἀπ' αὐτῶν, v. 38) in Pamphylia (Acts 13.13). The depth of the disagreement is reflected in the word παροξυσμός

---

peine de représailles, de toute forme de provocation' (C. Grappe, *D'un temple à l'autre: Pierre et l'église primitive de Jérusalem* [EHPhR, 71; Paris: Presse Universitaire de France, 1992], p. 135).

19. So too Grappe, *D'un temple à l'autre*, pp. 278-79: 'il faut envisager, nous semble-t-il, que Pierre n'est pas parvenu à convaincre Jacques et les siens et qu'il s'est soumis à leur appréciation ou à leur verdict en acceptant la promulgation du décret apostolique [...] la commensalité entre pagano- et judéo-chrétiens, telle que l'avait pratiquée momentanément Céphas à Antioche, n'était ni souhaitable ni possible'.

(v. 39), a word which suggests 'a severe argument based on intense difference of opinion'.[20] Behind the quarrel over Mark, there are very probably two irreconcilable visions about vocation and missionary collaboration, to the extent that the two men cannot work together any more, and they separate for good. According to Acts, their paths will never cross again, for Barnabas disappears from the story as he abandons Paul.

The argument recorded by Luke leads us to take note of the incident at Antioch (Gal. 2.13b) where Paul recalls precisely the hypocrisy of Barnabas who broke off table fellowship with the Gentiles for fear of the rigorist Jewish Christians. It seems that the separation of Paul and the Antioch community, of which Barnabas was a leading figure, could have been caused by the community's adopting the position of James, the brother of Jesus. E. Haenchen supports such a theory with good reason:

> Paul had publicly, before the congregation, defended 'his gospel' against Peter and Barnabas—and failed. The most important mentor of the Antiochian community, Barnabas, indeed the whole Jewish Christian part of the congregation (Gal. 2.13, cf. Acts 13.1) and the Apostle Peter himself were not persuaded. The authority of Paul, even though not formally contested, was shattered... How could Paul, after such a rebuff—a rejection of his gospel!—calmly stay on in Antioch as if nothing had happened, and invite Barnabas to join him on another tour?[21]

Such a reconstruction has the merit of both going beyond the Lukan framework of interpretation while using the elements provided by the story. But it runs the risk of hiding the mundane human side of any conflict: emotions also play their part in spiritual matters. The great Christian missionaries who let themselves be overwhelmed by uncontrolled emotions render a more human side to the history of origins.[22]

---

20. J.P. Louw and E.A. Nida, *Greek–English Lexicon Based on Semantic Domains* (New York: United Bible Societies, 1989), p. 440.

21. Haenchen, *Acts*, p. 476.

22. So the young K. Barth, 'Die Missionsthätigkeit des Paulus nach der Darstellung der Apostelgeschichte', in *Vorträge und kleinere Arbeiten (1905–1909)* (Zürich: Theologischer Verlag, 1992), pp. 148-243: 'Der Bericht und die Motivierung der Trennung lesen sich sehr natürlich und die ganze Sache—eine Menschlichkeit, wie sie eben auch im apostolischen Zeitalter vorkommen hatte— scheint eher für als gegen die Aufrichtigkeit des Berichterstatters zu sprechen, seine Stellung zu den Ereignissen mag gewesen sein, welche sie wolle' (pp. 165-66). Johnson, *Acts of the Apostles*, p. 288: 'We must as readers assume that a personal loyalty has here superseded a commitment to the work of the mission. This is

However, the seriousness of the rift suggests that the break is primarily at the level of how the mission is understood.

3. *Final Comments*

The analysis of some passages in Acts leads us to abandon the cliche according to which Luke has omitted all the conflicts from the history of the origin of the church which were not so complimentary, so presenting a story entirely moulded by unity and unanimity. I would say, on the contrary, that Luke more or less explicitly mentions the quarrels within the early communities and tries to resolve them in his narrative in various ways, whether it be by temporal changes (Acts 9.26, Paul's visit to Jerusalem), or by silence on certain facts (Acts 21.15-40, the collection), or by shifting the problem (Acts 6.1-7, from a theological conflict to one of charitable work), or by insisting on the happy outcome of the conflict (Acts 6.5; 11.18), or by letting us see only the minor features of the disagreement (Acts 15.37-40).

The book of Acts remains a precious document for the history of intra-Christian conflicts, but because of its undeniable theological tendency, it must always be confronted by other sources which are available to us. 'In his own way, Luke recaps Paul's inheritance. By placing him parallel with Peter in Acts, he has made his [Paul's] prestige all the greater. But in his concern to level out the differences, he paints Paul as rather softer than life.'[23] In this confrontation, the letters of Paul must take first place, but they in turn must be read critically. That is the only way of protecting ourselves against an excess of Paulinism which does not allow for the theological diversity in the New Testament (cf. the somewhat violent formulations of S. Schulz).

The image of the church which emerges from Acts is far from being irenic: the church remains riddled with divisions and tensions, more or less serious, and these can call into question its witness and its mission. But on the other hand, the church is sustained and guided by the Spirit, which intervenes directly in its affairs, without denying the negative consequences of the disputes (cf. the separation of Paul and Barnabas). Thus

---

particularly clear since Luke makes no mention of the two continuing any sort of evangelisation, and since Cyprus is Barnabas' place of origin.'

23. J. Anneau, 'Concurrent de Jésus?', in *Notre Histoire* 111 (1994): Dossier 'Paul, l'enfant terrible de l'Eglise', pp. 29-35 (30).

Luke's ecumenizing ecclesiology has not eliminated (or would not? or could not?) the differences which were rooted far back in time and which were still alive, although in different forms, towards the end of the first century.

LUKE, DISCIPLE OF THE DEUTERONOMISTIC SCHOOL*

Thomas Römer and Jean-Daniel Macchi

The Deuteronomistic Material

Ever since the publication of Martin Noth's *Überlieferungsgeschichtliche Studien*,[1] the deuteronomistic material has occupied a dominant place in Old Testament research. Noth had tried to show the unified nature of the body of material lying between Deuteronomy and 2 Kings, which, since then, has been called the deuteronomistic historiography. According to Noth, this great historical panorama was the work of a single author, writing in Palestine at a specific historical point in time, during the period of the Exile between 562 and 540 BCE. The theological aim of the writer was to provide an explanation of the tragic end of the Judaean kingdom in the light of Yahweh's history with his people. The exile was then understood as the definitive divine punishment against the people and their leaders for refusing to obey the law of Deuteronomy.

The deuteronomistic redaction is characterized by so-called 'chapters of reflection' which come at the end and at the start of an epoch and which summarize the way in which the Deuteronomist thinks of it. Thus there is the 'Testament of Moses' in Deuteronomy 32 with its introduction in ch. 31; similarly one gets the 'Testament of Joshua' in Joshua 23 with its introduction in 21.43-45. Then there is the introduction to the book of Judges in ch. 2, the 'Testament of Samuel' in 1 Samuel 12 which concludes the era of the judges, Solomon's great speech of the dedication of the Temple in 1 Kings 8, and the explanation of the Fall of

---

* We would like to express our gratitude to Ms A. Champendal for the English translation.

1. M. Noth, *Überlieferungsgeschichtliche Studien: Die sammelnden und bearbeitenden Geschichtswerke im Alten Testament* (Darmstadt: Wissenschaftliche Buchgesellschaft, 3rd edn, 1967); *The Deuteronomistic History* (JSOTSup, 15; Sheffield: JSOT Press, 2nd edn, 1991).

the Northern Kingdom in 2 Kgs 17.7-23. These sections are characterized by similarity in both style and thought.

According to Noth, the editing of the deuteronomistic work took place within a specific historical context. However, subsequent research on the deuteronomistic historiography has quickly altered this view of the matter, ascribing the work to a more extended chronological period. Despite important differences in interpretation and exegetical method which we cannot discuss here, both American[2] and German[3] scholarship has extended the period of the redactional activity of the Deuteronomist to cover the time from the Assyrian era to the Persian era, that is, from the seventh to the fourth century BCE.[4] However, one should go even further and note that deuteronomistic material is not confined to the editing of the books from Deuteronomy to 2 Kings.

Several scholars have pointed out that the so-called Yahwist (J), once considered the first document containing the narrative plot of the Pentateuch, also reflects a theology and a literary style close to that of the deuteronomistic school. Thus the Yahwist appears as a deuteronomist of the second or third generation.[5] In the prophetic literature, the

---

2. F.M. Cross, 'The Themes of the Book of Kings and the Structure of the Deuteronomistic History', in *Canaanite Myth and Hebrew Epic: Essays in the History of the Religion of Israel* (Cambridge, MA: Harvard University Press, 1973), pp. 274-89; R.E. Friedman, *The Exile and Biblical Narrative: The Formation of the Deuteronomistic and Priestly Works* (HSM, 22; Chico, CA: Scholars Press, 1981); R.D. Nelson, *The Double Redaction of the Deuteronomistic History* (JSOTSup, 18; Sheffield: JSOT Press, 1981).

3. R. Smend, *Die Entstehung des Alten Testaments* (ThW, 1; Stuttgart: Kohlhammer, 1978); W. Dietrich, *Prophetie und Geschichte: Eine redaktionsgeschichtliche Untersuchung zum deuteronomistischen Geschichtswerk* (FRLANT, 108; Göttingen: Vandenhoeck & Ruprecht, 1972); cf. also W. Roth, 'Deuteronomistisches Geschichtwerk/Deuteronomistische Schule', *TRE* 8 (1981), pp. 543-52.

4. E. Cortese, 'Theories concerning Dtr: A Possible Rapprochment', in C. Brekelmans and J. Lust (eds.), *Pentateuchal and Deuteronomistic Studies: Papers Read at the XIIIth IOSOT Congress. Leuven 1989* (Leuven: University Press and Peeters, 1990), pp. 179-90; N. Lohfink, 'Kerygmata des deuteronomistischen Geschichtswerks', in J. Jeremias and L. Perlitt (eds.), *Die Botschaft und die Boten* (FS H.W. Wolff; Neukirchen–Vluyn: Neukirchener Verlag, 1981), pp. 87-100 (= N. Lohfink, *Studien zum Deuteronomium und zur deuteronomistischen Literatur*, II [SBAB, 12; Stuttgart: Katholisches Bibelwerk, 1991], pp. 125-42).

5. M. Rose, *Deuteronomist und Jahwist: Untersuchungen zu den Berührungspunkten beider Literaturwerke* (ATANT, 67; Zürich: Theologischer

idea of a deuteronomistic edition of books such as Amos, Hosea and above all Jeremiah is almost universally accepted.[6] Some recent studies have even noted this style in very late prophets such as 'Deutero-Zechariah'.[7] Within the Writings, some psalms presupposing the final form of the Pentateuch (e.g. Ps. 106[8]), as well as the books of Chronicles,[9] clearly adopt a frame of reference inspired by the deuteronomistic ideology. As we shall see, such observations can also be made about texts from literature which is later still.

We see, therefore, that the deuteronomistic school cannot be restricted to a group or a well defined 'movement'; rather, it is a matter of a large current of thought spreading across the whole of Israelite intellectual history from the Assyrian period right up to the first centuries of the Christian era. This phenomenon can be explained by a style and a theology which are both attractive and also easily imitated.

The deuteronomist language has certain 'baroque' features and is characterized by a very stereotyped phraseology. Several scholars have drawn up lists—more or less exhaustive—of the deuteronomistic language.[10] Generally speaking, these formulae are connected with Moses' mediation of the law, a view of the origins of the true Israel based on the Exodus, and an exhortation addressed to the people to obey the divine precepts. Among other things, they serve to set the divine promises of the land or the covenant over against the perpetual disobedience of the

Verlag, 1981); 'La croissance du corpus historiographique de la Bible—Une proposition', *RTP* 118 (1986), pp. 217-36.

6. W.H. Schmidt, 'Die deuteronomistische Redaktion des Amosbuches. Zu den theologischen Unterschieden zwischen dem Prophetenwort und seinem Sammler', *ZAW* 77 (1965), pp. 168-93; W. Thiel, *Die deuteronomistische Redaktion von Jeremia 26–45* (WMANT, 52; Neukirchen–Vluyn: Neukirchener Verlag, 1981).

7. E.g. R.F. Person, *Second Zechariah and the Deuteronomic School* (JSOTSup, 167; Sheffield: JSOT Press, 1993).

8. H.J. Kraus, *Psalmen*, II (BK, XV/2; Neukirchen: Neukirchener Verlag, 1960), p. 728.

9. The situation is more complicated in the case of Chronicles, in that the author knew the books of Samuel and Kings and made a midrash from them. Cf. especially S. Japhet, *I & II Chronicles: A Commentary* (OTL; London: SCM Press, 1993); S.L. McKenzie, *The Chronicler's Use of the Deuteronomistic History* (HSM, 33; Atlanta: Scholars Press, 1984).

10. M. Weinfeld, *Deuteronomy and Deuteronomic School* (Oxford: Clarendon, 1972); W. Thiel, *Redaktion*.

people who are hardened, stiff-necked, and so on, but who are constantly warned by the prophets, the 'servants of Yahweh'.

Deuteronomist Ideology in the Christian Era

In view of what has been said above, it is not at all surprising that the deuteronomistic style and ideology can be found in still later writings. O.H. Steck[11] has shown that the deuteronomistic motif of the prophets being sent by Yahweh and rejected, even killed, by all the people (2 Kgs 17.13-14; Jer. 7.25-27; Neh. 9.26 etc.) is widely attested in rabbinic literature (*Pes. R.* 138a), in the intertestamental literature (*Jub.* 1.7-26; 2 Esd. 14.27-35), in Paul[12] and in the Synoptic Gospels.

Even the Koran is influenced by deuteronomistic ideas. Sura 5.70-71 says, 'We have taken the covenant of the children of Israel, and we sent to them messengers. Whenever a messenger came to them with what they themselves did not desire, some they accused of mendacity, and some they slew...so they were blind and deaf.'[13]

Luke and Deuteronomistic Influence

One of the authors most influenced by the deuteronomistic style is undoubtedly the evangelist Luke. The fact that he is the only evangelist to supplement his Gospel with a 'historiography' could be the first indication of deuteronomistic influence. Further, it has often been pointed out that it is the programmatic speeches, the so-called 'missionary speeches'[14] addressed to Jews and Gentiles, which give coherence to Luke's work and which enable him to express his major theological ideas through the mouth of one or another character. According to Conzelmann, the writing of Acts can be seen as a reaction to the crisis

---

11. O.H. Steck, *Israel und das gewaltsame Geschick der Propheten* (WMANT, 23; Neukirchen: Neukirchener Verlag, 1967); cf. also M. Barker, *The Older Testament: The Survival of Themes from the Ancient Royal Cult in Sectarian Judaism and Early Christianity* (London: SPCK, 1987).

12. J.M. Scott, 'Paul's Use of Deuteronomic Tradition', *JBL* 112 (1993), pp. 645-65.

13. Translation by M.M. Khatib, *The Bounteous Koran* (London: Macmillan Press, 1986).

14. U. Wilckens, *Die Missionsreden in der Apostelgeschichte: Form- und traditionsgeschichtliche Untersuchungen* (WMANT, 5; Neukirchen: Neukirchener Verlag, 1961).

which the delay of the parousia caused for Christians towards the end of the first century.[15] Even if this theory is today widely disputed, Acts still displays concerns which are similar to those of the deuteronomistic historiography. Like the Deuteronomists, Luke is trying to provide his addressees with a theodicy. The opposition faced by the preachers of the gospel should not discourage Christians: it is foreseen in divine teaching and confirms Israel's obduracy and the necessity of the gospel to move outside Jerusalem. In this connection, a comparison of the end of the two historiographies is extremely interesting.[16] Both 2 Kgs 25 and Acts 28 conclude with an end that is not an end. We find neither a final interpretation of the story, nor a clear happy ending. In both cases we are told what happens to a prisoner, a key figure in the story. These two prisoners obtain a privileged status: Jehoiachin is received at the King of Babylon's table, and Paul is in a position to preach the gospel. Nevertheless, the two remain subject to the control of a foreign power. In Luke, as with the Deuteronomists, we find the same literary strategy: an open ending which can therefore be interpreted in different ways. The reader is thus caught up in a dynamic hermeneutic which compels him or her to take a position in relation to this story.

Stephen's Speech in Acts 7

The parallels which we have outlined above can be confirmed by the Lukan speech which is placed on the lips of Stephen in Acts 7. This text occupies a key position in the understanding of Acts and can be regarded as a pivot. This important speech is inserted at a crucial moment in the history of the Church and is reminiscent of the deuteronomistic technique of marking turning points in Israel's history by great speeches.

Besides the problem of the sources used by the evangelist, many scholars have noted the very well organized structure of the speech. For example there is a development in the narrative which, between its beginning in v. 2a and its conclusion in vv. 51-53, is divided into four parts dealing with Abraham (vv. 2-8), Joseph (vv. 9-16), Moses

---

15. H. Conzelmann, *The Theology of St Luke* (London: Faber & Faber, 1960), pp. 95-97.

16. This comparison has been suggested to us by Professor P. Davies of Sheffield University.

(vv. 17-43) and then the holy place (vv. 44-50).[17] The text can equally well be structured according to the way in which the facts are presented, in one way 'objectively' (vv. 2-34, 44-47), in another way 'polemically' (vv. 35-43, 48-50).[18] However, J. Dupont is certainly right to point out the parallelism between Stephen's speech and the pattern of ancient rhetorical argumentation. The speech opens with a *narratio* (vv. 2-34), enclosed by two theophanies (vv. 2-4, 30-34), and giving a virtually neutral account of past events. This is followed by the *argumentatio* which is much more virulent after the turning point in v. 35. This *argumentatio* is divided into two main parts, one about Moses (vv. 36-43) and one about the temple (vv. 44-50).[19]

In each part within this structure, there are phrases and expressions which are frequently used by the Deuteronomists in the books of the Old Testament.

The oppression of the fathers in Egypt, mentioned in Acts 7.19, is a constantly recurring theme in the deuteronomistic credos (cf. Num. 20.15; Deut. 26.6 etc.). Then again, the image of the signs and wonders performed by Yahweh during the Exodus (Acts 7.36) is one of the most common in the deuteronomistic literature (Deut. 4.34; 6.22; 26.8; Jer. 32.21 and several other instances). We can, for example, compare Acts 7.36 ('He led them out of Egypt having performed signs and wonders in the land of Egypt') with Deut. 6.21-22 ('and the Lord brought us out of Egypt with a mighty hand; the Lord showed signs and wonders, great and grievous, upon Egypt').[20]

The disobedience of the people and their 'stiff-neck' (Acts 7.39, 51) is

---

17. J. Kilgallen, *The Stephen Speech: A Literary and Redactional Study of Acts 7,2-53* (AnBib, 67; Rome: Bibical Institute Press, 1976). Variants of such narrative approaches are mentioned by Dupont (see n. 19 below).

18. See M. Dibelius, 'Die Reden der Apostelgeschichte und die antike Geschichtschreibung', in *Aufsätze zur Apostelgeschichte* (FRLANT, 42; Göttingen: Vandenhoeck & Ruprecht, 1953), pp. 120-62 (ET in *Studies in the Acts of the Apostles* [London: SCM Press, 1956], pp. 138-85).

19. J. Dupont, 'La structure oratoire du discours d'Etienne (Actes 7)', *Bib* 66 (1985), pp. 153-67; this is adopted in part too by S. Légasse, *Stephanos: Histoire et discours d'Etienne dans les Actes des Apôtres* (LD, 147; Paris: Cerf, 1992).

20. Acts 7.36: οὗτος ἐξήγαγεν αὐτοὺς ποιήσας τέρατα καὶ σημεῖα ἐν γῇ Αἰγύπτῳ καὶ ἐν Ἐρυθρᾷ θαλάσσῃ καὶ ἐν τῇ ἐρήμῳ ἔτη τεσσεράκοντα. Deut. 6.21-22 (LXX): καὶ ἐξήγαγεν ἡμᾶς κύριος ἐκεῖθεν ἐν χειρὶ κραταιᾷ καὶ ἐν βραχίονι ὑψηλῷ. 22. καὶ ἔδωκεν κύριος σημεῖα καὶ τέρατα μεγάλα ἐν Αἰγύπτῳ ἐν Φαραω καὶ ἐν τῷ οἴκῳ αὐτοῦ ἐνώπιον ἡμῶν.

a cliche in the Deuteronomists' interpretation of the history of Israel (cf. Deut. 9.12; 2 Kgs 17.14 etc.).

In the structure outlined above, the *narratio* (vv. 2-34) and the *argumentatio* (vv. 35-50) are linked by the figure of Moses, whose life in Egypt in the wilderness is divided into three periods of 40 years (Acts 7.23, 30, 36). The third period is the time in the wilderness with the disobedience of the first generation (cf. Acts 7.42). This idea is clearly a direct reflection of deuteronomistic theology (cf. Deut. 1.3; 8.2; 31.2 etc.).[21]

Steck has shown how the deuteronomistic concept of prophecy survived into the Christian era, and this too is clearly present in Acts 7. Moses is the first of a long series of witnesses (Acts 7.37 citing Deut. 18.15) whom God has sent to his people to call them to repent. But each time these prophets have been rejected (Acts 7.52; cf. 2 Kgs 17.13; Jer. 7.25-26; 25.4 etc.). This idea is also reflected in Luke's Christology, where Jesus is the last of the series of the prophets. Already announced by Moses (Acts 7.37), he was rejected by Israel, like his predecessors (cf. Acts 7.52), but has been vindicated by God who raised him from the dead. This final rejection of God's messenger is clearly placed in parallel with the non-observance of the Mosaic Law (vv. 52-53).

Luke and the Fathers

Luke is the only New Testament author who uses the deuteronomistic expression 'God of the fathers'.[22] We find it in Acts 3.13; 5.30; 7.32; 22.14. Elsewhere it occurs 11 times in the book of Deuteronomy, and comes most frequently in the books of Chronicles (26 times).

Luke uses this phrase for God only in speeches addressed to Jews.[23] In this way he tries to show continuity in history, but at the same time discontinuity: the God of the Christians is the same as the God of the Exodus. This is particularly clear in Acts 5.30: 'The God of *our* fathers raised Jesus, whom *you* killed by hanging him on a tree'.

In Acts 7, Luke only speaks of the God of the fathers in citing

---

21. J.A. Thompson, *Deuteronomy* (TOTC, 5; Downers Grove: Inter-Varsity Press, 1974), p. 290.
22. Except Mk 12.8, quoting Exod. 3.6.
23. For the difference between speeches addressed to Jews and those addressed to Gentiles, see Wilckens, *Die Missionsreden*.

Exod. 3.6 (Acts 7.32). On the other hand, he often refers to 'the fathers', which is one of the most characteristic features of the deuteronomistic literature.[24] The frequent use of 'fathers' (Acts 7.2, 11, 12, 15, 19, 32, 38, 39, 44, 51, 52—i.e. 12 times[25]) can be paralleled with several deuteronomistic texts. But the range of semantic meaning of the word within the same text reminds us of another speech with a rhetorical structure of a *narratio* and an *argumentatio*, viz. Joshua 24. Indeed Acts 7 could have been largely inspired by Joshua 24, a speech which is post-exilic—probably Hellenistic—and provides the conclusion to a presumed Hexateuch,[26] and which clearly derives a great deal from a deuteronomistic heritage. As in Joshua 24 and other deuteronomistic historical summaries, Stephen's speech develops at length the history of the origins of the people up to the time of Joshua (7.45). Curiously, nothing is said in Acts 7 of the era of the Judges, and David and Solomon are only mentioned briefly in relation to the building of the temple.

A comparison with Joshua 24 may also explain the stress in Acts 7.16 on Shechem. The double mention of Shechem, linked to the idea that the 12 patriarchs were buried there, has been a puzzle for exegetes. Some have thought that this verse might reflect a Samaritan tradition.[27] Moreover, it seems to us that this verse can very well be explained in the light of Joshua 24. As Blum has shown, the speech of Joshua 24 can

---

24. T. Römer, *Israels Väter: Untersuchungen zur Väterthematik im Deuteronomium und in der deuteronomistischen Tradition* (OBO, 99; Freiburg [CH]: Universitätsverlag; Göttingen: Vandenhoeck & Ruprecht, 1990); cf. also 'Le Deutéronome à la quête des origines', in F. Haudebert (ed.), *Le Pentateuque: Débats et Recherches* (LD, 151; Paris: Cerf, 1992), pp. 65-98.

25. 'Father' in the singular occurs three times, referring to Abraham (v. 2), Terah (v. 4) and Jacob (v. 14).

26. Cf. J. L'Hour, 'L'Alliance de Sichem', *RB* 69 (1952), pp. 5-36, 166-84, 350-68; M. Anbar, *Josué et l'alliance de Sichem (Josué 24.1-28)* (BET, 25; Frankfurt am Main: Peter Lang, 1992); J. Van Seters, 'Joshua 24 and the Problem of Tradition in the Old Testament', in W.B. Barrick and J.R. Spencer (eds.), *In the Shelter of Elyon* (FS G.W. Ahlström; JSOTSup, 31; Sheffield: JSOT Press, 1984), pp. 139-58; C. Levin, *Die Verheissung des neuen Bundes in ihrem theologiegeschichtlichen Zusammenhang ausgelegt* (FRLANT, 137; Göttingen; Vandenhoeck & Ruprecht, 1985), p. 114-15; U. Becker, *Richterzeit und Königtum: Redaktionsgeschichtliche Studien zum Richterbuch* (BZAW, 192; Berlin: de Gruyter, 1990), pp. 69-70.

27. As cited by Légasse, *Stephanos*.

be understood as an appeal for the conversion of 'protosamaritans',[28] urging them to give up the worship practised by their fathers (Josh. 24.14) and to devote themselves to the true worship of Yahweh, the God of the Exodus. Similarly, Acts 7 brings about a break in the worship of the God of Israel, by dissociating from the behaviour of the fathers (Acts 7.51-52).[29]

Let us return to the 'fathers'. Acts 7 uses the word in the same way as Joshua 24. First there is Abraham, who is called 'father' like his ancestors (Josh. 24.23; Acts 7.2-4). On the other hand, nowhere in these two texts is this title given to Isaac or Jacob.[30] The term 'fathers' begins to be used more generally when the action is taking place in Egypt (Josh. 24.6ff.; Acts 7.11ff.). We are then fully into deuteronomistic terminology where the 'fathers' are the generation in Egypt (Acts 7.15; Josh. 24.26), the generation of the Exodus (Acts 7.36; Josh. 24.7), the generation of the revelation of the Law (Acts 7.38) and of the conquest (Acts 7.45).[31] In both texts there is a break between the ideal father, Abraham, and the more ambiguous fathers from the Exodus onwards. Basing himself on this line of fathers, who saw the miracles of Yahweh but nevertheless were not obedient (Acts 7.39), Luke can trace a line of constant refusal to hear the divine word as announced by Moses, the first prophet, right up to the murder of the last of God's messengers, Jesus. It is this murder which splits apart the common history of the Jews and the Christians. Thus at the end of the speech, 'our fathers'

---

28. E. Blum, *Die Komposition der Vätergeschichte* (WMANT, 57; Neukirchen–Vluyn: Neukirchener Verlag, 1984). Concerning the Samaritan schism, see J.D. Macchi, *Histoire d'une légende* (Le Monde de la Bible, 30; Geneva: Labor & Fides, 1994).

29. The idea that the tomb of the twelve patriarchs was in Shechem can be explained by a midrashic process. Since the Old Testament says nothing about what happened to the 12 patriarchs after their deaths (except in the case of Joseph), it is scarcely surprising that their tomb was located at the same place as that of their father and their brother.

30. In Acts 7.14 Jacob is called the 'father of Joseph', but this occurs in a context where no 'genealogical' link is made with the addressees of the speech. Cf. on the other hand Acts 7.2.

31. For the first Deuteronomists, the *'ābôt* are never the the patriarchs but either the Exodus generation or later ones. Cf. J. Van Seters, 'Confessional Reformulation in the Exilic Period', *VT* 22 (1972), pp. 448-59; *Prologue to History: The Yahwist as Historian in Genesis* (Louisville: Westminster/John Knox, 1992), pp. 227-45; Römer, *Israels Väter*.

(Acts 7.38, 39, 44, 45) become a reality distinct from 'your fathers' (Acts 7.51-52).

Acts 7 presents a good example of the influence of the deuteronomistic ideology at the time of the first Christians. Luke has often been regarded as the evangelist most strongly influenced by Hellenism. Our enquiry shows that he is also an heir of the deuteronomistic theology, certainly effective, but in some ways equally debatable.

WHY DID PAUL GET HIS HAIR CUT? (ACTS 18.18; 21.23-24)

Roger Tomes

In the Acts of the Apostles there are two references to cutting the hair or shaving the head in a religious context. In Acts 18.18 we read,

> After staying on [at Corinth] for a considerable time, Paul took leave of the brethren and sailed for Syria, accompanied by Priscilla and Aquila. He had had his hair cut[1] in Cenchreae, for he had taken a vow.

In Acts 21.23-24 James and the elders at Jerusalem suggest to Paul that he should take steps to allay the suspicions of the Jewish Christians.

> So do what we tell you. We have four men who have taken a vow ἐφ' ἑαυτῶν, upon themselves, or ἀφ' ἑαυτῶν, on their own initiative. Take them and purify yourself with them, and pay the expenses on their behalf, so that they may shave their heads.[2] Everyone will then know that there is nothing in what they have been told about you, but that you are observant and yourself keep the law.

Both passages raise a number of questions.

About 18.18 we have to ask, (1) Who had his hair cut? (2) Was the vow a Nazirite vow? (3) Was the hair cut when the vow was taken or when it was completed? (4) What was the significance of the cutting of the hair? (5) What may the motivation for the vow have been? (6) Why should Luke mention it?

About 21.23-24 we have to ask, (1) Was the vow a Nazirite vow? (2) What were the expenses Paul was asked to meet? (3) Why did he need to purify himself? (4) What purification rites did Paul and the others go through?

About both passages we need to ask, (1) Did Luke understand the customs he was alluding to? (2) Is it credible that Paul should have acted in these ways?

---

1. κειράμενος, aorist middle from κείρω.
2. ξυρήσονται, future middle, or ξυρήσωνται, aorist subjunctive middle from ξυρέω.

Acts 18.18

(1) Who had his hair cut? Here it is simply necessary to note that it is grammatically possible that Aquila is the antecedent to the participle κειράμενος. One Old Latin MS (h) takes it in this way (...*Aquila, qui votum cum fecisset*...). But Aquila is mentioned with Priscilla, and it would be slightly odd to add a clause which referred to only one of them. And so the Vulgate makes the words refer to both, ignoring the fact that the Greek participle is singular (*qui sibi totonderant in Cencris caput, habebant enim votum*). According to Ramsay, 'the natural emphasis marks Paul as the subject here',[3] and in Haenchen's opinion[4] there is not sufficient interest in Aquila for Luke to have mentioned his vow. We may take it that Paul is the subject here.

(2) Was the vow a Nazirite vow? It is generally assumed that it was, since this is the only kind of Jewish vow in which cutting the hair played any part. What would be envisaged here would not be the permanent Nazirite, who was not supposed to have his hair cut at all,[5] but the temporary Nazirite vow, the regulations for which are given in Num. 6.1-21. When the vow is completed,

> the Nazirite shall shave his consecrated head at the entrance to the Tent of Meeting, and shall take the hair of his consecrated head and shall put it on the fire underneath the peace offering (NRSV 'the sacrifice of well-being'; REB 'the shared offering')' (Num. 6.18 RSV).

There are, however, some difficulties about identifying the vow as a Nazirite vow. The law makes provision only for the hair to be disposed of in connection with a sacrifice 'at the entrance to the Tent of Meeting', in effect in the court of the Temple. According to the Mishnah, the Nazirites' Chamber was 'in the south-east corner of the Court of Women. There Nazirites boiled their peace offerings and threw their hair into the fire.'[6] While it was permissible to cut the hair anywhere in Jerusalem, it still had to be disposed of in connection with the

---

3. W.M. Ramsay, *St Paul the Traveller and Roman Citizen* (London: Hodder & Stoughton, 1895), p. 263.
4. E. Haenchen, *The Acts of the Apostles* (Oxford: Blackwell, 1971), p. 542 n. 4.
5. Samson (Judg. 13.5); Samuel (1 Sam. 1.11); James the Lord's brother (Eusebius, *HE* 2.23.4).
6. *M. Mid.* 2.5.

sacrifice in the Temple.[7] Hence the Nazirate might properly be practised only in the Land of Israel. Those who took Nazirite vows abroad had to return to the Land of Israel and live as Nazirites for the length of time they had vowed, or thirty days if the vow's duration had not been specified.[8] That this was current practice in the late Second Temple Period seems to be borne out by Josephus's account of Bernice

> visiting Jerusalem to discharge a vow to God, for it is customary for those suffering from illness or other affliction to make a vow to abstain from wine and to shave their heads during the thirty days preceding that on which they must offer sacrifices.[9]

Maimonides, in his classification of the rabbinic understanding of the Nazirite vows, adds that, while they were abroad, they had to observe all the conditions of the vow—not to drink wine, not to defile themselves by contact with the dead, and not to cut their hair—even though that time did not count towards its fulfilment.[10] It is therefore not easy to see how Paul could have completed a Nazirite vow by having his hair cut in Cenchreae.

(3) Was the hair cut when the vow was taken rather than when it was completed? The Western text (D H L P Ψ 383 614 *gig*, etc.) has an insertion which, if it were original, might suggest that Paul intended to visit Jerusalem for the express purpose of completing the vow. Before the words, 'I will return to you if God wills', Paul is made to say, 'I must at all costs keep the approaching festival in Jerusalem'. However, it is generally held that this is not part of the original text but a reviser's attempt to ease the difficulty about the vow.[11] Without relying on this textual evidence Kirsopp Lake suggested 'the possibility that just as in the Greek church a monk's hair is cut when he takes the vow, and is then never cut again, so a Nazirite cut his hair before beginning his vow'.[12] He had to admit, however, that he had 'no evidence that this custom of preliminary hair-cutting was a Jewish custom'. Conzelmann

7. *B. Naz.* 45a and b.
8. *M. Naz.* 3.6.
9. *War* 2.313.
10. *Mishneh Torah: Sefer Hafla'ah, Nezirut* 2.21-22.
11. B.M. Metzger, *A Textual Commentary on the Greek New Testament* (London: United Bible Societies, 1975), p. 465; W.A. Strange, *The Problem of the Text of Acts* (SNTSMS, 71; Cambridge: Cambridge University Press, 1992), pp. 47, 163.
12. *The Beginnings of Christianity* (London: Macmillan, 1920–33), IV, p. 230.

was surely right to hold that Luke thinks of the cutting of the hair as an element of the vow itself.[13] It is difficult to see what point there would be in reporting the preliminary to a vow rather than the completion of it.

(4) What was the significance of the cutting of the hair? This is not explained in Numbers 6, but it takes place in the context of the offering of a number of sacrifices. The Nazirite has to offer a male lamb as a burnt offering, a ewe lamb as a sin offering, and a ram as a peace offering (or offering of well-being) plus a cereal offering and a libation (Num. 6.14-15). Although the hair is not burnt on the altar of burnt offering but in the fire underneath the pot in which the peace offering is being boiled, it is probably intended as a kind of sacrifice. In the Mishnah the verb *galleah*, 'to cut the hair', is used to cover all the sacrifices which the Nazirite brings on the completion of his vow when he cuts off and burns his hair.[14] This again suggests that the cutting and burning of the hair is a sacrificial act. On the other hand, a Nazirite who contracts defilement through contact with a corpse also has to cut his hair because his consecrated head has become defiled and his vow has become null and void (Num. 6.9, 12). The Bible does not say what should be done with the hair in this event, but the Mishnah says that it is not thrown under the pot[15] and must be buried.[16] In this case it is not suitable as a sacrifice. Maimonides says that, if it is burnt, no use may be made of the ashes.[17] The burning is simply its destruction. Therefore the burning may not have positive sacrificial significance even in the rites at the completion of the Nazirate.

Since, however, the cutting of the hair in Acts 18.18 was not undertaken in the context of sacrifices in the Temple in Jerusalem, and there is no indication that it was carried out as the result of contracting defilement, we must consider the possibility that it had sacrificial significance in its own right. There is widespread evidence for the use of hair in offerings to deities. Much of it was assembled by Robertson Smith in *The Religion of the Semites*. Sometimes it was used in initiation rites. Thus Lucian says that 'young men and maidens in Syria cut off their flowing tresses and deposited them in caskets of gold and silver in the

13. *Acts* (Hermeneia; Philadelphia: Fortress Press, 1987), p. 155.
14. H. Danby, *The Mishnah* (London: Oxford University Press, 1933), p. 282 n. 4.
15. *M. Naz.* 6.8.
16. *M. Tem.* 7.4.
17. *Mishneh Torah: Sefer Hafla'ah, Nezirut* 6.14.

temples'.[18] But it was also used 'in connection with special vows and special acts of devotion, by which a worshipper seeks to knit more closely the bond between himself and his god'.[19] In Homer, 'the hair of Achilles was dedicated to the river-god Spercheus, in whose honour it was to be shorn on his safe return from Troy'.[20] The inscription on a ninth-century BCE bowl from a Cypriot temple is also cited in more recent discussions: it indicates that the bowl contained the hair of the worshipper, in connection with a petition to Astarte, which the goddess had heard.[21] The offering of hair was appropriate because it was regarded as 'a living and important part of the body' and less offensive than the offering of one's own blood.[22] It may be noted, however, that in the two instances quoted the hair is accompanied by other sacrifices.

(5) What may the motivation for the vow have been? Howard Marshall suggests that the vow may have been made either in thankfulness for past blessings (such as being kept safe in Corinth[23]) or as part of a petition for future blessings (such as safekeeping on the impending journey).[24] The vow might be taken conditionally or unconditionally. The Nazirite might vow to abstain from wine, avoid contact with the dead, and refrain from cutting his hair for a specified period after the prayer was answered or the benefit received. This seems to be implied in the passage from Josephus already quoted: 'it is customary for those suffering from illness or other affliction to make a vow to abstain from wine and to shave their heads during the thirty days preceding that on which they must offer sacrifices'.[25] But the Mishnah deals with cases in which a person might vow, 'I will be a Nazirite if a son is born to me', that is, a Nazirite 'in duty bound', and also with cases in which a person might vow to be a Nazirite 'of free choice', that is, without laying down a

---

18. W.R. Smith, *Religion of the Semites* (London: A. & C. Black, 3rd edn, 1927), p. 325; Lucian, *De dea syria* 60.
19. *Semites*, p. 326.
20. *Semites*, p. 325; *Iliad* 23.144ff.
21. B.A. Levine, *Numbers* (AB, 4; New York: Doubleday, 1993), pp. 233-34; J. Milgrom, *Numbers* (JPS Torah Commentary; Philadelphia: Jewish Publication Society, 1990), p. 356; idem, 'Nazirite', *EncJud*, XII, col. 908.
22. *Semites*, pp. 324, 334.
23. Cf. F.F. Bruce, *The Book of the Acts* (NICNT; Grand Rapids: Eerdmans, rev. edn, 1988), p. 355.
24. I.H. Marshall, *Acts* (TNTC; Leicester: Inter-Varsity Press, 1980), p. 300.
25. *War* 2.313.

condition.[26] Certain Nazirites 'who had completed their days', to whom the Maccabees appealed to help them against Antiochus Epiphanes (1 Macc. 3.49), could well have been people who had taken the vow unconditionally as an act of consecration. If Paul's vow was taken conditionally, and the cutting of the hair marked the completion of the vow, it would have to be related to prayers already answered. It could only relate to future benefits if the cutting of the hair was a preliminary to embarking on the vow. But there is always a possibility that the vow was taken unconditionally, as an act symbolic of personal consecration.

(6) Why should Luke mention it? Origen cites the passage as evidence that Paul observed Jewish customs, along with the reference to the circumcision of Timothy (Acts 16.3) and the incident in Jerusalem which we are to consider later.[27] Modern commentators agree.[28] If it could be assumed that in 21.23-26 Paul was completing this vow, which had only been undertaken or completed in a preliminary way in Cenchreae, that would give the mention here added weight. But that would be a doubtful assumption. As we have seen, it is likely that the cutting of the hair in Cenchreae is intended to signify completion. If Paul had intended to complete the vow in Jerusalem, the obvious time to have done so would have been on the visit to Palestine which immediately follows (18.22). (Incidentally, it is not clear whether Paul went to Jerusalem on this occasion: the NRSV has inserted the words 'to Jerusalem', which are not in the text.) In the references to Paul's intention to make the fateful visit to Jerusalem (20.16, 22; 21.13) there is no mention of completing the vow as a motive. And the suggestion that Paul should join others in completing their vows (21.23-24) comes from others and not from him.

The view that Luke is illustrating Paul's fidelity to the law should perhaps not go unquestioned. As we have seen, it is not clear that he was observing the law at all strictly. But since making vows that included an offering of hair was a more general custom in the ancient world, it may be that Luke wishes to present Paul to *Gentile* readers as a pious man.

---

26. *M. Naz.* 2.7-10.
27. *Comm. in Ioh.* 10.30; 13.111; *Comm. in Mat.* 11.8.
28. E.g. Haenchen, *Acts*, p. 543: 'One of the traits with which Luke illustrates the fidelity of Paul's piety to the law'; Conzelmann, *Acts*, p. 155: 'This indicates his faithful fulfilling of the Jewish prescription'. Cf. C.S.C. Williams, *A Commentary on the Acts of the Apostles* (London: A. & C. Black, 1957), p. 214; J. Munck, *The Acts of the Apostles* (AB, 31; New York: Doubleday, 1967), p. 180.

Acts 21.23-24

(1) Were the vows Nazirite vows? The fact that the four men were waiting to complete their vows in the temple, and that completion entailed the shaving of their heads, makes this virtually certain.

(2) What were the expenses Paul was asked to meet? The expense was essentially the cost of the sacrifices: three animals plus cereal offerings and libations. Although the verb *galleah*, 'to cut the hair', is used in the Mishnah for the whole group of sacrifices that had to be made, the NRSV translation, 'pay for the shaving of their heads', obscures the fact that more than a haircut had to be paid for. RSV, 'pay their expenses, so that they may shave their heads', was more accurate. Or we might follow Danby in his rendering of the equivalent expression in the Mishnah and translate, 'Pay their expenses, so that they may bring their hair-offering'. It was not unknown for Nazirites not to be able to afford these sacrifices which were needed to discharge them from their vows. They might have taken the vows without counting the cost. Or their circumstances might have changed: for example, the animals they had assigned for the sacrifices might have been stolen.[29] Therefore provision was made for others to pay for the sacrifices on their behalf. A person might vow to be a Nazirite himself and to 'cut the hair' or 'bring the hair-offering' of another Nazirite.[30] Or a person who was not a Nazirite at all might pay a Nazirite's expenses as a charitable act. The story is told of R. Simeon b. Shetah tricking Alexander Jannaeus (103–76 BCE) into paying for a large number of them.

> At the time of R. Simeon b. Shetah 300 Nazirites came to Jerusalem. In the case of 150 he found a reason for annulling their vows, but in the case of the others he found none. He went to his brother-in-law King Jannai and said to him, 'There are 300 Nazirites who need 900 sacrificial animals; you give one half, and I will give the other half'. So the king sent 450 animals.[31]

Josephus relates that when Agrippa came to Jerusalem he 'arranged for a very considerable number of Nazirites to be shorn'.[32] Other rabbinic

---

29. *M. Naz.* 5.4.
30. *M. Naz.* 2.5-6; *b. Naz.* 12b.
31. *Y. Ber.* 11b.
32. *Ant.* 19.294.

sources indicate that sometimes the community might bear the cost.[33] The background to the suggestion that Paul should assist these Jewish Christians is thus clear.

(3) Why did he need to purify himself? This is less clear. He could hardly undertake a new Nazirite vow himself in the seven days mentioned in v. 27. The minimum period was thirty days.[34] The same would apply if he was completing a vow undertaken abroad. On returning to the Land of Israel, according to the school of Shammai, he would need to continue as a Nazirite for another thirty days; according to the school of Hillel, he would need to begin the vow over again.[35] It has been suggested that anyone returning to the Land of Israel would be assumed to have incurred ritual defilement, and would therefore have to undergo the seven-day purification from levitical impurity before entering the temple, which would entail being sprinkled with 'the water for cleansing' on the third and seventh days (Num. 19.12; 31.19, 24). This would explain the seven-day period, but there is no evidence that those returning from abroad did have to undergo such purification, and Luke tells us that Paul purified himself immediately and went to the temple the next day, to give notice when the Nazirites' sacrifices would be offered (21.26). This would suggest the minor one-day purification prescribed after an emission of semen (Lev. 15.16; 23.10-11).

(4) What purification rites did Paul and the others go through? The completion of a Nazirite vow would not normally be described as purification. Therefore it has been suggested that the four men were 'contaminated Nazirites',[36] that they had contracted ritual defilement through contact with a dead body. In such circumstances they would have to go through a seven-day purification period; at the end of it they would have to shave their heads, and they would have to offer sacrifices: 'two turtledoves or two young pigeons', one as a sin offering and the other as a burnt offering, and a male lamb as a guilt offering. Then they would have to begin their Nazirate over again (Num. 6.9-12). While this explanation would account for the mention of the seven-day period and

---

33. *B. Tem.* 10a; *Sipre Zut.* on Num. 6.13 (ed. H.S. Horovitz, *Siphre ad Numeros adjecto Siphre zutta* [Leipzig: G. Fock, 1917; repr. Jerusalem: Wahrmann, 1966], p. 244); *y. Naz.* 5.3.

34. *Sipre Num.* §22 on Num. 6.2 (Horovitz edn, p. 26); Josephus, *War* 2.313; *m. Naz.* 3.1.

35. *M. Naz.* 3.6.

36. Milgrom, *Numbers*, p. 358.

the offering of sacrifice, the reason for paying their expenses would be weakened, since the sacrifices were less costly. It is also strange that the defilement should not be explicitly mentioned. As for Paul, one would have to assume that he could share in the rite though he had not shared in the defilement.

Paul is made to refer to these events in his address to Felix in 24.17-18:

> After a number of years I returned to my people to give alms and to offer sacrifices, during which they found me in the temple purifying myself.

This does not make any clearer what the reason for the purification was or what rites were involved. It merely suggests that Paul intended to offer sacrifices on his own account, as well as to pay the expenses of the Nazirites.

Conclusions

(1) We have found it difficult to equate the customs and rituals Luke alludes to with what we know from other sources about the Jewish Nazirate. As in the reference to 'their purification according to the law of Moses' in the narrative of the birth of Jesus (Lk. 2.22-24), Luke appears to conflate the rules about the redemption of the first-born and purification after childbirth, so in these passages in Acts he seems to refer to various customs without distinguishing clearly between them. The vow in 18.18 is reminiscent of a Nazirite vow in the mention of the cutting of the hair, but it ignores the requirement that such a vow cannot be completed anywhere else but in the Temple in Jerusalem. At first sight the vows in 21.23-24 seem to be Nazirite vows due for completion, but references to a seven-day period of purification are more appropriate to a vow which has become null and void through contamination. There are analogies for Paul's role in paying the expenses, but not for his joining in the purification. Unless Luke knew of variations in the customs of which we are ignorant, we may conclude that his knowledge of them was somewhat limited.

(2) It is accepted almost without question nowadays that Luke's portrait of Paul need not be compatible with the picture of Paul we construct from his letters. Those who stress his hostility to the circumcision party find it incredible that he should make such concessions to Jewish law and custom. Howard Marshall quotes Adolf Hausrath as saying apropos of Acts 21.23-24, 'It would be more credible that the dying Calvin would have bequeathed a golden dress to the mother of God

than that Paul should have entered upon this action'.[37] But it may be that Paul was not so scrupulously Protestant as that. He may indeed have made and fulfilled a vow in Greece, as part of his policy of becoming as one outside the law to those outside the law (1 Cor. 9.21); and he may have complied with the request of the elders in Jerusalem, because he did not wish to put a hindrance in the way of another (Rom. 14.13).

37. Marshall, *Acts*, p. 346, quoting A. Hausrath, *A History of the New Testament Times: The Time of the Apostles* (London: Williams & Norgate, 1895), IV, p. 112.

The Lukan Son of Man

Christopher Tuckett

Scholarly interest in the Lukan writings remains as intense as ever. So too discussions of the 'Son of Man' (= SM) continue to appear at an ever increasing rate. What is perhaps at first sight surprising is that the two spheres of interest have not often coalesced. In terms of 'the SM problem', the 'problem' has frequently been thought to lie at the level of determining what the phrase 'SM' might have meant in the earliest levels of the tradition, supremely on the lips of Jesus himself. What the term might have meant for each of the evangelists has often been regarded as something of a means to an end, in order to reach the true goal of interpreting the phrase at the level of the historical Jesus. On other occasions interest is shown in the use of the term SM by the earliest sources Mark and Q, perhaps more especially Q, since for Q 'SM' appears to have been one of the few Christological 'titles' explicitly used. However, the meaning of the phrase 'SM' for the later synoptic evangelists, Matthew and Luke, is less often discussed. And of these two, Luke has probably suffered more neglect than Matthew. Thus, for example, F. Bovon in an essay surveying 25 years' scholarship devoted to Luke's Christology over the quarter-century 1950–1975, gave only half a page out of 81 pages explicitly to discussions of the term SM in Luke;[1] similarly, in M. de Jonge's recent survey of the Christologies of the New Testament writers, only half a page out of 15 in the chapter on 'The Christology of Luke–Acts' is devoted to Luke's use of 'SM'.[2] And in a recent article discussing the Q text Q 12.8,[3] and the question of

---

1. F. Bovon, *Luc le théologien: Vingt-cinq ans de recherches (1950–1975)* (Neuchâtel: Delachaux & Niestlé, 1978), pp. 119-210 (195).
2. M. de Jonge, *Christology in Context: The Earliest Christian Response to Jesus* (Philadelphia: Westminster Press, 1988), pp. 97-111. 'SM' is treated briefly on p. 107.
3. Following the convention of using the Lukan chapter and verse numbers to refer to Q passages.

whether Luke's use of 'SM' here might be due to Lukan redaction (= LkR), P. Hoffmann argued his case almost exclusively in dialogue with Conzelmann's work on Luke, first published in 1954, and Tödt's work on the SM, published in 1959.[4] G. Schneider published an article on the topic of Luke's use of the phrase in the 1975 Vögtle Festschrift,[5] and chapters on Luke's use of 'SM' have appeared in the more wide-ranging books on the SM problem such as those by Lindars, Müller, Hare and others.[6] Generally, however, discussions of any possible specifically Lukan view of 'SM' have only been offered in passing. Commentaries seem just as concerned, if not more concerned, to deal with what are evidently regarded as the more interesting issues of the authenticity of the SM sayings as with any specifically Lukan view.[7] Individual verses (for example Lk. 22.69, above all Acts 7.56) have aroused much detailed discussion. Nevertheless, systematic analyses of 'the Lukan SM' have not been noted for their quantity.[8]

There may well be some good reasons for this apparent neglect. The

4. P. Hoffmann, 'Jesus versus Menschensohn. Mt. 10,32-33 und die synoptische Menschensohnüberlieferung', in L. Oberlinner and P. Fiedler (eds.), *Salz der Erde—Licht der Welt: Exegetische Studien zum Matthäusevangelium* (FS A.Vögtle; Stuttgart: Katholisches Bibelwerk, 1991), pp. 165-202; cf. H. Conzelmann, *The Theology of Saint Luke* (ET; London: Faber & Faber, 1960); H.E. Tödt, *Der Menschensohn in der synoptischen Tradition* (Gütersloh, 1959), ET *The Son of Man in the Synoptic Tradition* (London: SCM Press, 1965). References are to the English version unless otherwise stated.

5. G. Schneider, '"Der Menschensohn" in der lukanischen Christologie', in R. Pesch and R. Schnackenburg (eds.), *Jesus und der Menschensohn* (FS A. Vögtle; Freiburg: Herder, 1975), pp. 267-82.

6. B. Lindars, *Jesus, Son of Man* (London: SPCK, 1983); M. Müller, *Der Ausdruck 'Menschensohn' in den Evangelien* (Leiden: Brill, 1984); D.R.A. Hare, *The Son of Man Tradition* (Minneapolis: Fortress Press, 1990).

7. Cf. the commentary of J.A. Fitzmyer, *The Gospel according to Luke* (2 vols.; New York: Doubleday, 1981, 1985). Fitzmyer's section in his Introduction dealing with 'Lukan Christology' (pp. 208-11) is for the most part devoted to the problem of what the phrase meant on the lips of Jesus. Only two final paragraphs deal with the question of Luke's own understanding. Cf. too I.H. Marshall's *The Gospel of Luke* (Exeter: Paternoster, 1978), which discusses the term on its first occurrence in Luke (at 5.24) on pp. 215-16, but again primarily to discuss the question of historicity.

8. A search through the entry under 'Son of Man' in F. van Segbroek, *The Gospel of Luke: A Cumulative Bibliography 1973–1988* (BETL, 88; Leuven: Leuven University Press and Peeters, 1989), produced no more bibliographical material.

whole question of whether a titular approach to Christology is appropriate at all has been debated in recent years.[9] In particular, it may well be that Lukan Christology is less susceptible than some to such an approach,[10] bearing in mind too Luke's possible tendency to blur the distinction between some of the Christological titles.[11] Nevertheless the use of significant words or phrases (i.e. 'titles' in some sense) by a writer to refer to Jesus provides one possible access to that writer's Christology and hence such an approach may still have some value. In what follows, therefore, I look at Luke's use of the term 'SM' in his Gospel and in Acts, to see what it may tell us about Luke's own views of Jesus, as well as what it may tell us about the ways in which Luke used his sources.[12]

***

I start, as do so many contemporary studies of the Lukan writings, with Conzelmann. Conzelmann claimed:

> The use of 'Son of Man' is largely determined by the source (Mark)... It is not possible to prove anything either for or against a specific 'Son of Man' Christology.

Again,

> It is characteristic of Luke that although he develops a Christology of his own, he is no longer aware of the original peculiarities of titles such as 'Son of Man' etc. He has taken them over from the tradition and interprets them according to his own conceptions... In the main part of the Gospel and Acts the titles which are found most frequently are κύριος and χριστός.[13]

---

9. Cf. L.E. Keck, 'Toward the Renewal of New Testament Christology', *NTS* 32 (1986), pp. 362-77, repr. in M.C. de Boer (ed.), *From Jesus to John: Essays on Jesus and New Testament Christology in Honour of Marinus de Jonge* (JSNTSup, 84; Sheffield: JSOT Press, 1993), pp. 321-40.
10. Bovon, *Luc le théologien*, p. 189
11. G. Nickelsberg, 'Son of Man', *ABD*, VI, p. 146.
12. I assume here the two-document hypothesis without question: hence the sources used by Luke are assumed to be Mark and Q (possibly together with other source material available to Luke alone).
13. Conzelmann, *Theology*, pp. 170 and 171 respectively. Cf. too Fitzmyer, *Luke*, p. 211: 'Since the title was already in the gospel tradition, and Luke's use of it is scarcely distinctive, it is not easy to say just what he would have meant by it'.

This somewhat negative, or even agnostic, evaluation of the Lukan SM, however, is hard to square with all the facts. Luke's Gospel contains no less than 25 uses of the phrase 'SM', to which must be added the famous usage on the lips of Stephen in Acts 7.56, as well as probably Lk. 17.25, where the αὐτόν clearly picks a reference to Jesus as SM (Lk. 17.24). Simply in terms of numbers of occurrences, the phrase would appear to represent one of some importance for Luke.[14]

This is suggested too by the fact that, as far as we can tell, Luke preserves most of the occurrences of 'SM' in his source material: (a) in relation to Q, it is generally assumed that Luke has preserved practically all the uses of 'SM' in Q (cf. Lk. 6.22; 7.34; 9.58; 11.30; 12.8, 10, 40; 17.24, 26, 30).[15] On virtually all the 'standard' reconstructions of Q, there is at most one instance of Luke's deleting a reference to Jesus as SM. (The one instance may be Lk. 22.30 par. Mt. 19.27, where Matthew's version refers to the SM, and Luke's does not. However, the two versions are very different at this point and it is by no means certain what the Q wording was.)[16] (b) In relation to Mark, Luke preserves the vast majority of Markan SM references: cf. Mk 2.10//Lk. 5.24; Mk 2.28//Lk. 6.5; Mk 8.31//Lk. 9.22; Mk 8.38//Lk. 9.26; Mk 9.31//Lk. 9.44; Mk 10.33//Lk. 18.31; Mk 13.26//Lk. 21.27; Mk 14.21//Lk. 22.22; Mk 14.62//Lk. 22.69. There are a few Markan SM sayings which Luke does not have (Mk 9.9, 12; 10.45; 14.21, 41), but in each case the omission by Luke involves considerably more than simply deleting the SM reference.[17] These considerations alone suggest that Luke is

---

14. Cf. P.M. Casey, *Son of Man: The Interpretation and Influence of Daniel 7* (London: SCM Press, 1979), p. 201: 'If Luke used the term "Son of man" no less than twenty five times he felt no need to run away from it'.

15. There is neither time nor space to discuss each of these in detail; see the standard commentaries and discussions of Q such as S. Schulz, *Q—Die Spruchquelle der Evangelisten* (Zürich: TVZ, 1972); J.S. Kloppenborg, *The Formation of Q* (Philadelphia: Fortress Press, 1987), and others.

16. Nevertheless, Matthew's 'SM' is taken as original (i.e. in Q) by Schulz, *Q*, p. 331; A.D. Jacobson, *The First Gospel: An Introduction to Q* (Sonoma, CA: Polebridge Press, 1992), p. 247. The argument of Hoffmann ('Jesus versus Menschensohn') does not change the overall picture: Hoffmann argues that the SM reference in Lk. 12.8 is due to LkR. But even if this were the case, it would still not constitute an example where Luke had deleted a SM reference from Q. It would rather be an instance of Luke's adding a further SM reference to his traditions.

17. Cf. Schneider, 'Der Menschensohn', p. 273 n. 29. In any case Mk 10.45 and 14.41 may reappear in Luke in slightly different guises: see below.

certainly not negatively disposed to the term 'SM'. He appears to accept it very willingly when it appears in his sources and he displays hardly any tendency to replace it with another term. Clearly, in terms of numbers, the 26 or 27 uses of 'SM' do not rival the statistics for the Christological use of κύριος or χριστός in Luke–Acts.[18] Nevertheless, Luke's use of his sources suggests that Luke does have a positive interest in the use of the term 'SM' to refer to Jesus. In this respect, therefore, Tödt's assertion that 'Luke conceives of the Son of Man in a specific way'[19] has some a priori plausibility. What exactly the 'specific way' might be remains to be seen.

This theory grows in strength even more if one accepts the arguments of Schneider (and others) that all the remaining SM sayings in Luke, that is, those not derived from Mark or Q, are due to LkR. There are a number of such sayings (Lk. 17.22; 18.8; 19.10; 21.36; 22.48; 24.7; Acts 7.56) and a strong case can certainly be made for most, if not all, of these being LkR. Schneider has argued this in detail in his article (n. 5 above) in relation to most of the sayings, and others too have come to the same conclusion in relation to the individual sayings. Thus Lk. 17.22 looks very much like a partial anticipation of the language of 17.26, but redacted in line with Luke's own *Tendenz* to emphasize the necessity of the delay of the Parousia.[20] Lk. 18.8 and 21.36 both stress the fact that Jesus as SM will act as judge at the final judgment where all humanity, including Christians, will have to answer for their conduct. Lk. 18.8 looks very much like a secondary, redactional ending to the parable of 18.1-8, matching the almost certainly redactional opening exhortation in v. 1 encouraging persistence in prayer.[21] And Lk. 21.36 has a close

18. Figures for κύριος are uncertain because of doubt at times whether the term is referring to Jesus or to God; χριστός is used 12 times in Luke, 28 times in Acts.

19. Tödt, *Son of Man*, p. 108.

20. Tödt, *Son of Man*, p. 105; R. Schnackenburg, 'Der eschatologische Abschnitt Lk 17,20-37', in *Mélanges Bibliques en hommage au Béda Rigaux* (Gembloux: Duculot, 1970), pp. 213-34, on pp. 219-21; J. Zmijewski, *Die Eschatologiereden des Lukas-Evangeliums* (Bonn: P. Hanstein, 1972), pp. 417-19; Schneider, 'Der Menschensohn', p. 274. Others who disagree often do so on the basis of an almost a priori assumption that Luke does not create SM sayings: thus F. Rehkopf, *Die lukanische Sonderquelle* (WUNT, 5; Tübingen: Mohr, 1959), p. 56 (referring in part to MattR in Mt. 16.13, 21—though it is not at all clear how this relates to Luke!); C. Colpe, 'ὁ υἱὸς τοῦ ἀνθρώπου', *ThWNT*, VIII, p. 453 (also on the assumption that Luke never creates SM sayings).

21. Cf. Schneider, 'Der Menschensohn', p. 277; J.-D. Kaestli, *L'eschatologie*

thematic relationship with 18.8 so that the sections 21.34-36 and 18.1-8 form similarly structured units (opening exhortation—parable—concluding SM saying): hence 21.36 may also be a LkR creation.[22] Lk. 19.10 is in many respects a typically Lukan summary of the activity of Jesus (seeking and saving the lost) and may represent a LkR rewriting of Mk 10.45.[23] Lk. 22.48 may be simply a Lukan artistic rewriting of Mk 14.21,[24] and 24.7 is almost certainly LkR for Mk 16.7, with little evidence for the existence of a separate source.[25] And Acts 7.56 may well be Luke's remodelling of the trial scene of Jesus now applied to Stephen as the prototypical martyr.[26]

dans l'oeuvre de Luc (Geneva: Labor & Fides, 1969), p. 35; Lindars, *Jesus Son of Man*, pp. 136-37. Again, others who deny a redactional origin here do so often on the a priori grounds that Luke does not create SM sayings: cf. Colpe, ὁ υἱὸς τοῦ ἀνθρώπου', p. 437; Marshall, *Luke*, p. 676: 'Since Luke does not create "Son of man" sayings, there is a *prima facie* case that he has not done so here'. Cf. too J. Jeremias, *The Parables of Jesus* (ET; London: SCM Press, 1963), p. 155.

22. Schneider, 'Der Menschensohn', pp. 369-70; Lindars, *Jesus Son of Man*, p. 138. For a detailed argument that the whole of 21.34-36 may be due to LkR, perhaps in dependence on Paul's exhortation in 1 Thess. 5, see L. Aejmelaeus, *Wachen vor dem Ende: Die traditionsgeschichtlichen Wurzeln von 1. Thess 5.1-11 und Luk 21.34-36* (Schriften der Finnischen Exegetischen Gesellschaft, 44; Helsinki: Kirjapaino Raamattutalo, 1985), pp. 99-130; also my 'Synoptic Tradition in 1 Thessalonians?', in R.F. Collins (ed.), *The Thessalonian Correspondence* (BETL, 87; Leuven: Leuven University Press and Peeters, 1990), pp. 160-82, on pp. 173-76.

23. See R. Bultmann, *The History of the Synoptic Tradition* (ET; Oxford: Blackwell, 1968), p. 34; Schneider, 'Der Menschensohn', p. 278-79; Lindars, *Jesus Son of Man*, p. 137. *Contra* Colpe, 'ὁ υἱὸς τοῦ ἀνθρώπου', p. 456 (arguing again that Luke never creates SM sayings), Tödt, *Son of Man*, p. 133 (on the grounds that Luke never creates sayings referring to the present activity of the SM), and Marshall, *Luke*, p. 698 (again on the grounds that Luke does not create SM sayings).

24. Schneider, 'Der Menschensohn', p. 271; Fitzmyer, *Luke*, I, p. 448; M.L. Soards, *The Passion according to Luke* (JSNTSup, 14; Sheffield: JSOT Press, 1987), p. 98; Lindars, *Jesus Son of Man*, p. 133-34.

25. Schneider, 'Der Menschensohn', p. 272; Lindars, *Jesus Son of Man*, p. 134.

26. The origin of this verses is of course much debated. For the redactional origin, see M. Sabbe, 'The Son of Man Saying in Acts 7,56', in J. Kremer (ed.), *Les Actes des Apôtres: Tradition, rédaction, théologie* (BETL, 48; Leuven: Leuven University Press and Duculot, 1979), pp. 241-79, repr. in his *Studia Neotestamentica: Collected Essays* (BETL, 98; Leuven: Leuven University Press and Peeters, 1991), pp. 137-78, including an additional Note (pp. 176-78) with brief discussion of the most recent literature); Schneider was more uncertain at the time of

Clearly any one of these judgments is open to dispute; but even if one or two arguments here are wrong so that one or two of the non-Markan non-Q SM sayings in Luke were due to Luke's special source material, the overall situation would not be significantly altered: the result of the analysis indicates not only that Luke has retained the SM sayings from his sources, but that he has actually added to them by redactionally creating a significant number himself. Hence Luke is not only content to repeat the wording of his source material: he also evidently feels attracted to the language sufficiently to create a number of SM sayings *de novo*. This then suggests very strongly, *contra* Conzelmann, that Luke is not neutral about SM terminology: rather, Luke definitely seeks to promote this terminology positively.

What then of the *contexts* in which SM terminology is used? Do these indicate that Luke has a clear idea of what the phrase 'SM' signifies? As we have seen in part already, a number of different answers have been suggested to this question. For Conzelmann, Luke really has no idea of what SM 'originally' signified. He simply takes it over from his tradition and adapts it in the service of his own Christology.[27] Tödt, on the other hand, sees a clear definite idea reflected in the sayings where 'SM' is used, especially in the sayings to do with the future activity of the SM. According to Tödt, Luke sees Jesus qua SM as the advocate, pleading on behalf of Christians in the divine court; the SM is not, however, the judge himself.[28] Lindars is similar to Conzelmann: according to him, Luke is unaware of the meaning of 'SM' as used by Jesus:[29] rather, Luke is simply aware of the usage in the tradition as a self-designation by Jesus and he therefore adds the phrase in a number of places (e.g. 18.8; 21.36) as part of his literary artistry, but the term itself means very little for him. Hare goes even further along these lines: for Luke the term has virtually no connotative significance at all—it is simply denotative, a self-designation by Jesus but without any significance or overtones of meaning of its own.

---

his 'Menschensohn' article, but seems clearer about the redactional nature of the verse in his commentary, *Die Apostelgeschichte* (Freiburg: Herder, 1980), p. 471; cf. too A. Weiser, *Die Apostelgeschichte* (Gütersloh: Mohn, 1981), p. 193; others mentioned by Sabbe.

27. Conzelmann, *Theology*, pp. 170-71.
28. Tödt, *Son of Man*, p. 109.
29. Cf. *Jesus Son of Man*, p. 143. (For Lindars, the meaning on the lips of Jesus is a limited generic usage whereby 'SM' means 'a person in my position'.)

In considering the problem, the first point to make is that Conzelmann, Lindars and others are certainly correct in one way: Luke does take the term over from his source material and seems happy to accept virtually all types of SM sayings in his tradition. In terms of the (by now) traditional division of SM sayings into 'A' sayings (present activity of the SM), 'B' sayings (the suffering of the SM) and 'C' sayings (the eschatological activity of the SM), Luke preserves the full range of sayings from his sources. As we have seen, practically all the Q sayings are probably preserved by Luke; so are most of the Markan sayings as well, and any omissions of the Markan SM sayings are not focused on any one group of such sayings. Thus Luke has the full range of Markan B sayings, as well as the C sayings; and he preserves too all the sayings usually assigned to the A group.

The SM sayings which Luke takes from his sources are not, however, always simply copied verbatim. Some redactional activity takes place, although one must also note that not a lot of such activity is clearly identifiable. In relation to the Q material, it is generally assumed that Luke's version of the sayings in question is more original and that it is Matthew who has redacted: thus in Q 6.22; 12.8 it is probably Matthew who changes the form of the sayings into 'I' sayings, using the first person rather than the phrase 'SM'; in Q 7.34; 9.58; 12.10 Luke and Matthew are virtually identical and hence probably the evidence indicates that Luke (as well as Matthew) preserves the Q wording; in Q 11.30, Matthew's reference to the SM being in the belly of the earth is almost universally recognized as MattR of the more original form of the saying preserved in Luke; and in Q 17.24, 26, 30, Matthew's references to the παρουσία of the SM are again almost universally recognized as MattR. Only in 22.30 may Luke have deleted a reference to Jesus as SM.[30] How far Luke has 'redacted' the Q material by placing individual sayings in a different context is very difficult to determine, since we do not have the Q context available to check against. It is possible, for example, that Luke has placed the SM saying in 12.10 in a context which is not that of Q, so that blasphemy against the Holy Spirit is now related to a situation of persecution. However, this does not necessarily either explain—or even ease—the problem of the meaning of the phrase 'speaking a word against the SM' in Lk. 12.10 itself! Moreover, in many other places, it is generally assumed that Luke has preserved the order of the Q material more faithfully than Matthew has (Matthew

30. See n. 16 above.

having changed the order to collect related material into his five great teaching discourses). Thus in relation to the Q material, Luke appears to be a faithful and reliable transmitter of the SM sayings.

The case is not quite so simple in relation to the SM sayings adopted by Luke from Mark, for it is clear that at times a certain amount of rewriting has taken place, though the basic structure of most of the sayings is preserved. Thus the A sayings in Mk 2.10, 28 are retained by Luke with little change. (The changes are primarily of word order in the sayings, but it is not clear that these changes have very much, if any, significance.) In the case of the B sayings retained by Luke from Mark, some changes are made, but these are for the most part not enormous. In the second passion prediction (Lk. 9.44//Mk 9.31), Luke abbreviates the saying drastically by omitting the references to Jesus' death and resurrection. However, it is not clear whether this has any significance beyond a simple abbreviation, given that Luke has already recorded the fuller form in the first prediction in 9.22.[31] Luke also adds the verb μέλλει here to Mark which may introduce a note of (divinely determined) inevitability about the events predicted.[32] But this theme may well be anticipated already in the δεῖ of the first prediction in 9.22, a feature which Luke shares with Mark.[33] Hence Luke is simply underlining more strongly a feature which is present in Mark as well. That the passion of Jesus is determined by the will of God is brought out clearly in other SM sayings: the δεῖ governing the suffering of Jesus qua SM occurs in the (probably redactional) sayings in 17.25 and 24.7. And a similar motif comes to the fore in Lk. 22.22 where Luke replaces Mark's καθὼς γέγραπται with κατὰ τὸ ὡρισμένον. It is very unlikely that any change of meaning is implied here:[34] both Mark and Luke indicate that the sufferings of Jesus qua SM are part and parcel of the divine plan.[35]

---

31. Certainly there seems no need to postulate another source on this basis, as do Colpe, 'ὁ υἱὸς τοῦ ἀνθρώπου', p. 461, and Marshall, *Luke*, p. 394.

32. Cf. 9.31. See J.T. Squires, *The Plan of God in Luke–Acts* (SNTSMS, 76; Cambridge: Cambridge University Press, 1993), p. 169.

33. For the importance of δεῖ as expressing the divine will, perhaps as found in Scripture, see W. Grundmann, 'δεῖ', *ThWNT*, II, p.23; Squires, *Plan*, p. 169; B.P. Frein, 'Narrative Prediction, Old Testament Prophecies and Luke's Sense of Fulfilment', *NTS* 40 (1994), pp. 22-37 (29).

34. So rightly Hare, *Son of Man*, p. 73: 'There is no change in meaning'.

35. Cf. also D.L. Tiede, *Prophecy and History in Luke–Acts* (Philadelphia: Fortress Press, 1980), p. 99.

This then comes out most strongly in Luke's rewriting of the third passion prediction in Mk 10.33, whereby Mark's direct prediction that 'the SM will be handed over to the chief priests and the scribes' becomes in Lk. 18.31 'Everything written by the prophets concerning the SM must be completed'. At one level the force of the saying in Luke is quite clear and the saying represents a direct continuation of what we have been considering already. The sufferings of Jesus are in accordance with the divine plan, and represent the fulfilment of prophetic scripture. There is, however, considerable uncertainty about the more precise interpretation of the saying in Luke. In particular, it is not clear whether the dative τῷ υἱῷ τοῦ ἀνθρώπου should be related to the verb τελεσθήσεται or to the participle τὰ γεγραμμένα: in other words, does the Lukan verse refer to 'things written about the SM', or more generally to all Scripture being fulfilled in the person of the SM?[36] There is the question of what scriptures Luke had in mind here, which in turn is of course also connected with the problem of whether the OT has any idea of a suffering SM at all. Certainly Luke never spells out what particular prophecies he has in mind.[37] Hence it may be that Luke has no particular text(s) in mind at all and the situation may then be similar to the well-known Lukan emphasis on the necessity of the sufferings of the Messiah and the fact that these are predicted in Scripture (cf. Lk. 24.26-27; 24.46; Acts 3.18; 17.3; 26.23), even though it is all but impossible to find anything explicit in the OT to this effect.[38] The theme of the necessity of the Messiah to suffer is usually taken as a Lukan conjunction of two themes: the Messiahship of Jesus, and the suffering and death of Jesus as being part of God's plan. The link is the person of Jesus, resulting in the somewhat artificial scheme of the necessity of the suffering of the Messiah. Lk. 18.31 *may* be similar. However, the possibility remains open that Luke does have a specific text or texts in mind. The obvious candidate is Daniel 7. As is well known, there is much debate about whether Daniel 7 implies that the SM figure mentioned there is a suffering figure or not. So too there is debate about whether a first-century reader of Daniel 7 could have taken the text in this way. However, the problem is not only one for the

---

36. Cf. Marshall, *Luke*, p. 690, for the first; Fitzmyer, *Luke X–XXIV*, p. 1206, for the second.

37. Hence the comment of Squires, *Plan*, p. 141 n. 100: 'Precisely what ancient prophecies Luke has in mind remains a mystery'.

38. Tiede, *Prophecy*, pp. 100-101.

interpretation of Lk. 18.31. It is equally a problem for the interpretation of the δεῖ of Mk 8.31 and the καθὼς γέγραπται of Mk 14.21. Certainly Luke has redacted some of the suffering SM sayings in line with what is universally recognized as a powerful theme in the Lukan writings, viz., the importance of Jesus' death as part of the divine plan as foretold in Scripture.[39] Yet Luke has in this respect simply developed further what is clearly there already in Mark. Luke has thus not imposed anything fundamentally different on his Markan tradition.

The eschatological SM sayings in Mark also undergo a certain amount of revision by Luke. The rewriting of Mk 14.62 in Lk. 22.69 is frequently discussed. As is well known, Luke adds at the start of the saying the phrase ἀπὸ τοῦ νῦν and changes Mark's ὄψεσθε to ἔσται. He also omits the whole phrase in Mark which refers to the SM 'coming'. The net result is that the saying, which in Mark probably refers to the parousia, becomes in Luke a statement about the immediate position of Jesus as SM at God's right hand in glory. The way in which this relates to Luke's views on the delay of the parousia has been much discussed and needs no further elaboration here.[40] So too the changes made by Luke to Mk 13.26 in Lk. 21.27 are well known: the clouds of Mk 13.26 are reduced to a single cloud (ἐν νεφέλῃ) and the motif of the gathering of the elect in Mk 13.27 is omitted by Luke. The singular cloud is usually related to the cloud of Acts 1.9 which transports the ascending Jesus so that, according to the angelic commentator at the scene, the way in which Jesus is just seen to have departed will be the same as the way in which he will return (Acts 1.11).[41] Luke's use of the eschatological SM sayings in Mark is thus closely related to his own eschatological views and to the rest of his narrative. Thus for Luke, the eschatological SM sayings are pulled into the service of Luke's views on the present exaltation of Jesus as well as the parousia of Jesus. A certain shift of emphasis thus occurs (certainly in Lk. 22.69) and is undeniable. But it is not totally unrelated to the tradition Luke inherits.

I turn now to a brief consideration of the 'L' SM sayings, in other words, the sayings peculiar to Luke which, as we have seen, may well

---

39. Cf. Tiede, *Prophecy*; Squires, *Plan*; and more generally the programmatic essay of P. Schubert, 'The Structure and Significance of Luke 24', in W. Eltester (ed.), *Neutestamentliche Studien für Rudolf Bultmann* (Berlin: Töpelmann, 1957), pp. 165-86.

40. Conzelmann, *Theology*, p. 116; Tödt, *Son of Man*, p. 101, and many others.

41. Tödt, *Son of Man*, p. 101; Casey, *Son of Man*, p. 177, and others.

owe a lot, if not everything, to LkR. What is striking about these sayings is that they virtually all mesh closely with the themes and structures of the SM sayings as adopted by Luke from Mark and Q. Luke does *not* seem to expand significantly the range of ideas associated with Jesus as 'SM'. Thus Lk. 17.25 and 24.7 take up the theme of the Markan passion sayings and virtually repeat them verbatim. Lk. 22.48 is not far removed (in context or in substance) from Mk 14.41: in Mark Jesus as SM is the one who will be betrayed, and this becomes in Luke's more vivid scene a question by Jesus to his betrayer Judas, 'Are you betraying the Son of Man with a kiss?' If then it is justified to see the influence of Mk 14.41 on Lk. 22.48, and probably also the impetus for the formation of the Lukan verse (see above), then the SM of Lk. 22.48 is clearly again all of a piece with the Markan suffering SM: Jesus as SM is one who will be betrayed to death by others, the one who is to suffer and to die.

The eschatological sayings in Lk. 18.8; 21.36 are close in substance to the Markan and Q sayings (cf. Mk 8.38; Q 12.8) which speak of the SM's role in the final judgment. In this respect it may be worth noting that, *pace* Tödt, the SM's role here does appear to be more that of a judge than an advocate.[42] 'Standing before the SM' (21.36) suggests strongly a more judgmental role, as indeed is probably also implied by verses such as Lk. 9.26 and 12.9: 12.9 shows the same activity continuing from v. 8 (though it is now described with a passive verb, rather than an active verb with 'SM' as subject), and this activity clearly includes a negative, condemnatory activity ('denying'); the same is implied in Lk. 9.26 where Luke also heightens the status of the 'SM' by referring to 'his' (= the SM's) glory alongside that of the Father and the angels.[43]

The famous Stephen saying in Acts 7.56 is clearly similar to the SM saying at Jesus' trial in one way: indeed it is precisely this closeness which has suggested to many that the saying is due to LkR. The exact role played by the SM in Acts 7 is of course heavily disputed, and much depends on the precise significance to be seen in the fact that the SM is 'standing'.[44] Perhaps, however, the most convincing explanation is to

---

42. Cf. Hoffmann, 'Jesus versus Menschensohn', pp. 186ff., *contra* Tödt.

43. See Hoffmann, 'Jesus versus Menschensohn', p. 187-88. Cf. too A. Vögtle's review of Tödt's book in *BZ* 6 (1962), p. 137.

44. See the surveys of opinion, and suggestions, in Tödt, *Son of Man*, pp. 303-304; C.K. Barrett, 'Stephen and the Son of Man', in *Apophoreta* (FS E. Haenchen; Berlin: de Gruyter, 1964), pp. 32-38; also his *The Acts of the Apostles*, I

see the SM here as standing in the divine court to speak on behalf of the dying martyr to plead his cause, exactly as in Lk. 12.8.[45] If so, the picture of the SM from Acts 7 does not significantly extend the picture of the SM from the traditional SM sayings as they appear in Luke's Gospel. Lk. 17.22 may well be modelled in part for its language on the Q saying in 17.26 in speaking of the 'days of the SM' in referring to the coming of the SM.[46] The substance of the saying clearly reflects Luke's concern about the delay of the parousia. Yet the actual use of the phrase 'SM' itself indicates that for Luke the phrase is still being used in contexts similar to that of the source material, that is, to refer to future eschatological activity.

The one saying which is not quite so easy in one way to parallel is Lk. 19.10, 'The SM came to seek and to save the lost'. Further, *if* (as I

(Edinburgh: T. & T. Clark, 1994), pp. 384-85; E. Haenchen, *The Acts of the Apostles* (ET; Oxford: Blackwell, 1971), p. 292; Schneider, *Apostelgeschichte*, pp. 474-75.

45. So Schneider, *Apostelgechichte*, p. 475; also C.F.D. Moule, 'From Defendant to Judge and Deliverer', *Bulletin of the SNTS* 3 (1952), pp. 46-47; J. Roloff, *Die Apostelgeschichte* (Göttingen: Vandenhoeck & Ruprecht, 1988), p. 127; Hoffmann, 'Jesus und der Menschensohn', p. 192-93. Hoffmann's argument about Acts 7.56 does, however, make his claim about the redactional origin of the SM reference in Lk. 12.8 harder to accept. Hoffmann concedes that the picture of the SM as advocate in Lk. 12.8 is slightly at variance with the general Lukan picture of the SM at the Eschaton as judge (cf. above and his arguments—in my view justified—against Tödt). But this then makes it harder to see *both* Acts 7.56 *and* Lk. 12.8 as redactional creations by Luke. It seems more likely that one of these is given to Luke by a source, and the other a redactional echo. And the most likely candidate for the source, given the large number of Lukanisms in the context of Acts 7.56, is Lk. 12.8. Further, Hoffmann seems to imply that Luke interprets the SM saying in Lk. 12.8 as referring to a pre-Eschaton 'confessing' (this seems to be the logic of the close parallel he draws between the verse and its context, which does clearly relate to Christians under persecution [cf. above], and Acts 7.56), but this is then strange in the light of Lk. 9.26, where Luke clearly interprets Mark's parallel version of the saying (Mk 8.38) as a parousia reference.

46. The interpretation of this verse is also disputed. For the interpretation as forward-looking and eschatological, as here, see Schnackenburg, 'Eschatologische Abschnitt', pp. 227-28; Schneider, 'Der Menschensohn', pp. 274-75; Fitzmyer, *Luke X–XXIV*, pp. 1168-69; Marshall, *Luke*, pp. 658-59, also with a full discussion of the various possibilities which have been suggested. As Schnackenburg rightly says, the context, and the note about 'longing to see', are most naturally interpreted as implying a future, eschatological reference. Cf. too Müller, *Menschensohn*, pp. 133-34.

have tried to argue elsewhere) the 'A' sayings in Mark and Q (Mk 2.10, 28; Q 6.22; 7.34; 9.58; possibly 12.10) are in fact crypto-suffering sayings in that all refer—more or less allusively—to the rejection, and hence to the implied suffering, of Jesus,[47] then Lk. 19.10 does not quite fit this pattern. Nevertheless one may note the formal similarities between Lk. 19.10 and Q 7.34 as well as with Mk 10.45 (cf. above), so that Lk. 19.10 may well be Luke's rewriting of the passion saying in Mk 10.45. Moreover, the verse is not so dissimilar to the surface meaning of the other texts since any reference to the passion depends in part on the wider literary context in which these other verses are now placed.[48] In sum, therefore, the 'L' SM sayings in Luke fit in remarkably closely to the pattern of SM sayings which Luke adopts from his sources. Hence Luke does not really create new ideas and associate them with the figure of the SM.

The picture that seems to emerge is one of Luke as what might be described as a 'conservative redactor', with perhaps care needed to stress both halves of that description.[49] Luke is certainly a redactor. He does change his traditions a little—at times, one could argue, quite significantly. Lk. 24.7 is in one way a very radical rewriting of Mk 16.7: a prediction of a future event in Galilee becomes a reminder of a past statement by Jesus in Galilee. Similarly, Lk. 22.69 succeeds in shifting the emphasis of Mk 14.62 quite significantly away from any idea of a parousia event. Again, Lk. 18.31 represents quite a large rewriting of Mk 10.33, introducing the explicit idea of the fulfilment of Scripture (though the idea may well be already there in the δεῖ of Mk 8.31). In this sense Conzelmann is correct in saying that Luke has pressed the SM traditions to a certain extent into the service of his own ideas. The eschatological SM as a parousia figure in Mk 14.62 becomes the Lukan ascended, glorious figure in heaven in Lk. 22.69 and the advocate who in Acts 7 exercises that role now.

Nevertheless, Luke appears also to be basically 'conservative' in his

---

47. See my 'The Present Son of Man', *JSNT* 14 (1982), pp. 58-81.

48. This applies especially in the case of the Markan sayings in Mk 2—see the argument in my article cited in the previous note.

49. The phrase is taken from R. Pesch's description of Mark: see his *Das Markusevangelium* (2 vols.; Freiburg: Herder, 1975, 1976), e.g. on p. 53 (and implied throughout his whole commentary). However, as I hope is clear, I do *not* mean to imply by this that Luke is simply 'conservative' (as Pesch argues for Mark) in the sense of being one who simply preserves his sources largely unchanged. Luke is a conservative *redactor*.

treatment of his sources. He appears to be trying to be true to his sources and to retain, as far as possible, the categories and ideas supplied by his traditions. This is shown above all by the L sayings. Thus he takes up the idea of Jesus qua SM as eschatological judge or advocate from his sources; he retains some material (Lk. 9.26; 12.8) and he develops some sayings in his own way for his own purposes (cf. his redaction of Mk 14.62 in Lk. 22.69, and the possible creation of Lk. 17.22; 18.1; 21.36). But he retains the fundamental theme of Jesus qua SM as an eschatological figure. He also takes up the theme of Jesus qua SM as a suffering figure and adds at times sayings which mesh in perfectly with the grid of Markan suffering SM sayings. He takes over the present activity ('A') sayings with little noticeable change, perhaps adding one in 19.10 which may be his own adaptation of a Markan passion saying (Mk 10.45) to serve his purposes in providing a (Lukan) summary of the aim of Jesus' mission, but in a way that still remains formally (and substantially) close to existing SM sayings. Thus in his development of the SM sayings of his tradition, Luke shows himself to be (perhaps surprisingly) sensitive to his source materials: Luke does *not* introduce SM terminology into other contexts for which there is no justification in his sources. He does not, for example, use SM language in relation to Jesus' miracles. He does not use SM language in relation to Jesus' teaching. He does not seek to argue that Jesus SM is the fulfilment of Scripture via the resurrection. Rather, he keeps to the existing categories in which 'SM' is used in his sources.

Above all he keeps—with one famous exception—to the feature of his tradition which restricts 'SM' to sayings placed on the lips of Jesus. (Acts 7.56 is of course the exception to prove the 'rule'!) Thus Luke keeps to this 'convention' very closely. All the redactional SM sayings he (probably) creates are (excepting Acts 7.56) sayings of Jesus. Thus it is striking that, however much continuity Luke may be signalling between the SM of Lk. 21.26 and the Jesus of Acts 1 via the singular cloud, Luke does *not* develop 'SM' terminology at all in relation to the preaching of Christians in Acts, even in contexts where Jesus is referred to as the eschatological judge (cf. Acts 10.42; 17.31). Rather, as already noted, the dominant 'titles' used to refer to Jesus in Acts are κύριος and χριστός. The most that Luke seems prepared to do is to signal some link with the SM tradition via the parallel he creates with Acts 1 in Lk. 21.26 by reducing the plural clouds to a single one, but even this is fairly allusive—for example, Acts 1 does not use the term SM explicitly.

Hence Luke does seem aware of the fact that 'SM' is characteristic of the *Jesus* tradition.[50] Further, he seems aware of the range of contexts in Jesus traditions in which SM language is used. This range is wide, but not all-embracing. Luke then certainly explicitly exploits the width of the given range; but he does not really extend it. Conzelmann is surely right in one way to claim that Luke takes up 'SM' from his tradition and interprets the term in relation to his own ideas. Yet it is hard to agree with Conzelmann, or Lindars, that Luke is unaware of the 'original' meaning of the term. Much, of course, depends on what is meant by 'original' in this context. To expect Luke to know intimately the original Aramaic of Jesus' sayings is surely to ask the impossible. Luke's immediate precursors are Mark and Q, together with whatever other sources of information he had available (though in relation to SM sayings I have argued that no other sources are likely). Certainly in relation to Mark (and, I would argue, in relation to Q as well) it is clear that a key background for the meaning of the phrase 'SM' is to be found in Daniel 7. Whether this goes back to Jesus is of course a hotly debated issue, but it seems undeniable that, by the time tradition has reached the stage of (say) Mk 13.26 and 14.62, the link between 'SM' and Daniel 7 is secure. Luke certainly does not enhance the link between SM language and Daniel 7. Some, indeed, would argue that he significantly reduces it.[51] Nevertheless the linkage does not disappear. Luke's version of Mk 13.26 in Lk. 21.27 still keeps the clear Danielic imagery.[52] Luke's abbreviation in Lk. 22.69 can be interpreted as reducing the Daniel 7 imagery considerably, or even eliminating it completely.[53] However, there may still

---

50. Cf. C.F.D. Moule, 'The Christology of Acts', in L.E. Keck and J.L. Martyn (eds.), *Studies in Luke–Acts* (London: SPCK, 1968), pp. 159-85 (163-64); Lindars, *Jesus Son of Man*, pp. 138-39.

51. Cf. Müller, *Menschensohn*, p. 142.

52. *Pace* Casey, *Son of Man*, p. 177, who asserts that Luke's version represents a clear move away from the Danielic text. Cf. too Müller, *Menschensohn*, p. 125. However, despite any slight reduction, the Danielic allusion is undeniably still present in the Lukan version. In relation to the question of whether it is justified to see an allusion to Dan. 7 or not, reference is often made to G. Vermes, *Jesus the Jew* (London: Collins, 1973), p. 178, who claims that an indirect Danielic allusion should be allowed if there is mention of the SM's coming, glory or kingship, or of the clouds transporting him. In the case of Lk. 21.27 the reference to the cloud is surely enough to satisfy even Vermes's fairly demanding criteria.

53. So e.g. Casey, *Son of Man*, p. 184: 'his omission removed all definite trace of Dan. 7.13'. Cf. too Müller, *Menschensohn*, pp. 126-27.

be an allusion to Daniel 7 in some of the Q sayings in Luke, notably Lk. 17.26, 30, where the reference to the SM being 'revealed' should probably be seen as alluding to Daniel 7.[54] Further, Luke's use of Mark in Lk. 9.26 seems at least to preserve clear Danielic features from his Markan source (Mk 8.38) with the reference to the 'coming' and the 'glory' of the SM.[55] Indeed Luke could be said to enhance the allusion by referring to the SM's own glory even more clearly than Mark does (cf. above).[56] But this then makes it likely that, as far as Luke is concerned, verses such as Lk. 12.8-9 which speak similarly of the SM confessing/denying people in an eschatological context are also to be interpreted against the Danielic background. Similarly, Lk. 18.8, which also talks of the SM 'coming', probably alludes indirectly to Daniel 7.[57] Hence too the similar saying in Lk. 21.36 is probably to be taken in the same way.[58] Thus, despite the evidence of Lk. 22.69, it does seem to be the case that Luke is aware of the Danielic background, at least in relation to the eschatological sayings.

The ultimate origin of the idea of the suffering of the SM in the Markan tradition is heavily disputed. However, in my view a strong case can be made for this too coming from the Danielic background.[59] However, wherever it comes from, such an idea is present in Mark and Luke seems to take it over positively and enthusiastically (cf. above on Lk. 9.31; 18.31; 22.22). If then the Markan idea of the necessity of the SM's sufferings is derived from Daniel 7, and/or if Luke read Mark in

---

54. Rightly, in my view, Lindars, *Jesus Son of Man*, p. 95, *contra* Casey, *Son of Man*, p. 189.

55. Even Casey, who in general is highly skeptical of the existence of Danielic allusions in the gospel sayings, concedes the presence of such an allusion here: see his *Son of Man*, pp. 162-63.

56. Müller, *Menschensohn*, p. 129, is more doubtful and sees here simply dependence and use of Mk 8.38, rather than a use of Dan. 7.13-14. But are these two alternatives necessarily mutually exclusive?!

57. Vermes, *Jesus the Jew*, p. 179; Casey, *Son of Man*, pp. 196-97.

58. Vermes, *Jesus the Jew*, p. 179; Casey, *Son of Man*, p. 197.

59. See M.D. Hooker, *The Son of Man in Mark* (London: SPCK, 1967); C.F.D. Moule, 'Neglected Features in the Problem of the "Son of Man"', in J. Gnilka (ed.), *Neues Testament und Kirche* (FS R. Schnackenburg; Freiburg: Herder, 1974), pp. 413-28; also his *The Origin of Christology* (Cambridge: Cambridge University Press, 1977), pp. 11-22, and others (I am fully aware that this is not a universally held view!).

this way as well,[60] then this might make more sense of Lk. 18.31 diff. Mk 10.33: the sufferings of the SM fulfil 'all that has been written in the prophets' not only in a very general and unspecific sense (similar to the sufferings of the Messiah fulfilling Scripture), but in the sense of 'fulfilling' the specifically Danielic 'prophecies'. Thus Luke may well be aware of the significance of the term in the earlier stages of the tradition to which he has access.

In this respect Colpe's summary conclusion about Luke's use of 'SM' is justified: 'Lukas verwendet seine Quelle treu. Eine eigene Menschensohnchristologie ist bei ihm nicht erkennbar.'[61] Luke *does* reproduce his sources faithfully and he does not introduce new meanings. Nevertheless, the more negative side of what (I think) Colpe implies is perhaps more questionable. Luke is *not* agnostic about the term. His positive use of the term, going at times as far as redactional creation of SM sayings, indicates that he is not just a conservative, unthinking repeater of his sources: he is rather a conservative *redactor*. His ideas about SM largely coincide with those of his sources.[62] But this should cause no great surprise. The very fact that Luke has chosen to use his sources Mark and Q makes a significant degree of substantive continuity between Luke and his traditions a matter of no surprise at all.[63] On the other hand, Luke does not go overboard in developing his sources. He does add to them at times. But he respects his source material. He does not write SM references into Acts in a significant way at all. With the exception of Acts 7.56, he does not write SM references into Acts in relation to one key point where he does develop the SM terminology, viz. to refer to the position of Jesus at God's right hand in the post-Easter, pre-Eschaton era. Acts covers just this period of time, and Jesus' session at God's right hand during this period is of cardinal importance for Luke. The fact that Luke does not write SM references into his story in Acts is thus significant. Luke thus shows himself to be aware of the

---

60. The latter could be true without the former!
61. Colpe, 'ὁ υἱὸς τοῦ ἀνθρώπου', p. 462.
62. The greatest difference lies in his application of 'SM' to Jesus in his capacity as risen and ascended in the post-Easter, pre-Eschaton situation.
63. Cf. similarly in relation to Matthew and his sources, U. Luz, *Matthew 1–7: A Commentary* (Minneapolis: Augsburg, 1989), pp. 73-76. Perhaps modern gospel studies have gone too far in seeking to identify the distinctive features of each gospel writer by driving too much a wedge between the evangelists and their sources.

difference between the pre- and post-Easter situations and to be sensitive to his source materials.

The evidence reviewed here suggests that Luke is trying to remain true to the meaning of the term 'SM', at least as it is coming to him from his two main sources, Mark and Q. For those who think that the Markan and Q SM sayings are not so far removed from the historical Jesus, this may imply that Luke himself is not so far removed from the 'original' meaning. Such a discussion, however, would take us far beyond the limits of this present paper. Suffice it to say that Luke does have some kind of 'SM Christology'. It is perhaps not so distinctive in relation to other early Christian writers, in that it continues in a line of direct continuity the ideas associated with the term in his sources. Luke seems to feel constrained by his tradition to respect the parameters which the tradition implies; but insofar as he develops the SM tradition by adding to the fund of SM sayings, he can be said in one way to have a SM Christology.

By way of conclusion, I raise two questions, neither of which can be easily answered, but which may have wider implications for Lukan study. The first relates to a feature which Luke again shares with the whole gospel tradition in relation to the SM sayings, and yet which is perhaps more surprising in Luke than in the other Gospels. This is the fact that the term 'SM' is never explained for the readers of the Gospel. In relation to Luke, this is perhaps all the more surprising in view of the fact that most assume that Luke was writing for a Gentile readership for whom some of the more 'Jewish' elements would sound strange or inexplicable. ὁ υἱὸς τοῦ ἀνθρώπου as a Greek phrase would surely fall into this category: all agree that the phrase in Greek is a very strange, if not barbaric, translation of the Aramaic idiomatic *bar (')nasha* (with of course enormous debate about the significance of this Aramaic phrase). Yet Luke apparently never feels constrained to explain it for his (presumably) Greek speaking readers. In terms of a 'straight', 'literary' (or 'first') reading of the text of Luke's Gospel, 'SM' appears without warning in 5.24, is then used on several occasions, and is never explained. What does this say about the implied reader of Luke's Gospel? Perhaps a more interesting question for some, what does this say about the original readers? What would 'SM' (in Greek!) have evoked in the minds of Luke's first readers?[64]

64. Could one say that Luke's usage itself suggests that the term may have carried sufficient distinctiveness so as not to need explanation, at least for Luke's readers?

The second question arises from the fact that, if the analysis given earlier in this essay is correct, then Luke appears to have been far less free in relation to the SM tradition as it comes to him from Q than he was in relation to the Markan SM sayings. Luke seems to have preserved (almost) all the SM sayings in Q unaltered; yet he changed a number of SM sayings in Mark, at times significantly. Does this show that Luke had a greater respect for Q than for Mark? Is Luke's 'conservative' tendency in relation to his sources dependent on which source(s) he uses? And can such a 'conservative tendency' be shown elsewhere in the Lukan writings?[65] Such questions might repay further study.

---

65. As one possible example of such a 'conservative tendency', one might refer to the phenomenon of the so-called 'Wisdom Christology' of Q. As is well known, a number of Q passages seem to portray Jesus as one of the prophetic envoys sent by Wisdom (cf. Lk. 7.34-35; 11.49-51; 13.34-35 and pars.). Matthew in turn regularly upgrades the Christology by identifying Jesus with the figure of Wisdom: see M.J. Suggs, *Wisdom, Christology and Law in Matthew's Gospel* (Cambridge, MA: Harvard University Press, 1970); also my *The Revival of the Griesbach Hypothesis* (Cambridge: Cambridge University Press, 1983), pp. 148-66. But it is now striking that, on the usual reconstruction of the Q sayings, Luke has preserved the schema far more accurately. Yet Luke never elsewhere develops the idea of Jesus as Wisdom's envoy and hence the schema is not really a Lukan one. The schema is characteristic of Q and Luke has simply conserved the tradition relatively faithfully.

Another similar possible example of the same phenomenon may be provided by the composite citation of Isa. 61 + 58 in Lk. 4.18-19. I have argued elsewhere that Luke may here be preserving a Q tradition (rather than, as it is often interpreted, redacting freely). See my 'Luke 4,16-30, Isaiah and Q', in J. Delobel (ed.), *LOGIA: Les Paroles de Jésus—The Sayings of Jesus* (BETL, 59; Leuven: Leuven University Press and Peeters, 1982), pp. 342-54. Luke may be influenced by the citation a little in Lk. 4.31-44, and he certainly interprets it in Acts 10.38. But there is little other evidence of the influence of Isa. 61 in the Lukan writings, apart from the beatitudes in Lk. 6.20-21 and the reply of Jesus to the Baptist in Lk. 7.22, both of which are again Q passages, and where it may be significant that Luke may have redacted the beatitudes in such a way that the allusion to Isa. 61 is diminished rather than increased. (For details, see my 'The Beatitudes: A Source-Critical Study', *NovT* 25 [1983], pp. 193-207, esp. pp. 197-99 in relation to the second Q beatitude, where I have argued that Matthew's clearer allusion to Isa. 61.2 may be closer to the Q wording.) Thus Luke does not show any great redactional tendency to enhance the allusion to Isa. 61, and yet he preserves what may have been his tradition here faithfully.

Finally, is there any significance in the fact that the first of these examples is clearly, and the second arguably, Q material?

INDEXES

INDEX OF REFERENCES

OLD TESTAMENT

Genesis		15	88	*Judges*	
22.1-2	143	15.30	89	2	178
22.11-12	143	19	88	6	143
		19.21	195	13.5	189
Exodus		20.15	183		
3	143	31.19	195	*1 Samuel*	
3.6	184, 185	31.24	195	1.11	189
12	161			3.4-14	143
12.11	161	*Deuteronomy*		9–10	143
12.12	161	1.1	88	12	178
15.1	76, 77	4.34	183		
15.2	77	6.21-22	183	*1 Kings*	
15.10	77	6.22	183	8	178
15.22-26	76	7.26	89	17.17-24	76
18.21 (LXX)	62	9.9	142	22.19-22	143
34.28	142	9.12	184		
		18.15	184	*2 Kings*	
Leviticus		19.15	89	4.22-37	76
2.2	51	23	88	17.7-23	179
2.9	51	26.6	183	17.13-14	181
6.15	51	26.8	183	17.13	184
15.16	195	27–28	88	17.14	184
17–18	66	30.1-3	89	25	182
17.3	89	31	178	25.27	162
18.6-30	86	31.29	89		
19.19	89	32	178	*2 Chronicles*	
23.10-11	195			5.6 (LXX)	60
		Joshua			
Numbers		21.43-45	178	*Nehemiah*	
6.1-21	189	23	178	9.26	181
6.9-12	195	24	185, 186		
6.9	191	24.6	186	*Job*	
6.12	191	24.14	186	1.1 (LXX)	62
6.14-15	191	24.23	186		
6.18	189				

Index of References

Psalms		61.1	76	3.92 (Theod.)	162
79.11	162	61.2	217	3.95 (Theod.)	162
102.11 (LXX)	60			6	162
102.13 (LXX)	60	*Jeremiah*		6.23	161
102.20	162	1.4-10	143	7	207, 213, 214
106	180	1.7-8	152		
106 (LXX)	32	2.3	88, 89	7.13-14	214
107.14	162	7.25-27	181	9.3	142
142.7	162	7.25-26	184	9.25-26	75
146.7	162	25.4	184	9.25	75
		32.21	183	9.26	75
		40.4	162		
Isaiah				*Malachi*	
6	143			3.1	84
6.9-10	144	*Ezekiel*			
11.1-5	74	1–2	143	*2 Esdras*	
11.1	74	1.28	152	14.27-35	181
35	76	2.1	152		
35.5-6	76	2.3	152	*Ecclesiasticus*	
40.3-5	144			45.15	51
42.7	162	*Daniel*			
42.16	144	3	162	*1 Maccabees*	
49.6	144, 152	3.22	163	3.49	193
58	217	3.25	162		
59.9-10	144	3.26	161	*2 Maccabees*	
61	76, 217	3.28	162	9.5-6	157
61.1-2	159	3.90 (LXX)	61		

NEW TESTAMENT

Matthew		2.10	201, 206, 211	12.8	184
8.5-6	51			13.26	201, 208, 213
14.13-21	130	2.28	201, 206, 211		
14.25	163			13.27	208
14.28-33	163	6.12	157	14.2	160
14.29	164	6.30	157	14.21	201, 203, 208
15.32-38	130	6.32-44	130		
16.13	202	8.1-9	130	14.41	201, 209
16.21	202	8.31	201, 208, 211	14.57-61	160
19.27	201			14.62	201, 208, 211-13
23.15	51	8.38	201, 209, 210, 214		
27.51-52	163			16.7	203, 211
27.66	163	9.9	201		
28.2	160	9.12	201	*Luke*	
28.4	160	9.31	201, 206	1–4	146
		10.33	201, 207, 215	1.1-4	82
Mark				1.3	67
2	211	10.45	201, 203, 211, 212	1.4	67
				1.46-55	54, 77

1.50	54, 60	9.22	201, 206	17.30	201, 205, 214
1.52	157	9.26	201, 209, 210, 212	17.31	201
1.74	56		206, 214	18.1-8	202, 203
2.1	157	9.31	201, 206	18.1	212
2.22-24	84, 196	9.44	23	18.8	202-204, 209, 214
2.22	84	9.51	201, 205, 211	18.31	207, 208, 211, 214, 215
2.25	62	9.58	94		
2.30	144	10.7	84		
2.37	56	10.29-37	94, 95	18.35-43	159
2.46-49	84	10.38-42	92	19.10	202, 203, 210-12
3.2	23	10.39	92		
3.20	159	11.27	201, 205	19.45-48	84
4.7-8	56	11.30	94	19.47	84
4.7	56	11.37-52	217	21.12	159
4.8	56	11.49-51	214	21.24-25	66
4.16-21	75	12.8-9	198, 201, 205, 209, 210, 212	21.26	212
4.16	66	12.8		21.27	201, 208, 213
4.18-19	217			21.34-36	203
4.18	66, 76, 144, 156, 159	12.9	209	21.36	202-204, 209, 212, 214
5.24	199, 201, 216	12.10	201, 205, 211		
5.29	94	12.35	161	22.1	160
6.5	201	12.40	201	22.2	160
6.20-21	217	13.1	157	22.14-38	94, 96
6.22	201, 205, 211	13.11-16	76	22.22	201, 206, 214
7	51, 67, 68	13.25-27	161		
7.3-6	68	13.26	94	22.30	201, 205
7.3-5	68	13.31-32	159	22.33	159
7.4-5	51, 59	13.34-35	217	22.35-36	102
7.9-10	68	14	105	22.44	160
7.11-19	76	14.1-24	94	22.48	202, 203, 209
7.11-17	76	16.1-9	72		
7.16	76	16.8	72	22.69	199, 201, 208, 211-14
7.21	159	16.18	86		
7.22	75, 76, 217	17.11-19	85	23.2	104
7.34-35	217	17.14	84	23.6-12	159
7.34	94, 201, 205, 211	17.17	61	23.19	159
		17.22	202, 210, 212	23.25	159
7.36-50	94	17.24	201, 205	23.47	68
7.37	95	17.25	201, 206, 209	24.7	202, 203, 206, 209, 211
9–19	103				
9.4	94	17.26	201, 202, 205, 210, 214		
9.6	157			24.13-35	94
9.9	159			24.16	144
9.10-17	130			24.26-27	207
9.10	157				

Index of References

24.31	144	4.4	131	7.37	184
24.36-37	161	4.16-21	75	7.38	185-87
24.44	87, 88	4.24-30	109	7.39	183, 185-87
24.46	207	4.27	159	7.42	56, 184
24.47	66	4.32	73, 102	7.43	56
24.50-51	130	4.36–5.11	73	7.44	185, 187
24.52	56	5.1-11	104	7.45	185-87
27.51-52	163	5.17-40	131	7.51-53	182
		5.17-25	158	7.51-52	186, 187
John		5.20-21	84	7.51	183, 185
3.8	168	5.30	184	7.52-53	184
9.31	62	5.31	153	7.52	184, 185
12.20	69	5.36-37	157	7.56	199, 201, 202,
12.36	72	5.42	84		209, 210, 212,
18.3	161	6.1-7	169, 176		215
21	163	6.1-6	94	7.58	23
		6.1	169, 170	8–11	139, 140
Acts		6.2-4	169	8–9	139
1–14	84	6.2	73	8	139
1.8	17, 22, 145,	6.5-6	169	8.1-3	139
	146	6.5	50, 54, 69,	8.1	22
1.9-11	130		73, 169, 176	8.2	62
1.9	208	6.7	169	8.4-8	140
1.11	208	6.8–8.40	158	8.4	22
1.14	92, 158	6.11-14	160	8.20-23	140
1.32-35	74	6.47	54	8.26-39	167
2–5	130	7	160, 182,	8.26	140
2	30, 31, 139,		184, 185,	8.27-28	68
	154		187, 210	8.27	56, 85, 140
2.1–6.7	158	7.2-8	182	9	128-30,
2.1-41	131	7.2-4	186		135-42,
2.5	62	7.2	182, 185,		146-48,
2.9-11	30		186		151, 152,
2.10	50	7.7	56		154, 158
2.11	54, 69	7.8	51	9.1-30	134, 135,
2.42	73, 94	7.9-16	182		141
2.44	73, 102	7.10	162	9.1-2	135, 141,
3.1–4.4	130	7.11	185, 186		142
3.1-10	130	7.12	185	9.1	135, 141
3.1	51	7.14	186	9.2-34	183
3.11-26	131	7.15	185, 186	9.2-4	183
3.11	84	7.16	185	9.2	135, 141
3.12	56, 62	7.19	183, 185	9.3-12	140
3.13	184	7.23	184	9.3-9	135, 141,
3.18	207	7.30	184		143, 145
3.26	153	7.32	184, 185	9.3-4	142, 152
4–6	172	7.36	183, 184,	9.4-5	134
4.1-3	131		186	9.4	142

9.6	136, 142, 145	9.27-28	135	10.34-36	139, 146
		9.27	151, 174	10.34-35	66, 167
9.7-8	136, 138	9.29	135	10.34	146
9.7	129, 136, 143	9.30-34	183	10.35	51-53, 65
		9.30	135, 141	10.38	66, 217
9.8	142, 144	9.31–11.18	158	10.42	212
9.9	142, 150	9.31	135	10.45-46	146
9.10-19	138	9.32-41	160	10.45	51
9.10-16	135, 143, 148, 150, 152	9.35	183	11	130, 146
		9.36-43	183	11.1-18	169, 173
		9.40	144	11.1-3	146
9.10	142, 143	9.44-50	183	11.2-3	173
9.11-12	143	9.44-47	183	11.2	51, 158
9.12	143, 144, 148	9.51–19.27	84	11.3	51
		10–11	146	11.4-17	138
9.13-25	135	10	51, 54, 68, 101, 130, 139, 146	11.5-10	130, 137
9.13-14	140, 143, 144			11.11-14	130
				11.15	167
9.14-15	148, 150	10.1–11.18	66, 174	11.18	65, 67, 174, 176
9.14	150	10.1-23	138, 140		
9.15-16	136, 143, 151	10.1-11	167	11.19	158
		10.1-8	130	11.20	51, 68
9.15	66, 142, 145, 150	10.1-2	68	11.25	174
		10.1	51	11.28	157
9.16-17	136	10.2	51-53, 57, 62, 65	11.29–12.1	157
9.16	145, 148, 150			11.30	167
		10.3-6	146	12	22, 158-64
9.17-43	183	10.3	51	12.2	157, 159
9.17-21	150	10.4	51	12.3-4	160
9.17-19	135	10.6	33	12.3	159
9.18	144, 145, 150	10.7	51, 62, 68	12.4	161
		10.9-16	130, 137	12.5	160
9.19-30	135	10.10-16	146	12.6	158, 161
9.19-25	135	10.14-16	146	12.7	158, 161
9.19-20	150	10.17	140	12.8	161, 163
9.19	135	10.18	167	12.10	161
9.20-21	150	10.19-20	146	12.11	159, 162
9.20	141	10.22	51-53, 65, 130	12.12	92, 122, 158
9.21	150			12.17	158, 174
9.22	141	10.24-33	138	12.23	157
9.23-29	141	10.25-26	56	12.24	157
9.25	141	10.25	56	12.25	122, 157, 158
9.26-30	135, 167, 171	10.28-29	146		
		10.28	167	13–28	158
9.26-27	146	10.30-33	130	13–22	152
9.26	135, 140, 169, 171, 176	10.30	51	13-14	122
		10.31	51	13	22, 52, 65, 108, 131
		10.33	51		

Index of References

13.1-14	174	15	22, 82-84,	17.21	36
13.1-4	24		86, 167, 174	17.22-31	109
13.1-3	118	15.1-29	174	17.22	36
13.1	175	15.1	51	17.23	56
13.4	25, 32	15.3	193	17.31	212
13.5	158, 167	15.5	51	17.34	93
13.6	65	15.6	158	18.1-7	131
13.11	144	15.7-11	130	18.4	51, 58, 68,
13.13	122, 174	15.7-9	167		69, 167
13.14-50	122	15.10-19	167	18.5	53
13.14-15	54	15.12	73, 174	18.6	53, 56
13.14	52, 167	15.13	174	18.7	53, 55-57,
13.15	52	15.20	66, 86, 130		61, 62, 68
13.16-47	107	15.29	66, 130	18.13	57
13.16-41	53	15.30	73	18.18-21	167
13.16	52-54, 57	15.36-40	123	18.18	188, 189,
13.17-25	107	15.37-40	169, 174,		191, 196
13.26	52-54, 57,		176	18.20-23	24
	65, 107	15.38	123, 174	18.22	84, 167, 193
13.27-31	107	16	22, 31	19	135
13.28	174	16.1-3	122	19.8	167
13.32	107	16.1	51, 68, 69	19.9	73, 93
13.33-37	107	16.3	51, 68, 69,	19.10	51, 69
13.38-39	107		167	19.17	51, 69
13.39	108, 175	16.6-10	24	19.21	23, 31, 124
13.40-41	107	16.6-8	31	19.22	124
13.42-51	131	16.9-10	31	19.27	56
13.43	50, 53-55,	16.11	25, 32	20–28	124
	57, 59, 64,	16.13-14	92	20.1–21.16	124
	69, 108	16.13	53, 167	20.3-4	124
13.46-47	107	16.14	53, 55, 57,	20.3	32
13.47	152		61, 62, 68	20.4	124
13.48	55	16.22-40	158	20.5-15	123
13.49	55	17	52, 139	20.5-6	123
13.50	53-55, 57,	17.1-9	131	20.6	32
	68, 122	17.1-3	52	20.7-12	94, 123
13.51–41.5	122	17.2	167	20.9	96
14.1-6	131	17.3	207	20.13-16	32, 37
14.1	51, 58, 68,	17.4	51, 52, 54,	20.13	32, 123
	69, 122, 167		55, 57-59,	20.16	167, 193
14.5	122		68, 69	20.20-21	169
14.6-20	122	17.6	30, 36	20.21	51, 69
14.8-18	109	17.10-13	131	20.22	193
14.11-15	56	17.10	167	20.24-25	118
14.14-15	157	17.12	51, 54, 55,	20.25	121
14.19	122		68, 69, 93	20.29-30	119
14.26	24, 32	17.17	52, 54, 56,	20.38	32, 118, 121
			57, 61, 167	21.1-3	32, 37

21.6-7	32	22.14	148, 149, 184	26.19-21	141
21.10-14	118, 121			26.19	152, 154
21.13	193	22.17-21	135, 149, 151	26.21-23	151, 154
21.15-40	171, 172, 176			26.22-23	153
		22.17	149	26.22	153
21.15-26	84	22.18-21	152	26.23	153, 154, 207
21.17	23	22.18	149		
21.20-21	172	22.19-21	151	26.27	154
21.21	51, 66, 85	22.22	140	26.29	153
21.22	66, 73	22.25-29	68	27	32, 37
21.23-26	167, 193	23.6	153	27.1-2	37
21.23-24	188, 193, 194, 196	23.11	24	27.1	68
		23.16-22	172	27.4-8	37
21.24	85	23.17	68	27.6	68
21.25	66, 86, 130	23.18	140	27.9-10	37
21.26	195	23.23	68, 161	27.11	68
21.27	195	24.5	30	27.12-16	37
21.28-29	85	24.11	56, 167	27.21-26	37
21.28	51, 69, 147, 149	24.14	56	27.23	56
		24.17-18	196	27.30-36	37
21.29	124, 140	24.17	167, 172	27.31	68
21.30	140, 149	24.23	68, 172	27.43	68
21.31-36	140	25.13–26.32	159	28	110, 111, 121
21.32	68, 147	25.14	140		
21.40	147	25.23	140	28.2	36
22–26	141	26	127-30, 135-40, 147, 150-54	28.11-13	37
22	127-30, 135-40, 147, 148, 150, 151, 154			28.16-31	155
				28.25-28	65
		26.1-23	134	28.27	144
		26.1	141	28.28	145
		26.3	141, 153	30	135
22.1-21	129, 134, 149	26.4-8	135		
		26.6-8	153	*Romans*	
22.1	140, 141, 147	26.6	30, 153	14.13	197
		26.7	56	15	32
22.3-5	135	26.8	153	15.17-29	23
22.3	147, 149	26.9-11	135, 152, 154	15.19	24
22.5	147			15.25	23
22.6-7	150	26.13	152	15.31	172
22.7-8	134, 150	26.14-15	134	16	124
22.9-10	136	26.14	129, 136, 151, 152	16.23	124
22.9	129, 136				
22.10	136	26.16-18	136, 151, 152	*1 Corinthians*	
22.12	62			1.14	124
22.13	148	26.16	152, 154	9.21	197
22.14-16	154	26.17	152	16.3-4	23
22.14-15	148, 151	26.18	144, 151, 152		

Index of References

2 Corinthians		4.10	122	4.11	122
2.12-13	123			4.13	114-16, 123
11	32, 33, 36	*1 Thessalonians*		4.14	125
11.23-27	21	2.12	151	4.15	118
11.25	32	5.5	72	4.16-17	110
11.26	32			4.17	125
		1 Timothy		4.20	124, 125
Galatians		1.8-9	114		
1-2	167, 171	1.18	118	*Philemon*	
1.13-17	128	2.10	62	24	122
1.18-19	171	4.14	118		
1.18	171	6	116	*1 Peter*	
1.22-23	171	6.8	116	1.13	161
2	167			3.18-19	163
2.13	175	*2 Timothy*		3.19	163
		1.6	118	4.6	163
Ephesians		1.15	118, 125	5.10	151
5.8	72	2.17	125		
5.14	160	3.10-11	122	*Revelation*	
		4.6-7	118	3.20	161
Colossians		4.9-21	111, 113	21.1	36
1.12-14	151	4.10	118, 125		

JEWISH SOURCES

Pseudepigrapha		*4Q246*		62–64	80
2 Baruch			74	64–74	79
9.2	142			64–72	85
		4Q365 frag. 6		66	89
4 Ezra		2.1-7	76	70	89
12.2-13	143	2.4-7	77	75	86
				76	88, 89
Jos. Asen.		*4Q521* frag. 2		77	89
8.10	144	2.1	76	82	86
15.13	144	2.7-8	75		
		2.12-13	75	*4QMMT^c*	
Jubilees				6	89
1.7-26	181	*4QMMT^a*		10	87
44.5	143		79	11	89
				12	89
Odes		*4QMMT^b*		17–21	80
14.18-19	144	1–3	81	18–19	88
		3–38	79	21	89
Qumran		9	86	25–26	88
1QS		28–29	82	27	80
6.13-23	73	39–62	79		
		39–40	85	*4QpPs^a*	
		60–62	85	3-10 iv 7-9	83

11QMelch		*j. Naz.*		*Apion*	
17–18	75	5.3	195	2.123	58, 69
				2.210	58
Mishnah		Midrash		2.279	58
Bikk.		*Exod. R.*		2.282	58
1.4	55	18	161	2.284	58
Mid.		*Pes. R.*		*Life*	
2.5	189	138a	181	413	99
Naz.		*Sifre Num.*		*War*	
2.5-6	194	22		2.313	190, 192, 195
2.7-10	193	(on Num. 6.2)	195		
3.1	195			2.463	59
3.6	190, 195	*Sifre Zuta Num.*		5.185	84
5.4	194	6.13	195	7.45	58, 69
6.8	191				
		Jewish Authors		Maimonides	
Soṭ.		Josephus		*Mishneh Torah: Sefer*	
7–8	159	*Ant.*		*Hafla'ah, Nezirut*	
		2.2	64	2.21-22	190
Tem.		3.217	58, 69	6.14	191
7.4	191	11.8.4-5	144		
		14.7.2	64	Philo	
Talmud		14.110	61	*Spec. Leg.*	
b. Naz.		19.8.2	157	1.9.51	51
12b	194	19.294	194		
45a, b	190	20.2.5	56	*Virt.*	
		20.4.2	64	21.108	55
b. Tem.		20.8.11	64	179	144
10a	195	20.17	61		
		20.195	63	*Vit. Mos.*	
b. Yeb.		20.221	84	2.17	58
47a	51	20.34-35	61	2.20	58
47b	55	20.38	61	2.21-22	58
		20.41	62	2.23-24	58
j. Ber.		20.43-48	62		
11b	194				

CHRISTIAN AUTHORS

Acts of Pilate		Eusebius		*Praep. Ev.*	
2.1-4	55	*Hist. Eccl.*		9.27.12	156
		2.22.1-4	111		
Didache		2.22.2	115	Justin	
7.4	142	2.23.4	189	*Apol.*	
				1.161	142

Dial. Tryph.		Origen		Comm. in Mat.	
10.4	60	Comm. in Ioh.		11.8	193
24.3	60	10.30	193		
		13.111	193		

CLASSICAL

Aelius Aristides		7.5.8	34	Letter of Diogenes	
Or.		7.6.1-2	34	46	116
14	34	8.1	21		
		8.2.12	34	Letter of Socrates	
Aeschyles		8.3.1-11	35	6.2	116
Agamemnon		8.4.10	37		
1624	151	8.6.1-12	34	Letters of the Socratics	
				9.2	116
Agathemnerus		Dio Cassius			
1.5	26	Discourse		Lucian	
		8.9	94	De dea syria	
Arrian		27.2-3	95	60	192
Anab.		27.5-6	94		
3.7-8	27	32.9-12	94	Hist. conscrib.	
3.15-16	27	33.1-7	94	16	97
		61	95	39	127
Chariton				58	139
Chaereas and Callirhoe		Diogenes Laertius			
1.10.8–11.1	34	6.97-98	95	Philostratus	
1.11.6-7	36			Vit. Ap.	
1.14.9	34	Dionysius		8.30	156
3.3.8	34	Roman Antiquities			
3.4.17	34	8.50.4	104	Pliny	
3.5.1-9	34	11.12.3	104	Letters	
3.5.9	34			1.15	95
3.6.6	34	Euripedes		9.17.3	95
3.7.3	35	Bacchae			
3.10.8	34	443	156	Plutarch	
4.1.5-6	34		156	Sept. sap. conviv.	
4.2.1	35			148C–150B	95
4.6-7	21	Homer			
4.7.8	34	Iliad		Propertius	
5.1.3	35	23.144	192	e tabula pictos	
5.1.5-6	35			ediscere mundos	
5.2.6	36	Juvenal		4.3.33-40	25
5.3.1-10	35	Sat.			
5.4.5-6	35	6.434.41	95	Quintillian	
5.9.1	35	14.96-107	59, 60	Institutio Oratoria	
5.13.2-4	37			3.8.49	138
6.3.1–7.10	35	Letter of Crates		9.2.29-32	138
6.4	35	30	116		

Strabo		Xenophon of Athens		4.1.1-5	29
Geog.		*Anabasis*		4.1.3	29
1.1.6	29	4.7.20-27	33	4.1.5	29
2.1.1	26, 27			4.3.1	29
2.1.11	34	Xenophon of Ephesus		4.4	21
17.1.16	29	*Ephesiaca*		4.4.2	29
67–68	27	1.6-7	21	5.1.1	29
		1.10.3–11.6	34	5.2.7	29
Tacitus		1.13.1	28	5.4.5-7	35
Hist.		1.13.3	28	5.10-15	28
5.5	59	3.2	28	5.10.2	34
		3.10.4	34	5.15.1	34
		3.12.6	21		

INDEX OF AUTHORS

Achtemeier, P.J. 133
Aejmelaeus, L. 203
Aletti, J.-N. 146
Alexander, L.C.A. 22, 36, 82, 91-93, 95-97, 99, 103
Alexander, P.S. 25, 30, 81
Alter, R. 132
Anbar, M. 185
Anderson, J.C. 131, 133
Anneau, J. 176
Arnold, M. 31
Aune, D. 94, 96, 139

Bachmann, M. 149
Barbi, A. 153
Barker, M. 181
Barrett, C.K. 209
Barth, K. 175
Bauckham, R. 30, 102-104, 125
Baur, F.C. 166, 167
Bechtler, S.R. 128, 143, 151
Beck, N.A. 127
Becker, U. 185
Berger, K. 18
Bernays, J. 50
Betz, O. 75, 149
Blum, E. 185, 186
Bobertz, C.A. 94
Bovon, F. 66, 147, 198, 200
Braun, W. 94
Brenk, F.E. 38
Brinkman, J.A. 30
Bromiley, G.W. 170
Brooke, G.J. 73, 75, 77, 95
Brown, R.E. 163
Brox, N. 115, 117
Bruce, F.F. 129, 142, 192
Budesheim, T.L. 128

Bultmann, R. 168
Bunyon, J. 19
Burchard, C. 127
Burnett, F.W. 131
Burridge, R.A. 97-99

Callan, T. 60, 62, 63, 66
Calloud, J. 127, 144
Campenhausen, H. von 113
Casey, P.M. 201, 208, 213, 214
Chatman, S. 137
Cohen, S.J.D. 51, 55, 58, 59, 63, 64
Collins, J.J. 50, 51, 61, 62, 74-76
Collins, R.F. 128, 143, 150
Colpe, C. 202, 203, 206, 215
Conzelmann, H. 86, 129, 142, 169, 181, 190, 191, 193, 199, 200, 204, 205, 208, 211, 213
Corley, K.E. 94, 95
Cortese, E. 179
Cronje, J.V.W. 133
Cross, F.M. 179

Danby, H. 191
Davies, P.R. 182
Dibelius, M. 32, 128, 156, 166, 183
Dilke, O.A.W. 26, 34
Dillon, R.J. 157
Dombrowski, B.W.W. 78
Donelson, L.R. 115
Downing, F.G. 92, 97, 99, 101, 102, 106, 109
Dupont, J. 157, 161, 183

Eisenmann, R.H. 75, 81
Esler, P.F. 50, 51, 66-68, 92, 96, 101
Evans, C.F. 89

Feldman, L.H. 64
Feuillet, A. 112, 116
Finn, T.M. 50
Fitzmyer, J.A. 72, 74, 82-85, 199, 200, 203, 207, 210
Flusser, D. 77
Fowler, A. 99
Frein, B.P. 206
Friedman, R.E. 179
Funk, R.W. 128

Gager, J.J. 50, 62-64
Gagnon, R. 51, 67
García Martínez, F. 74, 78, 81
Gaventa, B.R. 128, 139, 141, 146, 153
Gempf, P. 92
Genette, G. 136
Gill, D. 135
Gilliard, F. 92
Gould, P. 26, 28
Goulder, M.D. 160
Grappe, C. 173, 174
Greimas, A.J. 145

Habel, N. 143
Haenchen, E. 54, 73, 129, 149, 151, 152, 167, 175, 189, 193, 210
Hägg, T. 17, 20, 25
Hamm, D. 128, 144, 152
Hare, D.R.A. 199, 204
Harrison, P.N. 112, 116
Hausrath, A. 196, 197
Hedrick, C.W. 127, 129, 145, 148, 151
Heidel, W.A. 26
Hirsch, E. 127
Hoffmann, P. 199, 201, 209, 210
Holmberg, B. 93
Hooker, M.D. 214
Huppenbauer, H.W. 73

Jacobson, A.D. 201
Japhet, S. 180
Jeremias, J. 156, 203
Jervell, J. 50, 65, 147
Jewett, R. 23
Johnson, L.T. 135, 142, 170, 172, 175
Jonge, M. de 198
Juel, D. 85

Kaestli, J.-D. 202
Kampen, J. 86
Käsemann, E. 166, 168, 171
Keck, L.E. 200
Kilgallen, J.J. 128, 183
Kloppenborg, J.S. 201
Kraabel, A.T. 50, 57
Kraus, H.J. 180
Kuhn, H.G. 51
Kuhn, H.-W. 72
Kümmel, W.G. 167, 168
Kurz, W.S. 128, 136, 138, 139, 148

L'Hour, J. 185
LaHurd, C.J. 128, 155
Lake, K. 50, 56, 60, 61, 64, 190, 191
Lausberg, H. 133
Légasse, S. 183, 185
Lentz, J.C. 93, 152
Lesky, A. 36, 37
Lestapis, S. de 112
Levin, C. 185
Levine, B.A. 192
Lieu, J. 50, 68
Lifschitz, B. 64
Liftin, D. 102
Lim, T.H. 75
Lindars, B. 199, 203, 205, 213, 214
Lindemann, A. 169, 204
Lohfink, G. 128, 145, 179
Löning, K. 127
Louw, J.P. 133, 175
Lüdemann, G. 23, 24, 171
Lundgren, S. 127, 147
Luz, U. 215
Lyons, J. 133

MacDonald, D. 125
Macchi, J.D. 186
Maddox, R. 22, 23
Malherbe, A.J. 116
Malina, B. 102, 106
Marguerat, D. 101, 103, 104, 107, 131, 146, 155
Marshall, I.H. 192, 196, 197, 199, 203, 206, 207, 210
Mason, S. 63
McKenzie, S.L. 180

Index of Authors

McKnight, S. 50, 54, 62, 65
McRay, J. 69
Meeks, W. 93
Metzger, B.M. 30, 190
Milgrom, J. 192, 195
Mitchell, A.C. 102, 105
Molinié, G. 18
Morgan, J.R. 17
Morgenthaler, R. 89, 130
Moule, C.F.D. 112, 114-17, 213, 214
Moxnes, H. 93, 105
Müller, M. 199, 210, 213, 214
Munck, J. 193

Nelson, R.D. 179
Neyrey, J.H. 102, 106
Nickelsburg, G. 200
Nicolet, C. 37
Nida, E.A. 133, 175
Nock, A.D. 59
Nolland, J. 67
Norden, E. 32
Noth, M. 178

O'Toole, R.F. 127, 152
Ong, W. 132
Overman, J.A. 50, 54, 57

Paassen, C. van 34
Palmer, D.W. 99, 103, 104
Pédech, P. 34
Person, R.F. 180
Pervo, R.I. 17, 95, 100, 103, 156, 165
Pesch, R. 129, 211
Plümacher, E. 98, 106, 165
Porter, S.E. 33
Praeder, S.M. 33
Puech, E. 74, 75

Qimron, E. 78, 86, 88
Quinn, J.D. 113

Rackham, R.B. 160
Radl, W. 132, 157, 160
Ramsay, W.M. 189
Reardon, B.P. 17, 18, 20, 21, 34, 35
Reymond, S. 128, 146, 152, 154
Reynolds, J. 60-63, 66, 69

Ricouer, P. 166
Riesner, R. 75
Rimmon-Kenan, S. 138
Robbins, V.K. 32, 33, 37
Robertson Smith, W. 191
Rohrbaugh, R.I. 105
Roloff, J. 150, 172, 173, 210
Römer, T. 185, 186
Rose, M. 179
Rosenblatt, M.-E. 128, 138
Roth, W. 179

Sabbe, M. 203
Said, E. 35
Sanders, E.P. 23
Sanders, J.T. 50, 62, 66, 159
Savran, G.W. 132, 137
Schiffman, L.H. 75, 80, 81
Schmid, J. 165
Schmidt, W.H. 180
Schnackenburg, R. 202, 210
Schneider, G. 129, 199, 201-204, 210
Schubert, P. 208
Schulz, S. 168, 169, 176, 201
Scott, J.M. 25, 30, 181
Segbroek, F. van 199
Sheeley, S. 156
Siegert, F. 62, 64
Smend, R. 179
Smith, D.E. 94
Snyman, A.H. 133
Soards, M.L. 203
Sohm, R. 168
Spencer, F.S. 92
Squires, J.T. 100, 108, 206, 207
Stadter, P. 19
Stalman, R.C. 73
Stanley, D.M. 127, 129, 152
Steck, O.H. 127, 143, 181
Stegemann, H. 75
Sterling, G.E. 99
Stern, M. 59, 60
Sternberg, M. 132-34, 136, 137, 145
Stolle, V. 127, 132
Stoneman, R. 17
Strange, W.A. 190
Strobel, A. 112, 116, 117, 161
Strugnell, J. 78-80, 86, 88

Suggs, M.J. 217
Suleiman, S.R. 133
Sussmann, Y. 78

Tabor, J.D. 74-76
Talbert, C.H. 131
Tannehill, R.C. 131
Thiel, W. 180
Thompson, J.A. 184
Tiede, D.L. 206-208
Tödt, H.E. 199, 202, 204, 208-10
Trebilco, P.R. 50, 51, 61, 62, 69
Tuckett, C. 203, 211, 217
Tyson, J.B. 50, 67, 68, 91, 92

Van Seters, J. 185
VanderKam, J.C. 87
Veltman, F. 140
Vermes, G. 74, 75, 213, 214
Vogels, W. 143
Vögtle, A. 209

Walbank, F.W. 34
Wehnert, J. 33
Weinfeld, M. 180
Weinstock, S. 30
Weiser, A. 129, 204
Wendt, H.H. 166, 167, 171
White, R. 26, 28
White, S.A. 76
Wikenhauser, A. 144, 165
Wilckens, U. 181, 184
Wilcox, M. 50, 53, 57, 60
Williams, C.S.C. 193
Wilson, S.G. 112-14, 117-19, 125
Windisch, H. 127
Winter, P. 77
Wise, M. 75, 76, 81
Witherington, B. 55
Witherup, R.D. 128, 130, 133, 136-39
Wittgenstein, L. 98

Yardeni, A. 78

Zimmerli, W. 143
Zmijewski, J. 202

GENERAL THEOLOGICAL SEMINARY
NEW YORK